MONSTROUS REGIMENT

Four Plays and a Collective Celebration
Selected and compiled by Gillian Hanna

SCUM by Claire Luckham and Chris Bond
MY SISTER IN THIS HOUSE
by Wendy Kesselman
ISLAND LIFE by Jenny McLeod
LOVE STORY OF THE CENTURY
by Märta Tikkanen
from the translation
by Stina Katchadourian
adapted by Clare Venables

NICK HERN BOOKS
London

A Nick Hern Book

Monstrous Regiment first published in 1991 as an original paperback by Nick Hern Books, a Random Century Company, 20 Vauxhall Bridge Road, London SW1V 2SA

Set in Baskerville by BookEns Limited, Baldock, Herts.

Printed by T. J. Press (Padstow) Ltd, Padstow, Cornwall

A CIP catalogue record for this book is available from the British Library: ISBN 1854591150

MONSTROUS REGIMENT is ——— company with twin sparks
at its centre: the complex nature of women's experience and the
dynamic culture of the theatre. It aims to produce contemporary
work that illuminates, entertains and moves the audience.
Founded in 1975 by a group of professional performers, the
company has explored a wide range of theatrical forms over the
years, including the epic, the straight play, musicals, real
performance pieces and cabaret. It has always been its policy to
provide work opportunities for women, whether as performers,
writers, musicians, designers, directors or technicians, although
both women and men have worked with the company.

Monstrous Regiment has commissioned a large body of plays
about women from such writers as Robyn Archer, Chris Bond,
Caryl Churchill, David Edgar, Bryony Lavery, Claire Luckham,
Rose Tremain and Michelene Wandor. The company has recently
taken a new direction by appointing its first artistic director, Clare
Venables.

GILLIAN HANNA is an actress and translator. Educated at
Trinity College, Dublin, where she took a degree in Modern
Languages, she has worked in theatre and television for over
twenty years. In 1975 she was one of the group of performers
who founded Monstrous Regiment and has worked with the
company extensively since then. She translates plays from French
and Italian and has published fourteen of her translations of
Franca Rame and Dario Fo's plays.

Cover picture: Helen Glavin in *Scum*. Photograph: Roger Perry

To the memory of Angela Hopkins and Ruth Marks

Contents

Gillian Hanna would like to thank Chris Bowler, Katrina Duncan, Diane Gelon, Mary McCusker, Cheryl Moch, Rose Sharp and Clare Venables for invaluable help in the preparation of this book.

Meditation on Monstrous Regiment, a.k.a. Monsters

'MONSTER': Oxford English Dictionary definition:

'Originally: a Divine Portent or Warning.
From 1710: a Prodigy or Marvel.'

(Plus all the other more obvious ones of animals of huge size,
combinations of 2 animals in one, etc., etc.)

DIVINE PORTENT, WARNING, PRODIGY, MARVEL

No wonder I have always loved their pet name more than their full
one. 'Regiment' frightened me.

CLARE VENABLES
Artistic Director, 1991

Prologue

This is a personal, partial – in both senses – record of some significant moments in the life of a theatre company. Even if I had wanted to, I am not the right person to write a scholarly document of social history. What I want to do here is to try and give some sense of what it felt like to be part of an enormous wave of social change. It isn't a minutely detailed account of The Monstrous Regiment's existence over the last fifteen years; more like a series of snapshots from the family album. So I apologise in advance to all those who will feel – who will *know* – that there are other versions of this story.

There is, of course, another history which underpins this one, the history which is rarely spoken of: the emotions, the rivalries, the quarrels, the love affairs licit and illicit that are part of any social group and especially a tightly-knit bunch of emotionally volatile idealists embarked on what they perceived as a life and art struggle to change the world. I am conscious that in omitting this vital thread of the company's life only part of the truth is visible. But that story, however crucial, belongs to those who lived it. I simply want to acknowledge its absent presence here.

What do I remember? How do I want to be remembered?

Scum: *Chalking 'Vive la Commune' on an upturned table as I listened to Helen Glavin playing her most beautiful song of all, 'Cherry Time' – dreaming of love and the spring while facing death. And there we were, with* our *dreams still intact.*

> CHRIS BOWLER
> *Company Member, Performer, Writer,*
> *Director, 1975 to the present.*

Soon after the question of writing this introduction was raised in the company, I had a dream that was so vivid I had to write it down. It surprised me because I'm not given to 'significant' dreams.

In the dream, the company had gathered together a group of women, many of whom I recognised as having worked with the company over the past fifteen years. We wanted some help with a difficulty we had got ourselves into: was it a hopeless task for women of our age and experience (early to late forties) to look for younger writers who could write about the concerns we wanted to see expressed on the stage? (This reflected an actual discussion the company was having at the time. We had been considering, for example, organising a conference on the issue.) There were some difficulties about the meeting itself. Some of us had agreed to meet in a building in Lower Regent Street, but we had got confused between Lower Regent Street and the Haymarket, so there was a terrible muddle; we thought that some women hadn't turned up, whereas in fact they had. We arrived in someone's house or flat. A private space, not public. There was difficulty in focusing the discussion. Every time a useful line of discussion got going, someone would move to another room, disrupting the flow, or someone would start another discussion on the other side of the room. There was a clear division between some of the younger women who couldn't see the point of the discussion and some of the older women who felt that these issues were now out of date and had no relevance to their lives. Someone said very loudly: 'I hope this isn't going to turn into a talking shop.' After a lot of talk and discussion – some useful some not – the meeting broke up. There was a general feeling that the younger women would not come back to another meeting. And in the dream I said to Cathy Itzin*: 'I started to panic when I heard that "talking shop" remark'. 'So did I', she said. 'And I couldn't bear it. I think I would die if the next generation didn't understand what we did and why, to the extent that it became necessary for them to start all over again as if we had never existed.'

While this short introduction cannot carry the burden of passing on all that we learned, I hope that it will make a contribution to the discussion that will begin when sufficient numbers of younger women perceive the hollowness of the premises of 'post feminism' and the next wave of feminism starts to take shape.

* Catherine Itzin, journalist and writer, author of *Stages in the Revolution* (Eyre Methuen, 1980).

When my mother started working at Monstrous Regiment I was all of about 5 years old. Now I'm 18, considered by many as a woman in my own right and shortly off to university. And believe me, it's as weird for me to see the Monsters grow up as I'm sure it is for them to see me. Sure, I've grown from being about 2 foot tall to a grand 5 foot 11 inches, but if you ask me, the Monsters have grown no less visibly. Whatever happened to that dingy office that was about 3 foot square in Essex Road? If you ask me my growing effort is measly compared to theirs! I see the name 'Monstrous Regiment' all over the place now and I must say I feel proud of their achievements.

So, what do I remember about the Monsters? I remember a few faces and even fewer names. I remember watching grown women, and the odd man, doing all sorts of strange things – screaming and 'relaxing'. I remember seeing every play the group did but not understanding a single word of any of them. I remember finding my first wobbly tooth at Chrissie Bowler's house, and designing flags for the company, and Bili the best dog ever, and eating lokshen pudding at Goswell Road. And my best memory is of Mary, Gillie and Chris singing me to sleep one bedtime.

Seriously though, the time I spent with the Monsters really was excellent fun. Of course I took it all for granted but in retrospect I'm sure that growing up among so many feminists helped form my opinions and attitude. I understand better than most girls my age the aims, achievements and implications of the women's movement, and also what still has to be fought for. I suppose I also take fringe theatre rather too much for granted, due to an overdose at an early age. The Monsters have contributed greatly to an upbringing that I'm grateful for.

When I played the child of the future in Shakespeare's Sister *at the ICA the most exciting thing for me was that I was allowed to stay up until way past my bedtime every night except Sunday. It was quite impressive to say that I was acting on a West End stage, but I actually couldn't have cared less. I did get £35 per week (half the real wage) but I didn't really understand money and I didn't even get a new dress as a costume. Still, I suppose it was fun to walk on stage every night, turn a record player off, walk to the front of the stage and read from some pieces of paper in a saucepan.*

Monstrous Regiment will never be a theatre company to me, as far as I'm concerned they are a group of 'aunties' and a part of my upbringing. Predictably, now I have no desire to go and see a Monstrous Regiment play (unless of course one of my monsters is in it) but I still keep an eye out for them and am absolutely amazed that it's 15 years. Now, at last my chance to say . . . 'HAVEN'T YOU GROWN!!'

Happy Birthday Monsters and Thank you.

Much love.

HANNAH BEARDON
Daughter of Sue and Star of the wonderful
Shakespeare's Sister, 1980.

———————

Introduction

The four plays in this volume cover fifteen years of Monstrous Regiment's existence – from *Scum: Death, Destruction and Dirty Washing,* the first show we produced, to *Love Story of the Century,* which toured in the Spring of 1990. Fifteen years, because although *Scum* did not open until May 1976, we had set up the company the previous August.

We are extremely glad to have the opportunity of getting some of the work we have performed into print. More and more women are writing plays and they are being produced, but they are rendered invisible because the texts are not published. It is important that people are made aware of the existence of women authors, beyond the handful that make it to the main stages of major mainstream theatres. *My Sister in This House* is well known in America but hardly at all in England, and the other three plays in this volume are almost unknown outside the comparatively small number of people who saw them in performance. One of the aims The Monstrous Regiment started out with was to create a body of work by and about women that could be performed by others, so we've always thought that making the texts publicly visible and available was of vital importance.

Because a major and crucial part of our existence is the creation and promotion of new writing, students often ask us what work method we use in the creation of our plays. We can never answer the question straightforwardly. The truth is that we have never evolved a 'work method' as such. Projects have been conceived and created in different ways. The work method fitted the talents and interests of the people who made up the company at any particular time. Or the desires of the author. It also reflected the state the company was in: in the early days, we demanded the involvement of every member of the company with the script at all stages and we continued to work at and shape the scripts through rehearsals and even on the road. At other points, when we commissioned authors, we pretty much left them alone, once the initial idea or scenario had been discussed and agreed.

Scum, which was created during a period of excitement and turmoil, involved a seemingly endless process of to-ing and fro-ing between the authors and the company to the extent that it is now almost impossible to know who wrote certain passages of the play (although, of course, it is Claire Luckham and Chris Bond's play). The development of *Island Life* followed a more conventional path. Jenny McLeod presented us with a choice of two scenarios. In discussion with her, we decided on one of them. She then went away and wrote the play. There were discussions and rewrites, of course, especially once the play went into rehearsal, but the process was a relatively conventional one, unlike *Scum.*

The change in approach reflects the material changes in the structure of the company and the world in which it works. So in 1975 we were a collective of eleven people, all of whom had the right and the burning desire to contribute to the making of the play. But by 1989, as a management of five, we were playing a more traditional, 'managerial' role.

My Sister in This House and *Love Story of the Century* represent another strand of the company's work. We have always felt that we needed to be in touch with what women were writing about in other countries – Sisterhood is Global – so we have produced plays from the USA, and translations from Italian, French, Spanish, and, in the case of *Love Story of the Century,* Finnish.

The First Fury: Creating the Company 1975–1979

Like many plays produced by the political touring companies of the 1970s, *Scum* came out of passionate commitment to principles, hard thinking about political objectives, explosive energy, careful organisation and near total chaos.

In 1970, a group of women had staged a much-publicised disruption of the Miss World contest. That was the same year in which the first Women's Liberation conference was held in Oxford. Germaine Greer published *The Female Eunuch* in 1972. The mythical American bra-burners were never out of the newspapers: women were back on the political agenda in a way they had not been since the days of the suffragettes.

More and more women were noticing that the famous sexual and political revolution of the 1960s just meant more better sex for the men; and that commitment to left-wing ideas meant more licking envelopes and making tea for the women. At best the revolution was passing women by; at worst it was rolling over them.

The atmosphere of the time was extraordinary: the shivering excitement in the air was almost tangible. Women felt they were throwing off the shackles of a thousand years or more and finding freedom. We were going to be the midwives for a whole new era of equality. The fact that our grandmothers had had the same feelings fifty years before was neither here nor there. The more we discovered what had been 'hidden from history', the more furious we became, the more convinced we were that this time we were not going to rest until the world was transformed. We were going to change things irrevocably, and our daughters and granddaughters would be able to learn from our successes and mistakes. Somehow we would pass on our knowledge, so that the next generation could take up where we left off instead of having to start all over again.

'Women are revolting', the badge said. Everywhere you turned, we were marching, writing, performing, striking, picketing, occupying newspapers and men-only wine bars, arguing with each other and everyone else. What's hard to grab hold of and pass on at a distance of twenty years is the sheer exhilaration and excitement of the times. The Buzz. The feeling – the knowledge – that what we were doing was *the* most important political and social movement, gave anyone who was part of it, however peripherally, a real sense of their own importance in the world. The movement was visionary and idealistic, but it was also practical: arguments about equal pay, equal rights, nursery care were raging.

In the context of this whirlwind of social change, it was inevitable that the ideas being debated so fiercely would find their way onto the stage. Some of the routes by which they did so are reflected in the diversity of the backgrounds of the women (and men) who became the Monstrous Regiment.

Perhaps some of the difficulties I find in relating to these accounts of the company are to do with class and education. I wasn't a member of the educated middle-classes, who came to socialism and feminism via the universities and polytechnics of the 60s and 70s. My own route was a different one. And often I resented my inability to compete with other members of the collective in articulating my thoughts in recognisable well-honed phrases.

The resentment and frustration will probably never quite disappear. But nor will my memories of the positive joy of being one of the Monstrous Regiment.

MARY MCCUSKER
Company Member, Performer, 1975 to the present, Executive Director, 1990–1991.

———————

During the afternoon of August 14th 1975, a freak rainstorm hit a very small area of north London. For three hours it poured down. Hundreds of people were left homeless as their basement flats were flooded, and in Gospel Oak, dinghies and rowing boats were being used to rescue the stranded. August 14th also happened to be the afternoon when a handful of disaffected and fed up actresses and musicians were supposed to be getting together to talk about setting up some kind of music theatre company. The meeting was in Gospel Oak. As the water level rose, and the one or two who had arrived before the storm really got going had to help to try and clear the blocked drain in the garden – to stop the water pouring in under the back door – we decided that this was one of those great ideas that had been rained off. No such thing. During the late afternoon and into the early evening, one by one, they all appeared: bedraggled and soaking wet, but they appeared. As we noted with glee, it seemed to be a wonderfully auspicious omen. It took us another eight months to get the company on its feet. Some of that original group left and others arrived before we opened the first production, but in the mythology of the company, The Afternoon of the Storm has always been the Beginning of the Monstrous Regiment.

———————

'Atmosphere' is so difficult to pin down in words. There was ups and there was downs; and life is complicated; and memory treacherous.

DAVID BRADFORD
Company Member, Performer, Director, different periods between 1975–1983.

———————

Who were we, and why were we there? The actors among us had been working in the professional theatre: Some were from 'straight' theatre and television; some had moved from that in the early 1970s into touring socialist companies or TIE (Theatre-in-Education) or radical experimental groups of one kind or another. We were musicians, too, singers and instrumentalists looking for a way to express something beyond the sexist platitudes of current popular music.

Each of us, in our individual situation, discovered that we wanted to marry our ideas and beliefs with the work we did every day. In an action that was partly conscious and partly unconscious, we were groping our way towards another way of looking at our work: we were questioning what 'the personal is political' might mean in the arena of our own working lives.

At some point, the tension between what we believed to be true about women, and what we were being asked to portray on the stage as being true about women, was too much.

Rarely were we able to play women who lived on stage in their own right. We were always someone's wife, mother or lover. (*Someone* being a man, of course.) Our theatrical identity was usually defined in terms of our relationship to the (more important) male characters. We only had an existence at all because we were attached to a man. The male protagonist gave us a reason for existing on stage. As Mary McCusker was often heard to murmur: 'If I have to play another tart with a heart of gold in a PVC skirt, I'm going to throw up.' And in bands we were required to be the attractive front; wear sexy clothes and sing. Musicians, real musicians, were axiomatically male.

If we ever questioned any of this, we were inevitably accused of 'whining'. Whether in straight theatre or left-wing groups, the Women's Movement was regarded with suspicion if not out and out hostility. (Trivialising women's aspirations was always one good way of trying to blunt the purpose of what we were up to. An interview we did with Erland Clouston for the *Liverpool Daily Post* started: 'You won't notice anything odd about the next play you go to, but that's just conditioning. "The average ratio's about six to two", the Monstrous Regiment sigh, filing their nails. Actors, they're talking about, men to women.')

———————

Critical response has ranged from the belligerent to the rapturous, stopping at many points in between, including the patronising and disdainful. A common reaction of critics to women's work (often, though not always, male critics) is total incomprehension. Unhappily there is only room here for a tiny selection of the classics that have come our way.

*'To use the Paris Commune as a vehicle for sentiments as simplistic
and modish as those of the Women's Liberation Movement might seem
to be politically irresponsible . . .'*

JEFF NUTTALL,
The Guardian *on* Scum: Death Destruction
and Dirty Washing, *1976.*

*'The Women's Lib movement, in spite of the considerable advances it
has made, is still at a stage where resentment dominates reason.
Because it keeps striving for the unattainable goal of happiness
through equality, frustration is its inevitable reward.* Teendreams *by
David Edgar with Susan Todd at the ICA theatre has the authentic
shrill note of so much writing about women's rights. When it is not
railing at men as oppressors, it is haranguing women for failing to
take part in the struggle. Being a mere male, Mr Edgar, as a
Women's Lib propagandist, has the disadvantage of seeing too many
sides of the argument.'*

MILTON SHULMAN,
the Evening Standard, *March 1979.*

*'The company – a feminist bunch who order up plays by women
writers – managed somehow to produce something that was about
people as much as women.'*

PHILIP KEY,
Liverpool Daily Post, *October 1981,
on* Yoga Class.

*'Sometimes you do tend to wonder if authors are losing their marbles.
The search for novelty at any cost gives rise to some curious
malformations.*

*Bryony Lavery's latest farce is a complete confusion. Miss Lavery
belongs to that modern breed of bellyaching feminist who protest the
role of women in what is believed to be a male-dominated world.
Which is nonsense.'*

RICHARD EDMONDS,
Birmingham Post, *November 1984,
on* Origin of the Species.

'Gillian Hanna is Calamity Jane, who maybe partly accounts for the success of the production by persuading the playgoer to forget for considerable periods that this is in fact an all-woman show.'

A.R.,
unidentified Scunthorpe paper, 1983.

We were mirroring the journeys of many other women at that moment: realising that we would wait till Doomsday if we were waiting for men to come through with anything beyond waffle about women's roles, we took action into our own hands. As we used to say in another context, the slave owners didn't give up ownership of their slaves willingly. Freedom has to be fought for.

The commitment with which we had engaged in the political struggle that was set in motion in the post '68 period helps to explain why women who came out of left-wing politics sometimes found it hard to embrace the full force of feminism. It was hard to face the idea that comrades with whom you had worked side by side were actually guilty of bad faith. Hanging on to their own male privileges, they retreated behind a wall and threw darts over the top with 'The Women's Movement is a diversion' written on them. Considering our delight when we discovered the idea of women organising autonomously, it's odd that some of us still hung on loyally to so many of the beliefs associated with our male dominated past.

Like all radicals nibbling at the edge of society we were up against an old problem: do you try and infiltrate ideas into the body politic of the ruling culture by working within the mainstream (and run the risk of diluting the radicalism of the politics) or act autonomously outside the mainstream and run the risk of being marginalised?

In 1975, a body of our peers seemed to be showing us that maybe this wasn't such a big issue: companies like Joint Stock, 7:84, Pip Simmons and The Freehold had been waving two fingers at the conventional theatre world. To those of us who had worked in such companies, whether in socialist groups like 7:84 or Belt & Braces, or in what Chris Bowler called 'the lunatic fringe', there wasn't really an argument. As we couldn't get anyone in the 'straight' theatre to take seriously the questions we were asking, forming our own company was the only road open to us.

And, of course, we had foremothers to look to. The Women's Street Theatre Group had been founded in 1970. In 1972 the

Bolton Octagon's TIE company had devised and performed *Sweetie Pie,* a play focusing on the 'four demands' of the 1970 Women's Liberation Conference. (Equal pay, equal education and opportunity, 24-hour nurseries and free contraception and abortion on demand.) Then in 1973, the Almost Free Theatre hosted a Women's Theatre Festival, out of which emerged two groups: The Women's Company and the Women's Theatre Group.

How our particular group came to be meeting in north London in the middle of a thunderstorm was through a theatrical accident: I had been working with the socialist touring company Belt & Braces. We were recasting a play about the Kent coalfields in the 1930s. Naturally enough, there wasn't an enormous number of parts for women in it. Two, in fact. And I had the only good one. The other one was a cough and a spit. At the auditions, I was amazed at the women who came to see us. They were so talented, so full of energy and ideas. It was outrageous that the scarcity of work for women meant that they were prepared to audition for what amounted to a 'bit part'.

Someone pointed out to me that I was always whingeing on about 'women' so, why didn't I put my money where my mouth was? So I contacted several of the women who had come to the auditions and asked if they would be interested in the idea of forming a women's company. Those who said yes were invited to a meeting. And that's where it began. In a thunderstorm.

There was never any question but that we would set ourselves up as a collective organisation. The company was always conceived as a performers' collective. Given the political climate of the time, the legacy of the libertarian politics of the 1960s and the fact that most of us had experience of some kind of socialist organisation, no other form of structure was considered. We felt too, that collective organisation was somehow the natural way for women to work. It was a period when women were emerging from their individual lives, sharing their histories and stories with each other. Collective work and action broke down the isolation individual women experienced and showed us that we weren't mad or bad.

Besides, there was the spur of feeling that the collectives we had experience of didn't really work. We wanted to do it better; to show that a collective could work efficiently, and honestly. Honestly in the sense that we were aware of the dangers of the 'hidden hierarchy' that can lie beneath the surface of a group, unacknowledged but nonetheless powerful and controlling. We wanted no one person to be so important that she could be considered to be the Artistic Director. Once the company had been established and was up and running, this issue of power and hidden hierarchies came up again and again. We were always conscious of it and struggled and argued and discussed the question endlessly, as the minutes of our company meetings show.

Item 8. Mouse Control

There are mice. Should we get a cat? Roger: Against it –responsibility and smell. Thinks we should get the Public Health Department. Gillie: Pro the cat. Much division. No decision taken.

Extract from the Minutes Book. September 7th 1977.

Although I brought together the women who came to the first meeting, I didn't really 'choose' them. They chose themselves (accidentally) by coming to the Belt & Braces auditions, and later re-chose themselves by staying with the group while others dropped out. At this very early stage there was one man involved with us. In the period between the first meeting and the opening of the first show nine months later we 'attached' other people to us in different ways. Some we knew of from other projects we had worked on. Some we found through auditions and interviews. Some just appeared.

Between August and December 1975 we formed the company proper. We were forced to work in a hand-to-mouth sort of way because we were scattered all over the country. We decided on the subject and title of the first play, commissioned it and invited a director to work with us on it; we named the company and began the process of setting it up as a legal entity. We drew up a 'shopping list' of possible future projects.

The First Blast of the Trumpet Against the Monstrous Regiment of Women is the title of a pamphlet written in 1558 by John Knox, the Scottish preacher and minister. There is some academic discussion as to whether 'Regiment' should more accurately be 'Regimen' meaning 'rule of', since the pamphlet was a virulent attack on Elizabeth I of England and Mary Stuart. We were unaware of any such controversy, and in any case we were rather taken with the image of armies of women driving around the country in battered Transit vans putting on plays. It always amused us to note the different responses we got to that name. To us, it was half comic – whole serious, but definitely intended to produce a smile. We were often astounded at the number of people who failed to get the joke.

The heatwave of summer 1976 peaked during our week of one-night stands for Southern Arts. One week I had booked included a performance at the West End Centre in Aldershot. We were very aware of being in a town dominated by the military – after all we were a regiment too. I was half expecting to be taken away and shot as a dirty feminist. The patriarchal machinery was all around us but we weren't afraid. It was blistering hot but we had women's work to do, getting the Scum *set (wooden flooring pallets and half-barrel washing tubs and a cast-iron stove) out of the van and into the theatre. We decided that swimwear was the order of the day, and of course our personalised carpenters' aprons and gardening gloves (the pallets were full of splinters). Yes, we were feminists, but we had bodies, and we didn't care who knew it. The W.E.C. didn't know what to do for the best. Should they comment, or stay mum and pretend that all their companies did get-ins in bikinis? Discretion won the day – or was it fear? Did they think we'd turn on them with our spanners and ratchet screwdrivers? After the show, one brave soul told me they'd expected us all to turn up in boiler suits and dungarees. So, victory to the Regiment. Another stereotype shattered.*

CHRIS BOWLER.
Company Member, Performer, Writer,
Director, 1975 to the present.

While we were involved with the practical job of setting up the company, at the same time we began the meetings and discussions which were to fuel its life over the next fifteen years; who are we? who do we want to be? what are we doing? who are we doing it for? More specifically, we embarked on the long investigation of our relationship to the two great social forces that motivated us: socialism and feminism.

An overview? I can't think of one.

Best thing; the company's ability to contain difference; the sort of rows and conflicts they had, in previous companies of my experience there'd have been sackings, scapegoating, all right-on justified of course . . . but not the Monsters. They went through it and survived, and I believe that is profoundly about them being women – mostly. I'd never experienced meetings with so much subtext, so much going on under the surface. But somehow it was all contained, and decisions were arrived at. Was this way to our advantage? Not always, for sure, but that was the way of it and the chemistry of it, and I came to love them for it.

Another best thing – the policy; 'We are a collective; we do plays; women's experience centre stage; never more men than women in the company.' Great. Easy to remember.

Favourite show I was in: Dialogue Between a Prostitute and One of Her Clients. *Favourite show I wasn't in?* Vinegar Tom.

JOHN SLADE
Company Member, Performer,
1979–1982.

In January 1976 we made two submissions to funding bodies: one application to the touring department of the Arts Council of Great Britain asking for a guarantee against loss to cover the first tour, and another to the Gulbenkian Foundation, asking for money to pay an administrator's salary for a year:

'We are a group of professionals (at the moment eight women and two men) who have an urgent desire to redress the balance of male/female status and opportunities in the theatre. At any one time, 91.5% of the Equity membership is unemployed. The latest survey shows that average annual earnings were £835; this average was based on male average earnings of £1,031, while for women it was £583. These figures force us to review the whole question of women in the theatre . . . These statistics graphically demonstrate the acuteness of the problem. Despite International Women's Year and the Sex Discrimination Act, we don't see any sign that directors and producers are even aware of the problem's existence, let alone that they are attempting to do anything about it. So we feel that we are forced to . . . The

imbalance that we have experienced is not only in the
scarcity of work but also in the quality of the work that is
offered: there is no challenge, no satisfaction and above all
no truth in representing women by an endless parade of
stereotypes . . . We can understand the motive behind the
commercial theatre's obsession with bare breasts and false
eyelashes, but even in those areas where subsidy is
supposed to foster a more intelligent approach we find too
much of the same kind of thinking . . . We have created a
nucleus of committed people . . . who will provide
continuity of policy, and who will be directors of a non-
profit distributing company limited by guarantee. However,
we know that there are many who will have valuable
contributions to make but who, because of other
commitments, (in the case of women these are usually
children) are unable to promise an undivided fifty-two
weeks a year undertaking. We do not think they should be
excluded because of this. We see as an important part of
our work the creation of a flexible group of writers,
performers, directors, etc. who will come together in
workshops . . . it is essential that we should become a forum
for ideas . . .

'We intend to start fairly conventionally by seeking to
establish ourselves on a well tried circuit and then to branch
out into more difficult directions. In this we are pursuing
the logical continuation of what we have been doing in our
various spheres up till now. (The Liverpool Everyman,
Incubus, the Combination, 7:84, Belt & Braces, etc.) As
individuals we have experienced the problems of trying to
reach a new audience and we do not underestimate them.
However we feel it is our task to try and expand these
efforts into new areas . . . we want to find that audience
which is to be found in launderettes or in front of television
sets. . . . Women in the past have tended to organise
themselves for social purposes, and we intend to tap these
organisations as well as those more usual ones structured
round places of work or local issues. We are already booked
to play in community centres around the Liverpool area
and we will be working hard to expand our work in this
direction . . .'

The Company

Linda Broughton: Bolton Octagon TIE, Glasgow Citizens Freeway, Birmingham Rep, Cockpit TIE. Writer/performer.

Chris Bowler: Combination, V Theatre Company, The People Show, Belt & Braces Roadshow. Performer/fire eater.

Helen Glavin: Black & White Minstrel Show, West London Theatre Workshop, RedBrass, Red Buddha, Edinburgh Festival rock opera 'Shylock', musicals, pantomime, Farnham. Musician/dancer/performer/singer.

Gillian Hanna: Liverpool Everyman, Newcastle University Theatre, 7:84, Belt & Braces Roadshow. Performer/admin.

Annie Hayes: Birmingham Rep, Sheffield Playhouse, Lincoln Theatre Royal, Palace Theatre, Watford. Performer/singer.

Claire Luckham: Ipswich, Watford, Royal Shakespeare Company. Stage manager/writer.

Mary McCusker: Young Lyceum, Edinburgh. Glasgow Citizens, Welsh National Theatre, Perth, Newcastle University Theatre, Liverpool Everyman. Performer/animal impersonator.

Pat McCulloch: American Conservatory Theatre, University of California Repertory Theatre, Committee Revue, San Francisco & New York, Voice, Incubus. Performer/musician.

Chris Bond: Victoria Theatre, Stoke-on-Trent, Royal Shakespeare Company, Liverpool Everyman, Belt & Braces Roadshow, Northcott Theatre Exeter. Writer/performer/director.

David Bradford: Lincoln Theatre Royal, Ipswich, Royal Court Theatre, London, Bolton Octagon, Leeds TIE, Community Industry, Liverpool Everyman, Belt & Braces Roadshow. Writer/performer/director.

Serious minded professionals trying to show that we had a sense of humour. Fire eating and animal impersonation, ho ho.

We did get our guarantee against loss from the Touring Department, largely thanks to Ruth Marks, an extraordinary woman who believed in encouraging ventures she thought had potential. She worked in the Arts Council at a time when what you were doing on stage was more important than The Business Plan. Her vision and courage in backing artistic talent was unusual and she had an enormous influence on many emerging companies. Ruth died at an absurdly young age, and she is badly missed.

In the 1980s the priorities of an arts administrator are shaped by considerations of funding, marketing and managerial efficiency. Arts funding bodies, guided by the prevailing monetarist philosophy of the present government, set stringent criteria for companies, based on their organisational effectiveness and ability to obtain a range of sponsorship. This is the age of the business plan, the consultant, the strategy, incentive-funding and expensive fund-raising training courses. The only growth area in the arts it seems and the only place anyone can make a decent living. Why fund an arts festival when you can fund a feasibility study on an arts festival. Why pay an artist when you can pay a consultant.

Of course efficiency and good management are important and were often less than they might have been in the 1970s. But if managerialism replaces commitment, excitement, the engagement of the arts and theatre with the deeply felt aspirations of both practitioner and audience, then theatre is empty and has nothing to say.

SUE BEARDON
Administrator, 1976–1978.

The genesis of the company's socialism is clear enough. Our individual histories had dictated it. Later on, as this amorphous group changed into the company that produced the first show and therefore became the founding members of Monstrous Regiment proper, we tried to clarify our relationship to the socialist movement. That commitment to looking for a new audience, already expressed in our first contacts with officialdom, became more concrete as we tried to forge links with the Trade Union movement. So we tried to express our politics both in theory and practice – in the content of the plays, in the way we organised our own working lives, and in our attempts to track down that elusive new audience.

How did this relate to our feminism? What was a feminist? Were we socialist feminists, or feminist socialists? We certainly weren't radical feminists. Indeed, we infuriated many women by insisting that we weren't separatist. How could we be, with men in the group?

———————

After the kind of huge rows and conflicts that there always are in groups like us, the resolution would generally be accompanied by tears, touching and hugging – the sort of thing, of course, that chaps just don't do as well. In any case, I think I was pretty good at keeping my head down and avoiding direct involvement in the huge rows and conflicts.

The most obvious way it was different was in the work itself. The world of the plays we did was female-driven. Even the simple fact of having a large majority had a huge impact. This meant that I was generally playing more supporting roles, although we were scrupulous in trying to avoid centering anything we did around one character. Curiously, I think this made it in some ways easier for the men than the women. Our presence as a minority on the stage was very noticeable. As MR wanted to explore the tensions in relationships between women and men, it often meant that the scenes involving men were exciting and dynamic because of that fact.

ROGER ALLAM
Company Member, Performer,
Musician, 1976–1979.

———————

At this very early stage our feminism was on the whole formally unexpressed. Although many of us felt we were part of the Women's Liberation Movement, we had very little idea of what that might mean in practice.

Feminism was leaping in our heads, of course. To be a woman in 1975 and not to have felt the excitement of things starting to change, possibilities in the air, would have meant that you were only half alive. But the Women's Liberation Movement was not a political movement in the sense that we had known politics up to that point. Those of us who came from a background of socialism knew how to join the I.S. (International Socialists) or the Communist Party (or even, God forbid, the Labour Party) but where did you go to join the Women's Liberation Movement? After all, the Women's Movement was everywhere and nowhere. There were no party cards, no enrolment formalities. Did buying *Spare Rib* make you a member? Were you a member because you read *The Female Eunuch* and agreed with Germaine Greer? Or had been to a Women's Liberation Conference? If you weren't in a consciousness raising group, did that mean you couldn't belong?

——————

In the sixties I was a very junior part of the establishment world of the theatre. It was rarely referred to that I was female, apart from the odd comment about how unusual it was for a woman to be doing my job. Any conflict was mainly unconscious, and if I felt particular stress, I just blamed myself and my 'Personality'. (In fact, I was aware that it was a bonus being 'rare'; it was more likely I would get noticed. When I applied for an Arts Council bursary, I was very pissed off that there was another women, Glen Walford, on the shortlist. So was she, I discovered years later.)

Late sixties, early seventies. Wow! Everything is up for grabs! Everything is changing! Not me. I read about it. That's ALL I did. I read about it. Monsters were there. They joined in. They were doing it. I read about them. They frightened me. I didn't know them. I saw them. To me they looked confident, sorted out, independent. They seemed to have no truck with the likes of me. Had I even faintly dared to get to know them, which I didn't, I KNEW that they would have found my fears, dependence, ambitions etc., completely stupid. I would be the subject of one of their plays, not a colleague.

CLARE VENABLES
Artistic Director, 1991.

——————

It is probably true to say that feminism crept up behind us and smacked us hard on the back of the head. The nature of the meetings turned out to be dramatically different from what we had imagined. Yes we were going about setting up a theatre company, in as businesslike a way as we knew how, but we were also raising our own consciousness as we went along. Our frustrations, our anger became inextricably tangled with our determination to get the project going. We set out at the very beginning to make theatre and over the weeks and months of discussions we discovered that we were involved in something much bigger than that: we wanted to change the world. At the time, this didn't seem like such an outrageous project. All around us, women in every area of the world we knew were doing the same thing. It seemed as natural as breathing.

But much more exciting than breathing. Exhilarating. The sense of being in the right place at the right time, in step with a great movement in history, *part* of history, making history ourselves. We were part of a huge wave of women and we were going to remake everything. It gradually dawned on us that we didn't have to go out and join any movement. We were already in it. We were the Movement.

Where did this leave us in relation to men? On the one hand, there was no question of not having men in the group. Our anger at women's position in the world was directed at 'men' in general, or patriarchy, the male-dominated system. We tried hard not to see the men we worked with as being part of the male conspiracy to keep women in their places (on their backs). Although we recognised that 'the personal is political', and although each individual woman was struggling in her own life to make sense of the political relationship between men and women, we always felt that in the context of the company, men were part of the problem, so they had to be part of the answer. If, as we often said, we wanted to dramatise the flashpoints between men and women, we felt that those flashpoints had to be visible on the stage. Our only stated position was the legal one we wrote into the company's Memorandum and Articles of Association: that Monstrous Regiment would never contain more men than women. Besides, our political backgrounds predisposed us to think of men as comrades. We looked on our project as a shared one: men and women working together to create a new kind of theatre, a new set of working relationships.

I recall walking into the rehearsal room on our first day of Alarms. *I was excited – for some time I had wanted to work with a women's theatre company. And yet I found myself surprised by my own reaction – surprised that I was surprised to see so many women in a rehearsal room. A female lighting designer, female director, female photographer, female playwright, female designer, female administrators, and only one male, who was an actor. I had known that this was likely to be the case, but the reality was nevertheless quite extraordinary, because during 13 years of working in theatre, I had never experienced this gender-ratio before.*

GERDA STEVENSON
Performer, Alarms, *1986–1987.*

In retrospect, it seems to me that the basic mistake we made was an organisational one. Given that we operated collectively, we went to extraordinary lengths to try and ensure that everyone's voice was given equal status. (When we found that some of us were being silent in company meetings, we discussed it and looked for strategies that would enable the person to speak.) We remembered how unvalued and silenced we had felt in male-dominated companies, and we were determined not to repeat the patriarchal pattern of dominance and submission. It was important to us that the men should feel an equal part of the company. In effect, we spent a lot of time making sure that the men felt comfortable, and falling head-first into the trap of mothering them. We were, as Helen Glavin says, 'too nice'. Not that the men found it an easy situation to be in. We were asking them to abandon the privileges of patriarchy and work side by side with women as equals. But the equality was blurred, in that it was informally clear that the women led and directed the company. Perhaps if we had been able to find a different organisational structure, things might have been easier; a structure in which women were formally recognised as being the leaders, having the power; in which the men were employed by the women. As it was, because we spent so much energy maintaining an equilibrium between the sexes, we scarcely had any left to examine the issue of relations of power between the women.

Male stage managers in theatres did usually walk straight up to the men in the company when we arrived, assuming we were in charge. After a few surprising interventions by suddenly tetchy women from the company I realised what a pain in the neck this was for them, and developed a blank, into-the-distance vagueness for those moments between the stage manager's approach and the woman's arrival. I

know I could have discussed it but I chose discretion and a dumb
look. Fortunately the women, like the cavalry, always arrived in time.

JOHN SLADE
Company Member, Performer, 1979–1982.

Scum: Death Destruction and Dirty Washing

From January to April 1975 we were more prosaically concerned
with booking a tour and getting a show on the road.

The composition of the company had begun to reshape itself
into its first public appearance: Claire Luckham and Chris Bond
would still write *Scum*, although new commitments in Liverpool
meant they couldn't be permanent members of the group; Susan
Todd agreed to direct the play. She was the perfect choice. Not
only did she have a great deal of directing experience in
mainstream theatre, but she had been a member of the Women's
Street Theatre Group, she had directed *Parade of Cats* at the
Almost Free Women's Theatre Festival and she had been part of
the Women's Company that came out of the Festival, directing
Pam Gems' *Go West Young Woman* at the Roundhouse in 1974.

Chris Bowler, Mary McCusker and I turned down all other
work we were offered and took on the administration of the
company and the organisation of the tour. Helen Glavin was
already writing music and songs. We advertised for and found a
stage manager, d. Wilson. Andrea Montag was designing the set.
With Susan we auditioned actors: Roger Allam, not long
graduated from the Theatre Arts Course at Manchester University,
and Alan Hulse, who had been working with The General Will in
Bradford.

> 'A musical celebration of the women of the Paris Commune
> written by Claire Luckham and C.G. Bond . . . "See
> Bismark do the can-can; watch a man wind himself through
> a mangle; savour the aroma of grilled elephant's trunk;
> thrill to the sound of 'Le Temps des Cerises' and a dozen
> more show-stopping songs; tremble before the final
> spectacle of Paris burning amidst a sea of blood." '

In our first press release we wanted to set the tone of what we
were about: serious, but joyful. Later, we emphasised the serious
a little more, in case people dismissed us as lightweight:

'On September 3rd 1870 a French army of 104,000 under
Napoleon III surrendered to the Prussians at Sedan. This
humiliation threw Paris into an uproar: Revolution, civil
war and the eventual establishment of the Commune
followed. It lasted only fifty-eight days, and ended with
Paris ablaze, and an estimated 25,000 Communards dead.
But although the Commune was destroyed, its example has
always been important to Socialists: When Lenin died his
body was draped in a red communard flag . . . for a brief
two months Paris celebrated the Festival of the Oppressed.
The sun shone as the scum of the earth sang and danced in
the streets. Those who had been reduced to eating rats
seized power and took the government of their lives into
their own hands. In the very forefront of this revolution
marched the Parisian women: exhorting, organising and
demanding everything from crêches to guns, defending the
barricades to the last.'

At some point we stumbled across a book in the Thames &
Hudson series, 'Documents of Revolution', *The Communards of
Paris 1871*. Reprinted in it was a selection of pamphlets, articles,
decrees and posters written by the Communards themselves. We
were amazed to read that not only had the women of Paris shown
incredible physical courage (confronting and disarming soldiers
sent to remove 'the people's canons'; later on, actually fighting
the French army sent in to regain control of the city for the
French government) but they had formed women's political clubs
to agitate for their demands. When we read the list of what they
were agitating for – equal pay, provision of crêche facilities for
working women, education for girls, equal opportunities for
women – we could see that we had a lot in common with these
women. We had the vote, to be sure, but it didn't seem to us that
a great deal more had been achieved in a hundred years.

———————

*We didn't change the world – in lots of ways things are worse for
women now than they were then. But I know* Scum *changed a lot of
women's lives (maybe some men's too). Some people hated the shows
– but they never failed to stimulate. That was because they were born
out of the real and often painful experience and feelings of the
company and their friends. It made life very raw at times and there
were casualties. There were times when I felt miserable.*

*But I doubt if I could have found any other job which I could
combine with the practicalities of being a single parent, which allowed
me to build my work life around my personal and political
preoccupations, gave me a solid grounding for my continued
involvement in the arts and provided me with lasting and valued
friendships.*

SUE BEARDON
Administrator, 1976–1978.

How did the script emerge? Certainly not as we had originally
planned it.

One of the questions that came up again and again in the
1970s was the breaking down of the division of labour and the
consequent hierarchy of skills. Why should an actor be considered
more important than a stage manager? Why should the writer be
God? Wouldn't it be more democratic to write scripts collectively?
If you were working in a collective, how could one voice represent
the ideas of the whole? We acknowledged some truth in this, but
there were some areas where we recognised it as bunk. Enough of
us (and I was one of them) had been through the painful
experience of writing shows collectively in other groups to know
that the skill of playwriting was one skill we wanted to
acknowledge. We also knew that women writers had to be found
and nourished. In one of our grant applications we had stated:

> 'We want to take the emphasis off collective writing, not
> because we are opposed to it as such, but because there are
> painfully few women writers actively involved in theatre and
> we want to encourage them.'

We were looking for a collective relationship with the writer. As it
turned out, there was no recipe for what that relationship might
be, and each one of our ventures with writers – whether it ended
happily or unhappily – was different from the others.

---

*I love words. I respect the skill that uses them to present eternal
truths and to share hard-won insights. But too often I find myself
resenting and distrusting how words have been used to turn my/our*

story into history – negating the process, the leapfrogging chaotic progress we made and are still making.

MARY MCCUSKER
*Company Member, Performer 1975 to the present,
Executive Director, 1990–1991.*

———————

Our original intention in commissioning Claire and Chris was to establish some kind of process whereby they would write and we would then discuss it with them. Or we would have discussions out of which they would go away and write. We were all reading and researching like mad. When they moved to Liverpool and consequently assumed the role of 'outside' writers, as opposed to being part of the group itself, that process was stretched in a way none of us had ever imagined. Claire took on the main burden of the writing – as Chris was trying to rescue a theatre (he had been appointed Artistic Director of the Everyman) – and travelled up and down to London to work with us as often as she could. Somehow, the thread between us never gathered the strength it should have had, and by the time we started rehearsals the company felt that parts of the script were still in an unresolved state.

The main structure of the play – written by Claire and Chris – the situation, the characters, most of the dialogue – was as we finally performed it. Mole and Madame Masson in all her horrendous glory jumped off the pages and onto the stage. Whatever wasn't working we thought we could sort out on the rehearsal floor. Which is what we did. Under Susan's direction, we improvised, we discussed, we argued, we went away and wrote scenes and bits of scenes. We also added more songs. It's almost impossible to say now who did what. Everything I wrote was thrown out as terrible. I think a lot of the scene in which they discover how much Masson had been exploiting them was Mary's. Everybody wrote something. Certainly as director, Susan shaped whatever we came up with and was the final arbiter of what worked and what didn't.

It's impossible to say how the play would have looked if Claire and Chris had been able to be at rehearsal all the time. When they were eventually able to see it on the road, they weren't at all happy with what we had done. Their view of what needed changing in the working script they had delivered to us was very different to ours. Looking back now, it seems to me inevitable that we would change aspects of the play in rehearsal, simply because of 'where we were at'. We identified with those women. We felt we knew them. We were trying to recreate our world just as they had. An interview in *Time Out* quoted one of us during rehearsals: 'It's important to us that we create this atmosphere of celebration, this release from toil . . . and create the kind of debate that went on. That's why it's interesting to us now. Women talking about marriage, day nurseries, women's education, equal pay.'

We, the company, were going through an experience which the writers couldn't be part of through an accident of physical separation. Just as we felt we were shattering everything that had gone before, so it was bound to be that we would want to shape the material we were putting on the stage in the same way. Life imitating art. Or was it the other way round? It was both; and somewhere in the middle and muddle a collision was inevitable.

The play opened in Cardiff at the Chapter Arts in April 1976 and then toured for over a year; we revived it in 1978.

The script that is printed here is the script as we performed it, with two changes that Claire and Chris have made in Act 2.

———————

Our recollection of the events surrounding the writing and rehearsal period of Scum *is substantially different from Gillie's. We were commissioned to write a play, not a 'working script', and that was what we delivered. That play was fundamentally altered in two ways: firstly because there were fewer performers available than we had agreed to write for, which was understandable; and secondly because the company wanted, in our view, to romanticise the story we had written, which was not. They did so without any consultation whatsoever, hence our surprise and anger on going to see the show.*

CLAIRE LUCKHAM & CHRIS BOND
Authors: Scum: Death, Destruction and Dirty Washing

———————

After the First Night

Where does the life of a theatre company truly begin? I suppose it doesn't really exist at all before it first appears in public, no matter how much work has gone into setting it up. So the founder members of the company in that sense are those who opened *Scum: Death Destruction and Dirty Washing* in Cardiff: Roger Allam, Chris Bowler, David Bradford, Helen Glavin, Alan Hulse, Mary McCusker, Susan Todd, d. Wilson and myself. But it wasn't as simple as that. Claire and Chris had been but were no longer 'members' of the company. Andrea Montag and Hilary Lewis who did the set and costumes were totally involved, but in as free-lancers. Pat McCullough dropped out at a fairly late stage, so for the first tour Susan played Eugenie as well as directing the show. She also 'joined up' as a full time member rather than as a visiting director. Linda Broughton was definitely a member although she wasn't in the first tour of *Scum*.

Imagine being on an endless bus tour with a family of nine, all with behavioural problems and none willing to submit to parental control. And accommodation that alternated between B & Bs with a week's supply of poached eggs in the fridge, damp sheets and bath taps you had to pay for (the landlady kept them in a safe place) – and hospitality (provided by friends of the theatre) with all nine in one room sleeping on narrow strips of foam and beating off the hungry mice.

Add on the activity of lugging the set upstairs (you'd be surprised how often we did), converting an ill-lit corridor into a dressing room, and attempting to persuade the caretaker not to close the building half an hour before the show finishes – and you have an average day. The ideal venues, the good B & Bs and the hospitality that provided delightful rooms free were as few as feminists in the Conservative Party, and that made you cherish them all the more.

MARY MCCUSKER
Company Member, Performer, 1975 to the present,
Executive Director, 1990–1991.

Over the next couple of years, one or two came and went, but by and large we were a fairly constant group. When the Gulbenkian Foundation gave us a year's salary for a full time administrator, Sue Beardon took over from David who had been looking after the office. She came to us from a background of working in the Labour movement, and her skills both organisational and creative contributed to the development of the company's work in a way that went far beyond the title 'administrator'.

We wanted to build a repertoire, so that while we were touring one show we could be preparing another. Our original submission to the Arts Council in January 1976 had described our plans for the first year and a half. After *Scum* we wanted to do: 'a show . . . at present untitled, the subject will be "Witchcraft – subversion and madness". We began research last September, and we are talking to several (women) writers about collaborating with us.' Then, 'as a contrast to the first two [plays] which will be "historical" pieces, a modern show set in an industrial context. Women at work. Probably including a (by then) retrospective look at how the Equal Pay and Sex Discrimination Acts are working. We are aiming to interest women in the organised Labour movement in this one, and we will be looking to bodies within that movement for substantial support.'

The untitled show turned into *Vinegar Tom* which Caryl Churchill wrote for us to produce and tour in the Autumn of 1976. Pam Brighton was the guest director.

We had been introduced to Caryl (in Hyde Park, after a march, NAC (National Abortion Campaign), I think) and she talked about how in researching her English Civil War play *Light Shining in Buckinghamshire* for Joint Stock, she had come across a mass of material relating to women and witchcraft, and wanted to write a play about it. Her ideas fitted with ours, and we commissioned her to write it. In terms of our relationship with a writer, it was one of the happiest we ever had. There was never any disagreement about the basic argument of the play, although we had long discussions with Caryl about the characters Jack and Marjory, the couple who represented the emerging bourgeoisie. As I recall, their first scene was the only one which was substantially rewritten. Other changes Caryl made were largely practical. A scene in which Jack and another man drag the drowned corpse of the cunning woman through the village and dump it while they go and look for a drink had to be cut because it had to immediately precede the witchfinding scene and Roger didn't have time to change. The part of Betty had to be written in such a way that Josefina Cupido, who had just joined the company as a musician, and who had never acted before, could have a part that wouldn't be too terrifyingly long.

Scum and *Vinegar Tom* toured in repertoire through the end of 1976 and the spring of 1977. At the end of that year we produced a cabaret, *Floorshow*, and a play with music about domestic violence, *Kiss and Kill*.

At some point in 1976 d. Wilson had left and Meri Jenkins had taken over as technician/production/company manager. Over the next eight years Meri worked with the company, taking time out now and then to go and pursue other work, but she was a rock on which we all leaned. She had an uncanny skill of seeing a problem and dealing with it almost before the rest of us had noticed the problem existed. She also had the invaluable ability of hiding 'contingency money' in a production budget to stop us overspending on the sets.

———————

I was 23, and a fledgling stage manager. In January, 1977 I joined Monsters as the Technical Stage Manager. I badly wanted the job. It was an awesome experience, taking care of everything for a group of people, majoritively women who had more experience than I, who appeared that articulate, that committed, who worked so hard, and were so hugely talented.

The company was still touring Scum. *A few weeks after I joined we went to the University of Sussex at the beginning of a twelve week tour. The theatre seats about 800. The control box is located at the back of the theatre – a kind of giant gold fish bowl. I was alone throughout the performance. In that situation, there are times when it is very difficult to feel connected to what is happening on stage, since the show is heard through a tinny intercom, and the performers are at some distance. I was just beginning to feel as though I had a handle on things – the show was becoming more familiar. At the end of the performance I went through the usual lighting and sound cues – blackout, hold five seconds, lights up to full for the curtain call, as the full company gathered on stage. I glanced up – to my sheer amazement, the audience had begun to stand. Not just the one or two as at other performances, but everyone there. The company stepped forward to applaud the audience, and as the applause echoed back at me, I had an intense feeling of exhilaration and mad joy at what was happening. I had no one to throw my arms around, so I danced around the gold fish bowl, alone.*

MERI JENKINS
Technical Stage Manager, Company Manager,
Different periods 1977–1985.

———————

Susan Bassnett,* in a paper she read at the British Theatre
Conference in Rostock, Germany, in April 1978 noted that, 'with
(*Floorshow*) the company has moved into new areas . . .
traditionally, the music business and the compèring of cabaret
acts have been male dominated and consequently by entering the
predominantly male preserve the company has been exploring
new ground. The role of women in cabaret has been that of
decoration or of servicing the male performers – hence the
scantily dressed assistants in conjuring acts, the pretty girls in
colourful costumes who assist compères and quizmasters, the
dancers whose routines serve as short interludes between the
main (usually male) acts. That is not to say, of course, that there
are no female comediennes, of course there are, but it is only
when one sees Monstrous Regiment's *Floorshow* with women
compères, women comediennes, women drummers, women
singers and the two men in very low-key positions that the extent
of their innovation becomes apparent. In terms of the costume
and design, the company have striven to escape the stereotype of
the women in star-spangled bikinis, and the costumes are a kind
of clown's overall, in brightly coloured satin, decorative but by no
means sexist.'

Now that cabaret has become a cliché of the alternative theatre
it doesn't seem like such an extraordinary thing to have done, but
at the time we knew we were taking a leap in the dark. We were
working with four writers – Caryl Churchill, Bryony Lavery,
Michelene Wandor and David Bradford – and not one of us really
knew what was going to work. We didn't even know if women
could stand up in front of an audience, without a character, and
be funny. So we wrestled endlessly over the problem of each
woman finding her 'voice', and the difference between a
performer's relationship to a 'persona' as opposed to a character.

A desire to discover if and how women could be funny; to
explore as many genres of theatre as we could; to find out if there
was such a thing as 'women's theatre' and was that any different
from 'theatre', which was always implicitly male. We were
searching and our theatrical curiosity pushed us into areas which
were new to most of us. Nudged us as well into cabaret because
of our good fortune in having three talented and accomplished
musician/performers in the company. Roger was primarily an
actor but had a wonderful trained tenor voice and could play a

* Susan Bassnett, Reader in Comparative Literature, University of
Warwick.

mean piano and guitar; Helen was equally accomplished in either art, but was a skilled composer. She had written the music for both *Scum* and *Vinegar Tom*. Josefina was a percussionist, drummer and singer. Cabaret would give us a chance to let them shine. We wanted to show them off.

I was always being asked at that time and since, what it was like to work with a majority of women. I never quite knew what to say. In certain ways it was easier for me than other men who worked with the company. I wasn't exactly a blank sheet of paper, but I was only twenty-two, it was my first job, so I did not have any previous working experience to question or reject. I was not politically involved at university but it seemed natural to be a socialist. I suppose I had been vaguely and completely unthinkingly sympathetic to the idea of feminism at university (only in theory of course, not in practice), so being confronted with seven older, articulate women in a sense helped to form my thoughts in a more concrete way. I needed to embrace some beliefs, and here were ones that seemed natural, idealistic and, very importantly for me, rejecting of my parents' ones. I can certainly remember becoming tense and defensive in social situations with friends who might joke about it, or say 'cunt', or comment on women's bums. Not to say anything seemed a betrayal; and if I did say something I always did it clumsily and felt upset and embarrassed. But inside the group I felt supported and loved in a way that I am sure wouldn't have been available to me in a male group, as there was a playful atmosphere I felt at home in. To this day, when I meet Gillian, we are roughly aged twelve.

ROGER ALLAM
Company Member, Performer, Musician, 1976–1979.

Cabaret would also give us the opportunity to try and move out of the theatres and arts centres and into other spaces in pursuit of that new audience we were always in search of. Set design and fairly complicated lighting had meant we found it frustrating when we performed the plays in non-theatrical venues. Without the technical facilities which theatres gave us access to we always felt the shows weren't being seen at their best. We were depriving the audience of the whole experience. A cabaret, on the other hand, would be more simple, designed to be flexible and play anywhere.

Kiss and Kill, written and directed by Susan Todd and Ann Mitchell, was an exploration of violence between men and women. Intended to be more experimental in form than anything we had previously done, it was almost a collage of short scenes exploring male violence, both domestic and 'public', and the relationship between the two. (One of the characters is a woman who has left her violent husband, but finds herself on the end of horrific abusive phone calls from him, another is an American living in London, a Vietnam veteran, who speaks graphically of the violence he saw and experienced in that war.) Musically, too, it was different from anything we had attempted before, in that it was largely improvised and therefore could change from night to night. Josefina sang, accompanied only by percussion.

We always thought it was an important play in the company's development, and were annoyed when people failed to recognise its experimental nature. Perhaps it was something to do with the subject matter – violence – that seemed to provoke violent reactions in the audiences. Love it or loathe it, it wasn't a piece that many people felt luke-warm about.

After the success of *Floorshow* we thought that the cabaret form was worth exploring still further, raising as it did questions about the female performer and her relationship to the audience. It seemed to us that no matter how skilled the performer was, or how strong the material, there was often an almost tangible sense of unease in the audience when the women performed; that when Roger or Clive Russell appeared on their own as opposed to one of the women, we thought we could often feel the audience relaxing. Was that a communal, unspoken, unconscious conviction that they felt safer when the men were centre-stage? Or were we somehow communicating our own fears that it still might not be legitimate for women to be confronting the audience in this direct way?

Time Gentlemen Please, written by Bryony Lavery, marked the first large change in the make-up of the company. Roger, Helen and Josefina left, so we auditioned musicians to replace them. We wanted to do a show about sex. And physical appearance. When Stephanie Howard was designing the costumes for *Floorshow* we discussed the appearance question endlessly. How could a woman look attractive without making herself into a sex object? We wanted, above all, not to deny our physical entities. Could we do this without exploiting our bodies? What was attractive anyway?

In the end, we went for bright, colourful, attractive yet sexless costumes. It was a solution, (although we were still attacked for them being 'too sexy') but somehow we all felt we'd avoided an issue rather than confronting it.

One of the objectives in *Time Gentlemen Please* was to try and challenge more directly the audience's (and our own) perception of female physical sexuality. Was a liberated woman allowed to be glamorous? Could women and men be equally glamorous? What might that look like?

These were questions which were as pertinent in our lives as on the stage. Perhaps because we mostly came from a background of professional theatre where we were used to costume and the idea of costume as something that was fluid and could be played with, we were personally never happy disowning our bodies under the androgynous uniform of dungarees. Of course we all wore dungarees at one time or another, but we were also the company that once did a get-out in cocktail dresses and high heels because we were on our way to a party and didn't have time to change.

In the written material of the show itself, the company was again challenging the received idea of female sexuality, and in particular female passivity in sexual relationships. (Not a new interest of ours. *Vinegar Tom* opens with a scene of a woman and a man having sex. We were insistent that the woman was very obviously *on top*.)

This was another occasion where a lot of people failed to get the joke. Or rather, failed to get the intensely serious purpose behind the joke. And, infamously, there was 'Leeds.'

A performance of *Time Gentlemen Please* at the Trades Club in Leeds was 'zapped'; literally stopped in the middle by a group of angry women and gay and left-wing activists. I wasn't in *Time Gentlemen Please*, but the descriptions of what happened were vivid. Angry women (and men) pulled the leads out of the amplifiers and speakers, climbed onto the stage and demanded that the performers get off. Chris refused to be terrorised into leaving the stage and finished the monologue she had been in the middle of. Mary then insisted on performing the last poem in the show. It was a traumatic experience: people screaming and shouting, arguing, crying. At the time, the reactions from both the zappers and the zapped was so emotional that it was impossible to make out exactly what it was that was being objected to. Confusing, too, because there seemed to be some kind of leftist factional in-fighting going on. Someone was screaming from the back, 'Tell me what your politics are and then I'll listen to you

. . . ' Someone else, infuriated by the interruption was shouting
'Doesn't anybody here understand irony . . ?' The company
offered to have a proper meeting in the next nearest venue so that
the debate could be thrashed out in a less fraught atmosphere.
Correspondence in *The Morning Star* attempted to clarify the issues
on both sides. In reply to an attack on the show Susan Todd, who
had directed the show, wrote that the women performers:

> 'deconstruct their traditional mode of stage presence and
> abandon coyness, terror and self-doubt for a direct
> expression of sexuality . . . that particular form of
> transformation was fought for very hard and it represents a
> victory for each woman over self-denigration.'
>
> (Letter from Susan Todd, 28 November 1978.)

The incident was in one sense simply part of the flavour of the
times. At conferences, women were often heckled or forced off
the stage. We frequently heard tales of other companies being
heckled or stopped. Intolerance and factionalism of the left was
rampant at the time. Nor was feminism immune. 'Get-it-
Rightism', one of the least savoury heirlooms passed on to us by
the patriarchs of the left, flourished. In the end, it proved to be a
poisonous heritage, encouraging the most narrowing kind of self-
censorship.

A performer or speaker puts herself in a position of power just
by being on a stage. An authoritarian figure, she is probably
experiencing herself at her *least* powerful and most terrified, but
the audience is unable to perceive this, unless she makes herself
obviously vulnerable. When one of the women in *Time Gentlemen
Please* was so upset by what had happened that she began to cry
(off-stage) one of her accusers immediately put her arms around
her and was clearly amazed that the performer should be so
distressed.

This event had a profound effect on all of us within the
company. In the preparation for the show, the company had
spent many hours discussing in detail and with great openness
their own sexual lives. Bryony wanted to work as much as
possible from the truth of the performers' experiences. So to be
attacked in this way was not simply an attack on the politics of the
show; they experienced it as an attack on themselves, personally.
There was probably no way the audience would have been able to
perceive this, because by the time it arrived on stage, the
experience had been turned into something other, more distant
from the performers' own lives by the process of making it into

art. Yet the show clearly hit some of the nerves it was meant to. One of the disrupters had been shouting, 'We talk about these things in our women's groups but we don't want it thrown at us from the stage.'

In *Floorshow* we had aimed at a kind of rough and tumble style, which confronted the audience directly. If they shouted at us, we could shout back at them. I remember at one point combing through joke books to memorise put-downs for hecklers. 'Oh here's one alcoholic who isn't anonymous.' *Time Gentlemen Please* was intended to be ironic and sophisticated, more of a theatre show than *Floorshow*, and had no space for any kind of audience participation built into it. Consequently, the performers were helpless when the heckling started. There was no mechanism in the structure of the show which would have enabled us to control the audience reaction.

Aside: there had been accusations that only the women were dressed glamorously. This was quite untrue. Clive wore a white tuxedo and looked so glamorous that at a performance to a weekend school for women shop stewards the audience reaction was uproarious to say the least.

And what did we do after the show, we supremely arrogant and disregarding actors? Well, we did the get-out of course. Back down the stairs and into the van. Then we went back to our extremely seedy digs and sat around on the floor in someone's room trying to work out what went wrong. I seem to remember sitting in the dark. Perhaps we were afraid that our fans had followed us. I remember being very cold and depressed, and when I finally got up to stumble off to my own room there was a click and my back went out – the end to a perfect day.

CHRIS BOWLER
Company Member, Performer,
Writer, Director, 1975 to the present.

A few days after the event, Beatrix Campbell, a great supporter of our work, wrote to the company:

'Dear Monstrous Regiment,
    This is a fan letter which I'm writing, having been

stunned to hear the news that people broke up your show
in Leeds the other night.

I'd at first assumed, clearly quite wrongly, that it was
some National Front or Festival of Light types, being
puritanical thugs, and was then stunned again to hear that it
was feminists who did it.

And that made me think a bit about why I'd so enjoyed
your show.

Now I'd like to tell you why I liked it, if it helps, because
you were probably shattered by the Leeds experience. The
first thing to say is that I've seen it a couple of times, with
largely feminist – lesbian and heterosexual – audiences who
loved it. Actually loved it. Why? Firstly I think because it is
very polished, very funny and very radical. And these days
you've got to go a long way to get that combination.

The second reason I think is because it takes sexual
politics back into a idiom which is *typical*, i.e. it takes it out
of the ghettos of men's culture, and it takes it out of the
feminist ghetto too, where too often we make massive and
inept assumptions about how the sexual contradictions are
lived among masses of people, and about how far we in the
Women's Movement have actually changed anything. I
don't think that's true of the mainstream of the WLM,
which is much more rooted in reality; I suppose I'd count
myself as part of that – and indeed I'd count the Monstrous
Regiment sisters as part of that Women's Liberation
mainstream as well.

So it was an enormous relief to have a feminist critique of
sexuality presented in a form that was a pleasure both to
self-conscious feminists, and to women who'd not identify
themselves in that way, but who nevertheless are fighting it
out.

Another important reason was that it was about
heterosexuality. By which I mean it made heterosexuality
problematic. The absence of a full homosexual dimension
is, I think, a problem.

I think homosexuality would have been incredibly
difficult to present in this show because for it to have been
problematic in an equivalent way to heterosexuality would
be extremely hard to get right; in other words it wouldn't
have been much cop to have nasty old heterosexuality
having its guts ripped out in *Time Gentlemen Please*, only to
have homosexuality immunised from criticism. I don't

think it would have been appropriate for a company like
you, however, to take on such a critique, not at this stage
anyway when gay politics and homosexuality in general in
this country is still relatively besieged, still a fragile flower.
If you'd had a confident gay caucus in the company then
that would have been different.

One of the problems with the show in my view is in fact
that the references to homosexuality are rather too bland
and sentimental. I'd rather have not had them, I think.
Much happier with the querying and parodying of
heterosexuality – this is the first show I've seen that dares to
take that on.'

I think Beatrix identified the collision correctly. In wanting to be
truthful about sex and sexual experience, the company felt it was
legitimate for them to deal only with what they knew personally.
As there were no lesbians or gay men in the company that
workshopped and performed *Time Gentlemen Please*, they decided
that it would be improper to speak of homosexuality on the stage.
What was intended as a subversion and explosion of
heterosexuality must have looked like celebration to lesbians and
gay men who were looking for affirmation and support in their
struggle against oppression. It also has to be said that when
people are angry, objectivity goes out of the window and the
angry groups in the audience were unable to see the intentional
irony of the show.

The issues highlighted by the events in Leeds reverberated in
the company for a long time. Towards the end of the tour we had
a painful meeting at which there was a clear difference of opinion
between those who were in the show and those who were not (of
whom I was one) as to what 'Leeds' meant in terms of the show
itself and the company in general. Because of what had happened,
and the emotions attached to the event, it was almost impossible
to have any objective discussion about it. Those who had been
there found that any criticism from other members of the
collective became tangled up with the emotion of the attack.
Looking back now, I think it is a measure of the company's
strength that we were able to agree (not without pain) to differ,
and that the incident didn't lead to a split or a 'putsch'.

In 1979 the company faced a major crisis, when certain
important links with the past were severed and it took a new
direction. At the beginning of the year we toured *Teendreams*, a
'retrospective look at ten years of the Women's Movement.' Susan
Todd and David Edgar wrote it and Kate Crutchley came in to

direct it. For the first time, we had no live music in a play. The idea was to use pop records as a means of tracing the passing of time over the ten years the play covered. Although we were happy with the piece, it didn't have quite the pzazz of previous work, and some of the critics thought it worthy but a bit dull. Perhaps we needed the cushion of live music to give us the bounce that the audiences had come to associate with the company's work.

We also had two projects in preparation. Caryl Churchill was commissioned to write another play. She was interested in seeing if there was any way of bringing together women from different historical periods and letting them talk to each other. In the minutes of our first discussion with her 'Dull Gret, Pope Joan, Pocahontas, a Japanese courtesan, Isabella Bird etc.' are mentioned. None of us had any idea how their meeting might be accomplished, but we hoped we might discover that in workshops. *Ms. Dante's Inferno* was floated as a possible title. When we came to do the workshops with Caryl we also introduced Florence Nightingale, Ruth Ellis (the last woman to be hanged in England) and Jane Anger (a possibly apocryphal contemporary of Shakespeare's who dressed as a man and went round fighting duels).

Then Susan Todd and David Bradford had conceived what we thought was the brilliant idea of following Caryl's play with a 'Season of Classic Plays'. We were getting very tired. Non-stop touring, crummy damp B & Bs, being away from home for weeks at a time were beginning to depress us. What about a season, in London, in which we would put on, deconstruct, three classics from the theatrical repertoire? It would mean we could stop touring for a few months while continuing to work. And as our ensemble was beginning to look a little ragged at the edges, it would mean we might be able to persuade actors who were interested in our work, but who wouldn't tour, or actors who had been part of the company but didn't want to tour any more, to join us on a temporary basis.

You called my bluff, backed me up. Much support, loving, chivvying all the way, but by the end I thought I'm too old to work in a rehearsal room where I can see my breath on a cold day.

PAOLA DIONISOTTI
Performer The Fourth Wall, *1983.*

We hired the theatre in the club attached to the Methodist Church in the Walworth Road, Elephant & Castle, and printed leaflets advertising '*Women Beware Women* by Thomas Middleton, *Phaedra* based on Robert Lowell's translation of Racine's *Phèdre* and Euripides' *Hippolytus*, and *The Man of Mode* by George Etherege.'

Then we made a disastrous foray into the grave labelled 'devised writing'. There is a gap in the minutes of the company meetings between March and September 1979, so there is no record of how or why we did it. A fit of communal lunacy probably. Caryl had hit a block. (The ideas she was working on eventually re-emerged in a different form in *Top Girls*.) But we had a tour booked, a schedule of gigs and no show. We had to come up with something fast. Of all the things we might have done, we abandoned all our principles about working with writers, and decided to adapt Anita Loos' novel *Gentlemen Prefer Blondes*. The idea itself was inspired. We were always looking to do the unexpected. This was certainly a candidate in that category. The notion of a feminist company adapting this particular novel struck us as highly amusing.

We were probably led astray by the success of *Scum*, forgetting that in that case, Claire and Chris had created a substantial basis of structure and narrative, a vision from which we worked. Here we were starting with a book. A very different proposition. The show was a glorious disaster. Real twenties beaded frocks, the Ritz Hotel Paris, the Statue of Liberty on roller skates. It had all the ingredients of an absurd farce, but it never worked. It was too long. It was incoherent. Too many people had a hand in writing it. We toured it during the summer, miserable, pretending that it was alright, but fraying tempers and a bad atmosphere in the van told us that it wasn't. That version of *Gentlemen Prefer Blondes* met its Waterloo at the Communist University Summer School in London University (where we had previously performed *Scum* to great acclaim) to an audience that not only didn't see the joke, but hated it. As the interminable torture of the evening dragged on for three bottom-numbing hours, (even after we thought we had cut half an hour out of it) and the only sound we could hear was the sound of people leaving, we realised it was the end of civilisation as we knew it. After the performance, a great friend and supporter of the company came into the dressing room and murmured 'Darlings . . . the curtain call . . . how brave . . . ' We knew it was curtains for us. Bad shows can have a disastrous effect on companies and this one was a stinker.

However bleakly funny it seems in retrospect, the show and particularly that performance was a watershed in that it provoked a major crisis which split the company and marked the end of the first phase of its life.

The great thing was, those early productions seemed to answer the hitherto unspoken needs of a large audience. It wasn't just the plays and their subject matter, it was also us – the women on stage. Everything seemed so very much in the present, nothing was reflective. The play and the costumes might be historical, but the electricity was now; *and the* now *was also us using the best of ourselves and our skills to map out a new place for women to be. We said it was centre stage, but there were occasions it felt more like the front line. We had no history, we only had a future.*

MARY MCCUSKER
Company Member, Performer, 1975 to the present.
Executive Director, 1990–1991.

The Second Stage: 1979–1989

Gentlemen Prefer Blondes (Mark Two)

The split centred on the issue of survival: had the company come to the end of its useful life? Did the disaster of *Gentlemen Prefer Blondes* mean we had nothing more to say? On one side the belief that the company should retire on its laurels and disband. On the other, the belief that to stop now would leave us all with a very bitter taste in the mouth. There's more to life than one rotten show. Besides, we had a thousand three-colour posters we had to do something with.

Rather shakily, we began to put ourselves back together. We weren't certain whether we could resurrect ourselves without the ones who had left. In particular, we weren't sure how we would manage without Susan Todd whose intellect and passion had been a guiding force in the first years. Bryony Lavery rescued us by going back to the novel and starting all over again. She had the idea of making the show a dialogue between 'then' and 'now'. It wasn't so much an adaptation of the book as a series of comic variations with music.

We went through a lengthy process of interviewing performers to join the company. We still identified ourselves as a functioning collective, and we weren't interested in actors who would come in and perform in one show. It was join up for fifty-two weeks a year or nothing.

Gentlemen Prefer Blondes Mark Two turned out to be one of the most popular shows we ever produced. We toured it through the autumn and into the following spring. Audiences loved it. When we performed for a week at the Citizens Theatre in Glasgow they had to open the gallery, so many people turned up. They may have been suckered into thinking they were getting some sort of version of Marilyn Monroe and Jane Russell, but once we started, who cared about those two dames?

Stylistically it was a new departure for us, which may explain why we made such a mess of it before when we'd tried to do it without a writer. Previously, the theatre shows had taken on serious themes in a sober style. The comic side of our work was expressed through the cabarets. Now we were trying to bring the two together.

The Season of Classic plays was abandoned, partly because all our energy had to be spent on getting the company up and running again, partly because it felt wrong to put on work which had been the brainchild of Susan who was no longer part of the company.

Ironically, although *Gentlemen Prefer Blondes* Mark Two was a great success, we were left at the end of the tour feeling completely demoralised. Some of this was plain exhaustion. To balance the books we'd had to tour it for longer than we really wanted to. (Mark One had spent a lot of money and made very little income.) We wore it and ourselves into the ground. Some of the depression came from sheer misery and grief. Angela Hopkins, the director of Mark Two, was killed in a car crash on her way to the show part way through the tour. We had to try and process the painful feelings surrounding that tragedy while we continued to tour. At the end of the run we decided to take three months off; to give ourselves the space to assess our situation and plan the future.

We began to think of how insular the English theatre can be, how little we knew about the sexual politics of other countries, other cultures. We also had nothing 'on the stocks'. The work we had to put into resurrecting *Gentlemen Prefer Blondes* and then its ferocious touring schedule had left us with no time to think about commissioning new shows. So we found three already existing plays and came up with the idea of making them into a 'foreign season'. A play from France, *Shakespeare's Sister*, written and originally performed by the Théâtre de l'Aquarium in Paris, *Dialogue Between a Prostitute and One of Her Clients* by the Italian writer Dacia Maraini, and *Mourning Pictures* by Honor Moore the American poet. I translated both of the foreign language plays. It meant we kept a measure of control over the work, and saved us money in that we didn't have to pay a commissioning fee or royalties as I was already on the payroll. The whole season was planned to fulfil a number of different needs, stylistic and practical.

Shakespeare's Sister was really a series of extraordinary visual images rather than a play. What text there was had been adapted from tape recordings of the voices of bored, trapped housewives the Théâtre de l'Aquarium had interviewed when they were putting the piece together. We had no experience of this kind of visual theatre, and realised we needed some expert help, so we asked Hilary Westlake, founder of Lumière and Son, to come and direct it for us. The show was not intended to tour because we wanted the freedom of designing a show that didn't have to fit into the back of a small truck. We were beginning to look for ways of getting off the rehearse/tour, rehearse/tour treadmill. We performed it for three weeks in December 1980 at the ICA.

―――――――

Gemma Jackson had costumed Gillian Hanna, Mary McCusker, Chris Bowler and Josefina Cupido in white bridal gowns with all the attendant paraphernalia of veils, headdresses, ribbons and bouquets. Just seeing these women wearing these outfits, gracefully gliding in an almost airborne fashion across Gemma's Ideal Homes (Fringe Budget) kitchen floor was memorable enough.

Hilary Westlake directed, peppering the evening with numerous bits of ironic business. At one point, shortly after Gillian successfully managed to make operational the very useful wedding gift of a brand-new stove (actually a cleaned up second-hand one), a maroon was detonated as if the stove containing the newly weds' first dinner had exploded. The maroon also ignited some grease left-over from the days before the stove made its theatrical début causing an unexpected and undirected but nonetheless impressive column of smoke and flame to belch forth from the cooker.

Completely un-fazed the four actresses gracefully glided in their stylized fashion to various corners of the theatre in search of fire-fighting equipment. McCusker swanned up the centre aisle to receive a fire extinguisher (in much the same way I imagine she would accept an Oscar) from Simon, the ready theatre technician, and elegantly returned to the set where she promptly doused the up-staging mini-conflagration out of existence.

This got a healthy round of applause and featured, if I recall properly, in more than one of the reviews the following day. It was so well choreographed that audience and critics alike thought it part of the play.

STEVE WHITSON
Lighting Designer, Shakespeare's Sister, *1980.*

———————

Mourning Pictures, written in free verse, was the autobiographical story of a writer's relationship with her mother who is dying of cancer. It was directed by Penny Cherns. This was the first play we ever produced in which we made absolutely no contribution to the text. In other respects *Mourning Pictures* fitted into our usual pattern of work. It brought back live music into the company, and we toured it like any other of our previous shows. Later in the year it was recorded for BBC Radio 4, and was broadcast as The Monday Play.

Dialogue Between a Prostitute and One of Her Clients, directed by Ann Mitchell, was a two-hander, the smallest show we had done so far. We wanted to have something flexible that would tour, but not in the usual way. It could be done in small or non-theatrical spaces.

Dialogue had caused sensation and riots in Italy. What attracted us was the author's direction that at certain places during the performance the actors had to stop, step out of their characters and engage the audience in a discussion of the ideas being brought up in the play. We wanted to know if we could get an English audience to let go of its inhibitions and talk in public about sex. We tested the proposition all through rehearsals, inviting all kinds of people, including working prostitutes, to come in and 'rehearse' being the audience. *Dialogue* was the first of our shows to tour abroad. We took it to Holland later that year.

———————

'What are men really looking for when they go to a prostitute?' the actress asks. Then suddenly, after only 15 minutes of performance, the show is stopped for the first of three inter-performance discussions with the audience. My immediate reaction was 'God, that's naff', swiftly followed by a feeling of having been ripped-off . . . fancy paying £1.50 in order to have a talk. In fact, the discussion turned out to be quite extraordinary, a genuinely integral part of the theatre experience. The intimacy and honesty of people's revelations about themselves and their sexuality astonished, intrigued and at times shocked me. To describe the show as 'thought-provoking' would sound like a Victorian understatement.

EILEEN FAIRWEATHER
Spare Rib, *November 1980.*

This season of work pushed us in interesting directions. None of them really said anything radically new about the condition of women in the world. We were often accused of being old fashioned and simplistic in what the plays *said* about sexual politics. That missed the point. We were a theatre company developing our craft. We were a 'political' company, yes, but theatre was our passion. Now that we had moved beyond the first flush of excitement and energy, we wanted to push artistic boundaries. Change or atrophy. We were trying to explore theatrical languages we were unfamiliar with: Visual language in *Shakespeare's Sister*, poetic language in *Mourning Pictures* and the relationship with the audience in *Dialogue*.

Chilly moments; taking my clothes off in Dialogue; *the Monsters' only male nude? It was all very sensitive of course, very tasteful. That show had discussions with the audience, and one audience, of right-on drama students, completely slagged us off from beginning to end. Our politics were garbage. A couple of them came up to me afterwards and said 'You've got a nice body though . . . Want a hand with the get-out?'*

Same show; in York the stage was invaded by irate public schoolboys. 'It seems very strange to us that everyone in this audience tonight who's spoken about sexual politics looks very like people who used to work for Monstrous Regiment.' Outrage and pandemonium from members of the audience who'd never seen us before. Exit public schoolboys.

> *Exit also, rather suddenly and surprisingly (for him), a drunk who insisted on sitting in on a women-only gig (same show) we did in Bristol.*

JOHN SLADE
Company Member, Performer, 1979-1982.

———————

The three plays taken together made a coherent whole; an attempt on our part to break new ground through an exploration of style. In retrospect, it seems to be significant that the discussion and analysis of sexual politics was taking a small step into the background. We were looking not so much at what we were doing, as how we were doing it.

1981 was too soon for any of us to have really begun to think through the implications of Margaret Thatcher's being in power. We knew she was no feminist or advocate of women's rights. But we had no sense of what was to hit us in the 1980s. If we thought about it at all, it was in materialist terms: we could see the attacks on women's economic interests as welfare cuts were implemented, we worried about cuts in arts funding. What we didn't see at that point was the spiritual gloom descending on us, as the very act of thinking about politics came to be seen as undesirable. We had always seen ourselves as riding on the crest of the wave of feminism. It buoyed us up, gave us strength and ideas and energy. We were part of the Movement. We were the Movement. We didn't foresee what would happen when apathy and paralysis overtook both the left and the Women's Movement under the onslaught of Thatcherism.

In 1981 we didn't see anything sinister in our desire to explore other theatrical styles. We didn't in any way identify it as having anything to do with a retreat from our feminist roots. And in one sense, of course it wasn't. We still wanted to ask tough questions about women's role in society. We couldn't know that this was going to become harder and harder to do in the context of a prevailing ideology trying to abolish the very idea of 'society'. It is no coincidence that the theatre groups that 'failed' in the 1980s were the political ones; and that the successful new companies were the ones that abandoned any attempt to analyse or question the world in which they moved in favour of explorations of style.

The season of foreign plays saw another change in the company's practice. Up to this point, it was always the assumption that, as a collective of performers, everyone was in every play. There had been exceptions, of course, when someone felt tired and needed a break, or when members went off and did something else and then came back. It meant that when other actors came to work with us, they either 'joined up', or there were so many 'core' company members in the show that the relationships were relatively easy to negotiate.

Now, however, we started to think that we didn't all want to be in every play. It was another reaction to the touring treadmill. In practice this meant that it was now possible for full members of the company to be outnumbered on the road by performers who were not permanent members. What we hadn't yet begun to grasp was the implications of this situation. Having identified ourselves for so long as members of a collective, we had great difficulty in seeing ourselves as employers.

So when we toured Rose Tremain's *Yoga Class*, Chris Bowler and John Slade found themselves in a minority, and uncertain how to deal with that. The rest of us weren't much help. We hadn't even begun to formulate a structure to deal with this new situation. The essence of the problem was that the non-company members didn't know who was 'in charge'. Was it the director, as it would be in a conventional theatrical situation, or was it the two members of the collective? Nobody, not even Chris and John, was sure. The associations of that word 'employer' were so distasteful we failed to observe that it was possible to employ someone without exploiting them. In practice it often meant that we unwittingly refused to take responsibility where we should have done, and it was sometimes the (unidentified) source of tension between us and those who came to work with us.

We had been looking for new writers to work with, knowing that we wanted to get back to an engagement with the ideas of feminism. *Yoga Class* was one of a series of commissions we made at the beginning of the 1980s with this in mind. It was beautifully written and toured quite successfully, but it was somehow unsatisfactory. By placing the characters in the confining space of a yoga class we domesticated them in a way that was foreign to the nature of the company's work. We had always identified ourselves as dealing with 'big' issues: Women's lives, women's concerns, women's demands. In our work we aimed to be woman-identified, but we always strove to locate ourselves and the women we portrayed in a highly visible setting. We didn't want to be pushed and parcelled into the ghetto labelled 'women's work'.

We rehearsed at Elder Street, their then headquarters in the City. It was an amazing Dickensian-type warehouse building, with winding stairs, dusty corners and plenty of space for rehearsal. I used to walk to Spitalfields Market during my lunch break and with other bag ladies, help myself to perishable goods discarded by the greengrocers. I called them street vegetables. I was introduced to Yoga, which I have enjoyed ever since. I had to open the play standing on my head and when I told Chris I had never done it in my life she just smiled and said, 'You've got five weeks' rehearsal.' I mastered the skill and count it as a great achievement.

JOANNA FIELD
Performer Yoga Class, *1981,* Island Life, *1988.*

———————————

It was a tricky course to walk and took some balancing. We never equated the domestic, the female with 'second rate'. When we spoke with admiration of the 'epic', we saw the dangers of the subtext: 'male therefore admirable'. Experiencing our energy as having been bottled up and thwarted for too long, our vision encompassed the whole world. At the same time we recognised that the domestic arena is where many women spend their lives and we felt that 'reclaiming' the domestic should be part of our agenda. Just as in our organisational practice we tried to include women traditionally left out by incorporating child care into our budgets, so we wanted to break the patriarchal view that regards women's domestic lives as trivial and unimportant.

This conflict between confinement to the small and small scale and the desire to act on a wider stage was reflected in much of the company's work in the 1980s, and coincided with, or perhaps was triggered by, the shrinkage of funding in that same period. Having found our 'voice' in the 1970s and early 1980s, we had to struggle to find it again, or find a new voice later on against a background of cuts in the real value of our grant.

The cloudy relationship between form and content embodied that struggle. Our instinct was never to trust naturalism. While resenting the use of the words 'televisual' or 'soap opera' to describe women's writing (what male critics defined as soap opera we thought of as fractured and episodic, reflecting the nature of women's lives), we always wanted to escape the stifling effect of the naturalistic. Music was the clearest instrument for breaking it up. By the time we produced *Yoga Class* we no longer had actors who were also musicians in the company, and inflation meant we couldn't afford to have a band. There was music in the play but not enough to push it out of its naturalistic mode.

When we commissioned a play from Melissa Murray, and she proposed to write about the revolutionaries who assassinated Tsar Alexander II, we fell on it as if it were cool water in a desert. We saw it as a return to our roots. *The Execution*, a vast historical panorama in which women were seen to be making and shaping history. These were the women who took advantage of the first wave of liberalism in Russia, went abroad (mostly to Switzerland) to get an education and then returned home to try and destroy the corrupt system personified by the great patriarch, Alexander.

We were betting our bottom dollar on the show being a huge success. Our intention was to tour it in England and then take it abroad. We had been in contact with an Australian arts festival who were making encouraging noises. After the success of *Dialogue* in Holland, Europe looked also enticing. More encouraging noises there. It was a chance, too, to revitalise and enlarge the collective. We were hoping that the new company we assembled would become the collective that would work together on subsequent projects. We were in expansive mood, out to conquer the world again.

When disaster strikes, you wonder afterwards why you never saw it coming. Our grand touring plans began to unravel before the play opened, an ominous sign, as we had been budgeting for a substantial income from that source, and we were already committing large amounts of money to the production. Then we began to nudge up against problems with the production itself. *The Execution* was too long, three acts, but it had patches of real brilliance. Melissa had written in a heightened, 'nineteenth century' style, trying to reflect the characters' era in the way they spoke. No naturalism there. We wanted music, and Sue Dunderdale, the director, wanted it to be grand and sweeping, so we commissioned Lindsay Cooper to write a taped score that would accompany the text.

Rehearsals were hard work but exciting and although we had nagging worries about the length of the evening, we never seriously doubted that it would work. As soon as we got in front of an audience, we began to fall apart. Of course, there were a few discriminating souls who enjoyed the play, but by and large audiences didn't. We got to the point where we would peer at the audience in the second interval to see how many we'd managed to keep for the third act. Perhaps we had never found the right style of acting that would have made it work. We were certainly never able to cut it to a manageable length.

After three weeks in London and a short tour (originally intended to be the first leg of a year's travelling with it) the whole company collapsed in exhaustion, misery and recriminations. This was the second major crisis in the company's life, and again it provoked a period of reassessment and a change of direction.

The story of 'the company' is stamped with the personalities of those involved. Without them it is just a name. The choices made came from those people wrestling with their differences and coping with their weaknesses – and eventually agreeing, believing, and achieving. And much of what the histories and analyses of the company attribute to political judgment and artistic intention in fact owed more to good reflexes, theatrical sense and sheer necessity.

I find it impossible to chart some ordered passage through those memories of meetings and productions that make up the tangible history of the company. It sometimes appears to be more like a piece of patchwork than a finished garment, a series of stepping stones as opposed to a well laid-out road. I do remember the people, the emotions and the traumas; and the talent, dedication and singlemindedness that were invested in every aspect of the company's work.

MARY MCCUSKER
Company Member, Performer, 1975 to the present,
Executive Director, 1990–1991.

The Third Stage. Learning to be a Management, 1982–1991

The sense of failure and demoralisation was so acute, it was impossible to think of working on another show. In the meantime the company couldn't be allowed to fold. If the company is going to go under, we said to each other, we want it to be on our own terms, and not because we've made a mess of something.

We had a couple of commitments to fulfil. We revived *Shakespeare's Sister* for a third excursion, with a cast that was part company members and part employed performers. The conditions in which we had to work (including a dress rehearsal at three in the morning because the venue where we were performing at the Edinburgh Festival was in a state of chaos and

couldn't cope with the needs of all the groups they had booked)
did nothing to help the morale.

Providentially, Penny Cherns, who had directed *Mourning
Pictures*, and Paola Dionisotti, approached us with the idea of
doing an evening of Franca Rame and Dario Fo's one-woman
plays. We offered to produce it and I translated the text from the
Italian. It had to be done on a shoestring since we had invested
so much in *The Execution* that we hardly had any money left over
for the rest of the financial year.

The Fourth Wall toured in the spring of 1983 and fulfilled all the
criteria of the best Monstrous Regiment shows. It tackled sexual
politics head-on; the two pieces about the women of the Baader-
Meinhof gang dealt with terrorism and the state; the other two
with women's sexuality. Musically, it was extraordinary, in that
Paola performed the pieces with Maggie Nichols, who sang
unaccompanied in counterpoint to the text. Because the music
was improvised (within strict limits worked out in rehearsal) no
two performances were ever the same. It was one of our best
shows.

The breathing space that *The Fourth Wall* gave us enabled us to
take time to analyse our position. We tried to face up to the
causes of our failures and came to some difficult decisions.

Numerically we were reduced to five women. Three
performers, our lighting designer/technician Ronnie Wood and
our administrator, Diane Robson. John Slade who had joined the
company for *Gentlemen Prefer Blondes* Mark Two wanted to stop
touring completely. The rest of the cast of *The Execution* who might
have formed the basis of a renewed collective clearly wouldn't
want to be caught talking to us at a bus stop. Reluctantly we were
forced to admit that the full time collective was a dead duck. We
also had to face the fact that financially it had become impossible
to maintain. With inflation eroding the value of our Arts Council
Revenue grant almost month by month, we simply couldn't afford
to pay eight or nine people for fifty-two weeks a year any more.
Actually, we could only afford to pay one person for fifty-two
weeks a year. Administrator excepted, we had all come off the
payroll after *The Execution*. We would never again go back on it on
a permanent basis. From this point on, apart from the
administrator, we were all paid like any other performer or
technician the company employed: when we were in a show we
were paid the company wage. When we weren't, we worked
elsewhere. All the administrative and managerial work we did
from this point on we did unpaid, apart from basic expenses.

Perhaps this is as a good place as any to make a short digression on the role our administrators have played in the company's life. When I talk about 'we', I mean 'we the company', and that included Sue Beardon, our first full-time administrator and then Gus Garside who took over from her. Until this point in the company's life, when the full-time collective became impossible to maintain, it was hard to differentiate between company members. We were simply The Monstrous Regiment. We had different jobs, of course. Performers performed and administrators administrated. But we tried to break down the barriers set up by the traditional hierarchy of skills. We had a system of 'committees', including a finance committee to assist the administrator. We recognised that running a company is a skilled operation, and some people are better at, or are trained to do, some jobs rather than others. That was why, for example, we happily asked Gus to join us: he was the only candidate with the relevant professional qualifications. The contribution that both Sue and Gus made to the company's life went far beyond the usual administrative function. They were an integral part of all decisions, both administrative and artistic. When the company faced the fact that it could no longer operate as a full-time collective, the role of the administrator changed dramatically, and during the 1980s our administrators had to deal with a wholly different relationship to the company.

Joining the Company in 1983 as a young (!) administrator was a major turning point for me, bringing in to sharp relief my career, my love of the theatre, my politics and my life and moulding all four together.

The original collective had fragmented by this point (as much for financial reasons as any other) and almost every remaining member had begun pursuing individual careers outside of the Regiment again. This, of course, meant that attention and creative energy were not necessarily focused on Monstrous Regiment and I rapidly learnt the joys and horrors of the collective way of working.

The administration continued to be the last bastion in which the collective spirit was also translated into collective practice. All of the group would do a 'stint' in the office – some kind of ancient penance for actors whose first love belonged in front of the footlights and not in

front of the typewriter – although everyone did the latter with good
grace!

SANDY BAILEY
Administrator, 1983–1988.

———————

If we weren't a collective any more, what were we? Slowly,
painfully, we accepted the fact that we were now a management.
But to reflect the fact that we still had no Company Director or
Artistic Director, we called ourselves a collective management.

We also had to face the fact that although we all wanted to
continue to be part of Monstrous Regiment, we had differing
needs in relation to the company. Mary and I still wanted the
freedom to initiate shows, but basically we were performers,
actors, and that's what we wanted to do. Chris, on the other
hand, was losing interest in performing and wanted to write and
direct. Without ever really putting it into words, we recognised
that we were going in different directions and we tried to make
room for that in the work.

In the period 1983-1985, Mary and I performed in two shows
written by Bryony Lavery and directed by Nona Shepphard:
Calamity, a three-woman wagon train across the mythical history of
the Wild West (Jane Cox joined us to play Quiet Kate) and *Origin
of the Species – a Love Story*, in which Mollie Starkey, famous
archaeologist and raconteuse digs up her five-million-year-old
ancestor, Victoria. *Calamity* reintroduced live music and was
invited to play at the Women's Theatre Festival in Rome.

The name Bryony Lavery crops up often in the history of the
company. Of all the writers we've worked with she's the one with
whom we've had the longest relationship. Not only has she
written three plays and a cabaret and a half for us, she has also
run writers' workshops and organised readings. She has got us out
of a lot of scrapes when we were in trouble of one sort or
another, and we've had many of our best times with her.

Calamity also introduced Nona Shepphard to the company. She
rescued us by agreeing to direct the show at the last minute, and
has worked with us regularly ever since. Another woman who has
got us out of some tight corners.

———————

The blessing of being able to use the collective to my advantage. A
sure way out of an awkward telephone situation would be to suggest
I had to consult The Collective (always capital letters at this point). I
would hang up; ruminate by myself for a few minutes and then call

back delivering the verdict that 'The Collective had decided that . . .' A skill I continue to use, in one way or another, still!

SANDY BAILEY
Administrator, 1983–1988.

Origin of the Species marked a new phase in the company's work in that it was our first co-production with a mainstream theatre. We produced it with the Birmingham Repertory Theatre. As we continued to struggle for our financial existence during the 1980s, co-productions with larger institutions became a lifeline in the maintenance of our artistic standards. They gave us access to resources and facilities (workshops, wardrobe departments) beyond our own means. However, small entities taken under the wing of large institutions are in danger of being swallowed whole, and we felt we were constantly juggling our economic needs against our desire to work on our own terms.

During the same period, Chris pursued her interest in visual theatre, taking up a thread we had begun to explore in *Shakespeare's Sister*, by devising and directing *Enslaved By Dreams* (1984) celebrating the life of Florence Nightingale and *Point of Convergence* (1986), set in an indeterminate time and place, exploring the clash between two very different groups of young women. This show was originally produced with the Cockpit Theatre, and had six professional performers and fifteen unemployed women aged between fifteen and twenty-five in it. The show was rewritten for a subsequent tour so that it could be performed without the fifteen young women.

Two other fundamental changes in our working practices emerged at this period. Firstly, and most importantly, we became an all-women group. We're often asked about this, and how we came to the decision not to work with men. In fact, we never actually sat in a meeting and made a decision. The shift from a mixed group to an all-woman's group was more of a process than a decision. It evolved over a period of time.

All the men who had been in the collective left after *The Execution*. We had been forced to give up our collective identity and there was no reason at that point to expand the collective management. Thinking about the shows, we realised that we had never worked in an all-women, as opposed to women-dominated, environment and we wanted to explore that. We found that it gave us a different kind of freedom to anything we had experienced before and we enjoyed it.

Did I change? Would I have changed anyway? When it comes to it, was I really just there to represent the patriarchy? Or was there more to it than that? One thing is dead certain; it made my life more difficult.

Did it make my life richer? I think I know the answer to that question; I hope when I'm old I'll know I know the answer.

JOHN SLADE
Company Member, Performer,
1979–1982.

We discovered that we had often given too much energy trying to prevent the men from feeling like 'token' men (as we had been made to feel like token women in other companies). Often we had, in fact, fallen into the old trap of mothering them and this had prevented us from fully exploring our relationships between each other as women. We were aware of the problem, as the minutes of our meetings reveal, but we were unable to resolve it. Issues of power, control, guilt, unresolved problems with the mother/daughter relationship, were never adequately recognised or sorted out. Would we have been able to manage the company better through its first seven years of life if we had been able to explore the conflicts between the women? Our joy at the discovery of the power of sisterhood masked the very real differences (political and aesthetic) we had. When the depth of those differences started to appear they frightened us and the presence of men in the group probably inhibited us when trying to deal with them. We had no mechanism for exploring conflict which excluded certain members of the group (the men). There are issues and conflicts which women simply do not want to air in the presence of men. At one point, for example, we sought the assistance of the Women's Therapy Centre who helped us sort through some of the group dynamics that were causing difficulties, but even there, we worked as a whole group, and I don't think we ever managed really to reach a deeper understanding of the specifically 'female' sources of the conflicts between women. I think it was the first (perhaps the only?) time the Women's Therapy Centre had had men coming through their doors.

It's possible that some of what prevented us from dealing with, or in some instances even acknowledging the existence of, those conflicts came from the need for us to see ourselves as 'superwoman' in front of the men. To openly admit to jealousy and rivalry would somehow have been a betrayal of sisterly solidarity. As someone said in another context, we talk about those things in our women's groups.

———————

As a very long-haired composer, musical director, musician, actress and reluctant set lifter, I enthusiastically carried the Regiment's banner up and down the motorways of the land. People were often wary of our name. Would we be monsters, harridans, devourers of men; well no, actually I think that we were very nice, too nice perhaps. At that time there were usually two male actors in the company and they were treated with an abundance of respect and fairness, one might almost say that they were spoiled. Despite the great physical strength of these fellows, when we did 'get-ins' they would always be ironing or sewing whilst the foolish women would fight for the privilege of carrying two tons of wooden set up three flights of stairs.

HELEN GLAVIN
Performer, Composer, Musician,
1975–1978.

———————

Gradually, over a period of time, at the beginning of the 1980s we came to the conclusion that we would be a women-directed company performing plays with all women casts except when the play absolutely required male characters, in which case we would employ male actors.

Secondly we came to the conclusion that from now on, we the performers would not have an automatic right to be in all productions. We were coming into the ambit of more conventional theatre rules, which meant for example, that we would have to cast plays taking the age of the characters into account. We would also have to be sensitive to the fact that guest directors might think Mary or I, the only performers remaining in the collective, weren't suited to a part even if we wanted to do it.

This issue surfaced several times between 1986 and 1988: Susan Todd came back to work with us and direct *My Song is Free* (1986) which both Mary and I had wanted to be in. But in the end we decided with Sue that we weren't right for the parts. And in *Waving* (1988) a co-production with the Sheffield Crucible Theatre, which Carol Bunyan had actually written with Mary and me in mind, we reluctantly had to concede that the play would work better cast with performers who really were the same age as the characters.

Mary had been in *Alarms* (1986), a play wc commissioned from the American writer Susan Yankowitz which dealt with the post-Chernobyl landscape. This one did have male characters in it. In addition to touring England, we were invited to the Boston Women's Theatre Festival in the United States where it was a great success.

Taking our production of Alarms *to the USA, where we were participating in the Boston Women in Theatre Festival, 1987, was an exhilarating experience. I had never attended such a festival before – a broad mixture of women performers playing to predominantly female audiences, which were hugely rumbustious and enthusiastic in their response to most of the work on offer. Our play was written by the American poet/playwright/novelist, Susan Yankowitz, and I felt that it was really only in the USA that the humour and particularly American voice of the play was communicated and understood – this despite the fact that we were performing* Alarms *in British accents. My abiding memory of the festival was the hunger of its audiences – woman who were there in force on a small but rich harvest which bore the fruit of their own experiences. We were given the most warm reception by our American hosts and audiences, who seemed to respect* Monstrous Regiment *as something close to a grandmother of women's theatre from over the Atlantic.*

GERDA STEVENSON
Performer, Alarms, *1986–1987.*

Both Wendy Kesselman's *My Sister in This House* (produced 1987) and Jenny McLeod's *Island Life* (1988) were plays with which we were closely involved as producers but which had no actual members of Monstrous Regiment performing in them.

During the 1980s the company was in a constant state of balance/friction in our dealings with the writers we commissioned. We were often uncertain ourselves about how to deal with the changing world around us. This blurring of our own certainties coupled with a desire not to trample on the writers' creative process I think meant we often didn't give them a clear enough sense of what the company's philosophy and ideas were. So when we approached writers we were interested in, we usually simply asked them to write about what they wanted to write about. A radical change from the days when we breathed down the writers' necks for months on end. In the argument about whether a play is a feminist play just because it is written by a woman and speaks of woman's experience, we were taking the side that said 'yes'. It was a change that we were only partially conscious of. In the absence of a clear picture of where the Women's Movement was going, we were as confused as everyone else as to what the plays we were performing should be saying. Our feeling was that if we couldn't point with any certainty to the way forward, then we had simply to support and encourage women writers. Keeping women's work in the public eye is no easy task in itself.

In the mid to late 1980s we were trying to reflect the changing world as we were experiencing it. Nothing new there. But we were experiencing it as painfully hard. As I've already mentioned, politically it was a nightmare, and feminism, in retreat like the left, was having to do some pretty fast footwork just to stay in the same place. Writers, of course, were no more immune from the feeling of confusion than we were. So the writing of the period reflects the withdrawal from the arena of public struggle. The dilemma for a company such as ours is how to balance the desire to take on the whole world against a desire to rescue the domestic lives of women from the dustbin marked 'trivial, unimportant'.

One of the issues we were becoming concerned with was the question of growing older. We noticed that opportunities for women performers get very thin on the ground after the age of forty or so, and we began to think that one of our concerns should be consciously to produce work about and for women of our own generation. The shift in emphasis can be seen in the change from *My Song is Free* and *Alarms*, both produced in 1986, one about women in detention in Pinochet's Chile, and the other tackling the destruction of the environment, to the plays we produced in the following two years which dealt with more personal, individual concerns.

We had been looking for an already existing script. In the changing economic climate, theatres were beginning to want to read the script of a show before they would book it. The birth process of a new play doesn't always conform to the strict timetable required by administrators and bookers, and we wanted to have a script we could let people read while we developed our commissions.

My Sister in This House had been performed several times in America by the time someone sent us the script. We couldn't understand why it had never been seen in this country. It is an extraordinary piece of drama: dense, claustrophobic, creating, second by second, the tiny mind-numbingly boring details of a suffocating provincial society. The play is based on an actual event that took place in France. The same actual event that Jean Genet used as the springboard for *The Maids*.

My Sister in This House was co-produced with the Leicester Haymarket Theatre, did a short tour and then played at the Hampstead Theatre. It provided us with a wonderful example of the pitfalls waiting for small scale alternative companies when they get involved with mainstream organisations. One of the reasons we had picked this particular play was we knew that it was a tried and tested piece of theatre. It was the most mainstream play we had done for a while, and we wanted to use it as a means of putting the name Monstrous Regiment back in the public eye. We achieved much of what we set out to do. Nancy Meckler directed a stunning production which had excellent reviews. However, we didn't manage to get the name of the company onto the London poster in large enough print, with the result that everyone thought that it was a Hampstead Theatre production, the critics referred to it as such, and we were rendered totally invisible.

'In the Spring of 1986 we rehearsed Wendy Kesselman's play My Sister in This House. *Set during the thirties in a provincial French city, the play took its story from real life events. Two sisters, live-in servants since their adolescence, brutally murdered and severely mutilated their mistress and her daughter after serving them faithfully and devotedly for seven years. Within the confines of a rigidly bourgeois social framework, Wendy's play examined the minutiae of these four women's lives. Amazingly Madame and Isabelle Danzard manage to conduct their lives virtually without speaking to the two girls who serve their every need.*

The rehearsal process became a fascinating journey for us all. Susanna Hamilton and Maggie O'Neill, playing the sisters Christine and Lea, were sent out to spend a day with professional cleaners (who turned out to be sisters!). Each morning while Maggie Steed, Tilly Vosburgh and myself had coffee, Susanna and Maggie scrubbed and cleaned the rehearsal room. Countless improvisations inspired by clues in the text and an extended interview with a psychiatrist made it possible to create a palpable history and milieu for each of the four women. What were the circumstances of life and character that could push these shy, gentle, loyal women to perform acts of such extreme violence? The more questions we asked, the more aware we became of the passionate nature of each of the four women, and their inherent sense of loneliness. We saw how their needs, when thwarted or unfulfilled, could manifest themselves in a desperate, possessive kind of loving. It was then we began to glimpse how the final tragic events in the play could have come to pass.'

NANCY MECKLER
Director, My Sister in This House, *1986.*

In 1988 we produced *Waving* by Carol Bunyan and *Island Life* by Jenny McLeod. *Waving* reflected our interest in the process of growing older, the characters being around fifty. As one of them remarks, 'Well, Joan Collins is fifty, but not the same sort of fifty'.

We knew of Jenny McLeod through her prize-winning play *Cricket at Camp David*. She was then in her very early twenties and the quality of her writing was so impressive that we asked her to write a new play for us. We had been thinking about working from both ends of the spectrum as it were, reflecting the concern of our own (mid-forties) generation, and at the same time looking for younger women authors, of a different generation, to see what they were thinking about.

We were amazed to find that what Jenny most wanted to do was to write a play about old ladies. The process by which the play was produced was relatively conventional. Once we had agreed on the subject with her, she went away and wrote it. Thereafter Jane Collins, the director, worked closely with Jenny on subsequent drafts and rewrites.

Island Life, set in the wilderness of an old people's home, spends a weekend with Emmy, Sophia and Vera as they go about setting up an experiment to recreate or visit the (non-existent?) past. Their ritualised relationship is shattered by the intrusion of Kate, an accidental tourist in their fantasy life. The resulting mayhem as 'truth' clashes with 'illusion' is both comic and heart rending. *Island Life* is certainly no naturalistic examination of the problems of old age. More, it is a kind of metaphysical meditation on the nature of truth and illusion. But it isn't didactic either. The characters are drawn in exuberant detail, and the language of the play is rich in the vocabulary and history of each of the women.

The play was a co-production with the Nottingham Playhouse,

first performed in a new studio space the theatre was opening. It made for appalling working conditions for the performers and the director, not to mention the set designer, Iona McLeish, trying to open a new (and difficult) play against a background of last minute furious building work. Later in the year, the production did a short tour and played in London with two changes in the cast.

A Common Woman (originally produced by the Sheffield Crucible Theatre), an evening of three short plays by Franca Rame and Dario Fo and *Beatrice* by Ian Brown, two one-woman shows we produced in 1989, brought Mary and me back into performing with the company (*A Common Woman* won a 1989 Time Out/01-for London Award) and at the beginning of 1990 we produced *Love Story of the Century*.

Love Story of the Century is a long autobiographical poem by Märta Tikkanen whose husband, a celebrated Finnish writer, was an alcoholic. The poem describes, sometimes in harrowing detail, the story of their life together, from the day they fell in love-at-first-sight, through their marriage, as he, always a heavy drinker, gradually descends into a pit of alcohol and destroys their relationship.

What is remarkable about the poem is its almost clinical recording of every nuance of feeling they went through: passionate love to loathing and every emotion in between. Nor does the author spare herself. Although alcoholism is plainly held responsible for the chaos of their lives, she acknowledges and charts her own unconscious participation in the mayhem.

Once we read the poem, we were shocked at our own insularity in never having even heard of it. It had originally been published in 1978, and since then had been dramatised and performed all over Europe (more than twenty productions in ten years.) There was, as far as we knew, no one theatrical version. We knew that it was sometimes performed as a one-woman show; we also found out that a production in Sweden had used three women and a man. We asked Clare Venables (who directed *Beatrice* and is skilled at cutting and shaping a text in rehearsal) to direct a dramatised version of the poem. She said she would, but only if we commissioned an adaptation first. She didn't want to cut and shape this one in rehearsal. In the event, her commitments elsewhere meant that she couldn't be with us during the rehearsal period, so we asked her to do the adaptation. Debbie Shewell directed it.

In deciding to construct a play with two performers we were wanting to explore the idea of the woman as divided self. She often knows what she 'ought' to do but cannot. In the later years of the marriage she is constantly at war with herself: should she leave him or not? Is she capable of leaving him? The poem is not as simplistic as this, however, and when we were working on it in rehearsal we found the division of text between the two voices didn't always fall into that obvious kind of inner conflict. When we came to patches in the adaptation that we didn't think worked, we went back to the poem and took out or put back verses or sections. The text printed here is the text as we eventually performed it.

When Märta came to London for the first night, we discovered to our horror that there was in fact an authorised dramatisation already in existence. In all the correspondence with her Swedish agent they had never thought to mention it, and we had never thought to ask. Fortunately she liked what we had done, and it is with her permission that our version is printed here.

We have included our stage directions to give readers some idea of what the production looked like. They are by no means an integral part of the text, and anybody performing the play will want to find their own style of production.

In 1990 the company produced *More Than One Antoinette* written and directed by Debbie Shewell, an exploration of the life and death of the first Mrs Rochester, drawing on Charlotte Bronte's *Jane Eyre* and Jean Rhys' *Wide Sargasso Sea*. We also produced Marivaux's one-act play *The Colony* with a second act or companion piece, *The Colony Comes a Cropper*, written by Robyn Archer. The latter was a co-production with the Salisbury Playhouse, directed by Nona Shepphard, music composed by Lindsay Cooper.

Hanging on in the Eighties

What had the Monstrous Regiment set out to do in 1975? Among other things we wanted:

> To produce great shows.
> To discover and encourage women writers.
> To explore a theory of feminist culture. 'What is a feminist play?'
> To resurrect women's 'hidden history'.

To give women opportunities for work – especially in
technical areas which had always been male preserves.
To put *real* women on the stage. No more stereotypes.
To be a consciousness-raising group.
To attempt a theory and practice of collectivity.
To find a new audience.
To explore the relationship between music and theatre.

And where did the 1980s leave us?

Post feminism and the free play of market forces. While red-
braced Porsche-driving yuppies were let loose to roam the floor of
the commodities market, and successful career women were
falling over themselves to deny they even knew what that nasty
word 'feminism' meant, what place was there for these old lady
dinosaurs who would keep banging on about sisterhood and
solidarity? What place was there for the word 'sisterhood' itself
when the cult of unrestrained individualism told us that any
woman could be Prime Minister if she had the guts and worked
hard enough?

Against a backdrop of cuts in arts funding, rampant inflation
that eroded the value of what grants we did get, and the
dismemberment of the political theatre movement, survival was
the name of the game. On the practical day-to-day level, running
a theatre company became more and more of a struggle. We
fought to maintain our standards of production, which, ironically,
often caused painful tensions with women who came to work with
us: from the outside we looked like a glossy company with a huge
internal support network. From the inside, we looked like what we
really were: a tiny group who didn't have enough women to do
the work and didn't have the money to pay other people to come
in and do it.

In such a difficult material position, the only way to continue to
grow and develop is with the support of the community in which
you are rooted. But in the 1980s our community fell apart. The
Women's Movement retreated in confusion and we all suffered
under the backlash of so-called 'post feminism'. (An interesting
note. In her book *The Demon Lover: A Study of the Sexuality of
Terrorism*, Robin Morgan found the expression 'post-feminist'
being used as far back as 1919. So the idea that women should
shut up and go home because they've fulfilled all their aspirations
is not a new one.) Post-feminism is a spurious concept. As Naomi
Wolf has recently pointed out 'no one speaks derisively about
post-democracy'. Ten years of Thatcherism have shown us that

our democratic rights are not sacred. They have to be defended
and fought for and a society that cares about its political
institutions has to be constantly vigilant in defence of those rights.

This scramble for survival has meant that there has been very
little chance to evaluate the theatrical implications of our work. In
our continuing championing and performing of women's writing,
the actual producing of the work has been such a battle in the
1980s that we have been forced to put one of our primary aims
on the back boiler. The conscious exploration of what 'women's
writing' is or might be has had to be postponed. This is still a
project of some urgency. There seems to be a growing consensus
of opinion that 'new writing' is in crisis, but the articles and
papers which talk about this crisis never mention women's
writing. As usual the dominant (male) is deemed to include the
less visible female. It never seems to cross male critics' minds that
women are not a special interest group, not a caucus, not a lobby.

We are not even a minority. Women make up just over half the
human race, and it is inevitable that we begin to explore what
might constitute a specific female vision. Not just in terms of
content, but in the structure of the drama we write. In June 1991
I attended the 2nd International Women Playwrights' Conference
in Toronto and I was struck by the way many of the women
writers talked about their work. They are consciously thinking
about what makes their plays different from the classical (male)
form. They are acutely aware of having embarked on an
exploration. Of course we have continued to commission and
champion women's work of all kinds, but economic conditions
force us into a conservative position. We have had to form a
relationship with establishment theatre which I suspect has not
always been to our advantage. In commissioning plays we have
had to use the traditional model, but we have none of the
safeguards that traditional methods provide: almost without
exception we have tried to produce every play we have
commissioned, whether we thought it was ready or not, because
we never had enough money to build up a body of work in
preparation. In contrast, mainstream theatres may have up to
twenty-five commissions in various stages of development at any
one time. Out of those commissions, each theatre may go on to
produce only four or five.

Where does a company such as ours find its place in the
theatrical community, when mainstream, male-run theatres such
as the Royal Court provide a more visible stage for women
playwrights to work on? Indeed, it's probable that none of the

writers in this volume would like to be thought of as 'women writers', laden as that description is with resonances of the marginal and, by extension, the second rate.

Yet women are writing for the theatre. More now than ever before. But by and large they are still as invisible as they ever were. They are not being nurtured. With the closure of many studio spaces and smaller venues a traditional testing ground for new writing has been lost. Additionally, new writing itself has become harder and harder to put on as cuts in arts funding and a recession push bookers and producers into a more conservative position of producing safe plays. When critics like Michael Billington wail at the 'crisis in new writing' they never seem to grasp the obvious correlation between the 'crisis' and the economic situation in which theatre operates.

Not enough has changed in the last fifteen years. We were a group of performers and we started out looking for women writers as a way of making ourselves visible on stage. Enlightened self-interest. Mel Gussow, distinguished American critic and writer, recently wrote a long profile of Michael Gambon for *The New Yorker* (28 January, 1991). The article mentions the stars of the English stage: Ian McKellen, Alan Howard, Derek Jacobi . . . and on and on . . . and the new generation . . . Daniel Day-Lewis, Antony Sher, Simon Callow, Kenneth Branagh . . . Not one woman. You'd think Oliver Cromwell was still in Whitehall and women banished from the stage altogether.

It is still the case that for most theatrical purposes the male shall be deemed to include the female. As long as the male vision of the world is taken to be *the* vision of the world then women's writing will be identified as marginal. And many women will want to wriggle out of the identity their gender imposes on them. Understandably.

Fear of being marginalised: an issue that comes full circle again. What is the point of a women's theatre company? Shouldn't we rejoin the mainstream and try and infiltrate what we've learned into the body theatrical.

Being a woman designer I found it very comfortable working in a company that takes the concerns and interests and struggles women have seriously. The writing for women, by women with good parts for women of different ages. They are not separatist or judgmental but simply care for and take the art of women particularly seriously. When I work for them I feel appreciated and enabled. There may not

*be a fantastic budget to work with but I feel valued and that is
enhancing.*

*Recently I have approached them for new plays to run a project with
new design students at Central St Martin's Theatre Design degree
course. Young designers work on unperformed, maybe unfinished,
plays. It can be helpful for a writer to see their play visualized and
set in a proposed space before completing it. I hope this will be an
ongoing relationship.*

JENNY CAREY
Designer, Origin of the Species *1984,* The Colony
Comes a Cropper, *1990.*

Part of the problem of women's theatrical invisibility has to lie in
the classical foundations of our repertoire. Shakespeare pre-
eminently, but also Marlowe, Jonson, the Jacobeans, the
Restoration playwrights. The model theatre company, the ideal, is
one which can tackle and scale these heights of the English
cultural experience. And a company which is geared up to do
Macbeth (21 male characters, 5 female) or *Hamlet* (At least 20 male
characters, 2 female) is hardly likely to be considering how they
might employ more women.

Interestingly enough, two of the most celebrated examples of
'tinkering' with gender in classic texts were the National Theatre's
As You Like It (1968) and *The Oresteia* (1981) both of which were
performed by all-male casts. In other words, even with so few
parts in the classical repertoire for women, what few there were
were taken from them and given to men. Why? The rationale was
that these plays were written for men to perform at times when
women were not allowed on a public stage. But what was the real
reason? Are men inherently more interesting than women on
stage? Are they better actors than women? Does the deep
authoritative male voice appeal to the audience more than
women's voices? Or do they make more convincing women than
women themselves? I was told a story about how Samuel Beckett
reputedly refused to allow *Waiting for Godot* to be performed at all
in Holland because a certain theatre, contrary to his wishes,
performed it with an all-female cast. What terrible damage could
four women inflict on this play that such a punishment should be
meted out to an entire nation? Had they fouled it, besmirched it,
somehow rendered it invalid? If Shakespeare can survive strobe
lighting, motor bikes and Sherman tanks, can Beckett not survive
being performed by women?

The physical invisibility of women on stage is only the manifestation of our invisibility in the whole theatrical edifice. That is why the women's theatre companies have to keep fighting for their right to exist. Fifteen years ago, we were looking forward to the day when we could pack up and go home knowing that women's experience, women's vision, women's culture had become an acknowledged part of culture in general. Unfortunately we can't pack those cases yet.

A New Beginning

To have survived for fifteen years is an achievement. The bigger achievement will be survival for the next fifteen years.

ROBERT BRECKMAN
Company Accountant, Advisory Committee Member 1975–1991.

In 1991 the company has taken a radical leap in a new direction. The structure of the company has always been the motor which carried the artistic policies forward. Towards the end of the 1980s we started to admit that the collective management model was not working well. For each of us to earn a living, as the company couldn't support us, we had to take work wherever we were offered it. This created a situation where it was possible for the company to be in pre-production or rehearsal for a show and for the administrator to be the only member of the company who was physically present. The result was that the process of taking major decisions of policy became inefficient and occasionally haphazard. This left the adminstrator with the burden of taking many decisions alone which should have been taken collectively. Additionally, the management collective had dwindled to three (Mary, Chris and myself) plus Rose Sharp, our administrator, the only one of us on the permanent payroll.

We tried to tackle the problem by setting up an Advisory Committee. The Committee has made an important contribution to the company's life, supporting and challenging our activities, but it was never intended to be a management body, and as it meets only quarterly, it couldn't really help to resolve the problems of the day to day running of the company.

I have already talked about the vital role the company's

administrators played in the early days of its existence. The nature of that role changed radically during the 1980s when the full-time collective ceased to exist. The nature may have changed but the vital importance of the administrator did not. If anything, it became more crucial still. After Diane Robson left us, first Sandy Bailey, then (briefly) Ferelith Lean and currently Rose Sharp have all had to cope with the problems posed by our attempts to keep the spirit and artistic standards of the company going without the full-time support of a collective that characterised the early days.

I had never heard of a business plan, a feasibility study or an arts strategy. I had no experience of marketing or financial management. But I was (still am) a committed feminist with ideas about how women on stage could blow a hole in the patriarchal hold on imagination and drama. I was actively involved in the Women's Movement and a whole range of cultural political groupings and activities. I was naive. misguided in many ways, but I was motivated, energetic and a fierce campaigner. I like to think that was why Monstrous Regiment asked me to work for them.

SUE BEARDON
Administrator, 1976–1978.

We gradually realised that we were 'ipso facto' forcing the role of artistic director on our administrators, who didn't want it. So when, in 1990, the Arts Council made continued funding dependent upon our appointing an Executive or Artistic Director, we were not greatly surprised. Nor, when we came to discuss it in depth, were we as aghast as we might have thought we would be.

Mary agreed to take the role of Executive Director for nine months while we sorted out how best to proceed. The work she did in those months was invaluable, indeed we probably wouldn't have survived at all if it hadn't been for her energy and skill. On the artistic side she oversaw the production of *The Colony* (with Rose) and organised workshops and rehearsed readings throughout the following six months in partnership with Tash Fairbanks, who was our first writer-in-residence. At the same time she produced a series of study papers which became our blue-print for survival.

Our discussions were guided by Sue Beardon, our very first administrator, now a management consultant, who came back to help us to work through what we wanted to do. While still believing fiercely in the collective principle, we saw that in our situation, the renewal of the company and the company's work was the only thing that mattered. And perhaps 'collective' has other meanings than the one we had always assumed. We have always tried to be flexible at moments of crisis, to look for a course of action that would ensure the survival of the company and the ideas it stands for. So rather than cling on to a power it was no longer feasible for us to exercise, we decided that the appointment of an Artistic Director who would work side by side with the administrator, offered us an exciting chance to put the company back on its feet to face the challenges of the future. Consequently, in April 1991, we appointed Clare Venables as our first Artistic Director. She had just spent nine years as Artistic Director of one of the largest regional theatres in England, The Sheffield Crucible, and we could hardly believe our luck when she agreed to work with us. Her relationship with the company over the years meant that she was familiar with our work, and with us. She had been on the Advisory Committee since its inception and had worked with us on two productions in the last couple of years. She had co-produced *Waving* when she was at the Crucible. We had also planned together (until we discovered that neither party could afford it) for the company to become resident in the Crucible Studio for a season.

It will take many different forms over the years, but their first principle of majority is more important than is ever stated; in this 'post-feminist' era there is a danger that people can feel many battles have been won, and that we do not still need women's companies, rather in the way that women's pages in newspapers are now questioned by men and women alike. It is short-sighted. Perhaps life might be technically easier for our daughters (though actually I doubt even that) but until we are as confident in our female perspective as in our male, whether we are men or women, we need groups of women, working and exploring together. Not individual women struggling or conquering alone, but groups, sharing and conquering, and eventually welcoming the male principle because the female principle has become strong enough to match it.

CLARE VENABLES
Artistic Director, 1991.

With the addition of Katrina Duncan, who had known the company since 1979 when she worked with us on placement from the City University Arts Administration Course, and had been on the Advisory Committee, we formed ourselves into something approaching a conventional Board of Directors. I say 'something approaching' because I don't think any of us really sees what we are in the process of creating as a traditional structure. The word 'collective' may not look anything like it looked to us in 1975, but the resonances of the ideas it represents are still as strong. The last twenty years has had a profound effect on women's perception of ourselves. As Carolyn Heilbrun* says: 'What became essential was for women to see themselves collectively, not individually, not caught in some individual erotic and familial plot, and, inevitably, found wanting . . . I suspect that female narratives will be found where women exchange stories, where they read and talk collectively of ambitions, and possibilities, and accomplishments.'

We think we are ready to start telling the story all over again. Several years ago, David Bradford, one of the original group, told me about an expression he had found in a book on evolution. Apparently it is a technical term used to describe a species that is in the process of evolving. At a certain point in its development it is not possible to predict whether it will be successful or not. In the meantime, it is called a 'hopeful monster'. I think that isn't a bad way to describe how we feel about the company as we move into the 1990s. We are evolving into something quite different from what we have been. We acknowledge and salute that history and every person who contributed to its successes. At the same time, we recognise that we have to change in order to move on. We want to build on the past not live in it. We want the next fifteen years to be as extraordinary as the last fifteen have been. As we look into the future with anticipation we feel that we are indeed, 'hopeful monsters'.

* Carolyn Heilbrun: Writing a Woman's Life. WOMEN'S PRESS. 1989.

Monstrous Regiment Productions

SCUM
by Claire Luckham, Chris Bond and the company

VINEGAR TOM 1976/77
by Caryl Churchill

KISS AND KILL 1977/78
by Ann Mitchell and Susan Todd

FLOORSHOW 1977/78
by Caryl Churchill, Bryony Lavery, Michelene Wandor and David Bradford

TIME GENTLEMEN PLEASE 1978
by Bryony Lavery

TEENDREAMS 1979
by David Edgar with Susan Todd

GENTLEMEN PREFER BLONDES 1979/80
by Bryony Lavery

DIALOGUE BETWEEN A PROSTITUTE AND ONE OF HER CLIENTS 1980
by Dacia Maraini. Translated by Gillian Hanna

SHAKESPEARE'S SISTER 1980
by Théâtre de l'Aquarium
Translated by Gillian Hanna

MOURNING PICTURES 1981
by Honor Moore

YOGA CLASS 1981
by Rose Tremain

THE EXECUTION 1982
by Melissa Murray

THE FOURTH WALL 1983
by Franca Rame and Dario Fo
Translated by Gillian Hanna

CALAMITY 1983/84
by Bryony Lavery

ENSLAVED BY DREAMS 1984
devised by Chris Bowler

MACBETH WORKSHOPS 1984
Devised and directed by Bettina Jonic

ORIGIN OF THE SPECIES —A LOVE STORY 1984/85
by Bryony Lavery

POINT OF CONVERGENCE 1985
Devised/Directed by Chris Bowler

MY SONG IS FREE 1986
by Jorge Diaz
Translated by Paloma Zozaya
Adapted by Nigel Gearing

ALARMS 1986
by Susan Yankowitz

MY SISTER IN THIS HOUSE 1987
by Wendy Kesselman

WAVING 1988
by Carol Bunyan

ISLAND LIFE 1988
by Jenny McLeod

A COMMON WOMAN 1989
by Dario Fo & Franca Rame
Translated by Gillian Hanna

BEATRICE 1989
by Ian Brown

LOVE STORY OF THE CENTURY 1990
by Märta Tikkannen. Adapted by Clare Venables
Translated by Stina Katchadourian

MORE THAN ONE ANTOINETTE 1990
by Debbie Shewell

THE COLONY COMES A CROPPER! 1990
Act I The Colony by Marivaux. Translated by Gillian Hanna
Act II Comes a Cropper by Robyn Archer

Administrators

Sandy Bailey
Sue Beardon
Katrina Duncan
Gus Garside
Ferelith Lean
Di Robson
Rose Sharp

Artistic/Executive Director

Mary McCusker
Clare Venables

Choreographers

Eve Darlow
Karen Rabinowitz

Costume Makers

Hilary Lewis
Pam Tate
Marion Weise

Designers

Hildegard Bechtler
Jenny Carey
Moggie Douglas
Stephanie Howard
Gemma Jackson
Annabel Lee
Claudia Mayer
Sue Mayes
Iona McLeish
Andrea Montag
Geraldine Pilgrim
Di Seymour

Directors

Chris Bowler
David Bradford
Pam Brighton
Penny Cherns
Jane Collins
Kate Crutchley
Sue Dunderdale
Caroline Eves
Angela Hopkins
Bettina Jonic
Angela Langfield
Nancy Meckler
Sharon Miller
Ann Mitchell
Jan Sargeant
Nona Shepphard
Debbie Shewell
Susan Todd
Clare Venables
Hilary Westlake

Graphic Designers

Jo Angell
Carol Carter
The Drawing Room
Sophie Gibson
Claudine Meissner
Chris Montag
Alan Rickman
Lee Robinson
Jude Rugg
Angela Stewart-Park

Lighting Designers

Inigo Espejel
Beth Hardisty
Peter Higton
Meri Jenkins
Tina MacHugh
Geoff Mersereau
Charles Paton
George Tarbuck
Steve Whitson
Veronica Wood

Musicians/Composers

Paul Abrahams
Diane Adderley
Roger Allam
Richard Attree
Lindsay Cooper
Jane Cox
Josefina Cupido
Helen Glavin
Sylvia Hallet
Tony Haynes
Joanna MacGregor
Keith Morris

Performers

Diane Adderley
Richard Albrecht
Roger Allam
Jenifer Armitage
Denise Armon
Diana Barrett
Hannah Beardon
Ian Blower
Abigail Bond
Chris Bowler
David Bradford
Linda Broughton
Angela Bruce
Vivienne Burgess
Georgia Clarke
Angela Clerkin
Norma Cohen
Nora Connolly
Jane Cox

Stephen Crane
Sally Cranfield
Josefina Cupido
Cotchie D'Arcy
April de Angelis
Paola Dionisotti
Joanna Field
Andrew Frame
Susan Franklyn
William Gaminara
Tim Gatti
Iain Glass
Helen Glavin
Aviva Goldkorn
Celia Gore-Booth
Tony Guilfoyle
Suzanna Hamilton
Gillian Hanna
Gay Harding
Ann Haydn
Tamsin Heatley
Joan Hooley
Alan Hulse
Irma Inniss
Pauline Jefferson
Paul Kiernan
Pamela Lane
Stephen Ley
Jane Lowe
Stella Maris
Mary McCusker
Marilyn Milgrom
Marsha Millar
Ann Mitchell
Maureen Morris
Maggie Nichols
Maggie O'Neill
Carlene Reed
Sue Rogerson
Clive Russell
Mary Shand
Rosamund Shelley
Corinne Skinner-Carter
John Slade
Geraldine Somerville
Maggie Steed
Gerda Stevenson

Stella Tanner
Susan Todd
Marcia Tucker
Yolanda Vazquez
Lynne Verrall
Frances Viner
Tilly Vosburgh
Natasha Williams

Photographers

Sarah Ainslie
Sheila Burnett
Dee Conway
Phil Cutts
Howard Gibbins
Jane Harper
Sean Hudson
Gerry Murray
Raissa Page
Roger Perry
Mark Rusher
Mary Tisserand
Pamela Toller
Val Wilmer
Nigel Wright

Technical

Liz Ainley
Janet Ball
Alison Bullivant
Janet Cantrill
Lesley Chenery
Sheryl Crown
Valerie Dew
Inigo Espejel
Jessica Higgs
Meri Jenkins
Deirdre Malynn
Gill McBride
Greta Millington
Mel Nortcliffe
Tessa Panter
Lizz Poulter
Nancy Secchi
Sheila Sloane
Christine Thornhill
Debra Trethewey

d. Wilson
Veronica Wood

Writers

Jo Anderson
Robyn Archer
Chris Bond
Chris Bowler
David Bradford
Ian Brown
Carol Bunyan
Caryl Churchill
Ellen Dryden
David Edgar
Monica Gazzo
Nigel Gearing
Gillian Hanna
Stina Katchadourian
Wendy Kesselman
Bryony Lavery
Claire Luckham
Dacia Maraini
Jenny McLeod
Ann Mitchell
Honor Moore
Melissa Murray
Franca Rame & Dario Fo
Debbie Shewell
Théâtre de L'Aquarium
Märta Tikkanen
Susan Todd
Rose Tremain
Clare Venables
Michelene Wandor
Susan Yankowitz
Paloma Zozaya

Monstrous Regiment
Advisory Committee – 25 June
1991

Sandy Bailey
Simi Bedford
Robert Breckman
Beatrix Campbell
Caryl Churchill
Leonora Davis

Diane Gelon
Cathy Itzin
Helena Kennedy
Ann McFerran
Susie Orbach
Veronica Wood

Monstrous Regiment Plays in Print (in English)

Vinegar Tom by Caryl Churchill (published in *Plays by Women Volume One*, Methuen)

Teendreams by David Edgar with Susan Todd (published in *Teendreams & Our Own People*, Methuen)

Origin of the Species by Bryony Lavery (published in *Plays by Women Volume Six*, Methuen)

Mourning Pictures by Honor Moore (published in the USA in *The New Women's Theatre: Ten Plays by Contemporary American Women* by Vintage)

The Fourth Wall by Franca Rame and Dario Fo, translated by Gillian Hanna (published in *Woman Alone*, Methuen)

A Common Woman by Dario Fo and Franca Rame, translated by Gillian Hanna (published in *Woman Alone*, Methuen)

Alarms by Susan Yankowitz (published in *Female Voices* by the Playwrights Press)

Production Photographs

1. Monstrous Regiment: The Company, 1976/77.
2. Gillian Hanna in *Scum: Death, Destruction and Dirty Washing* (1976).
3. Ian Blower, Roger Allam and Linda Broughton in *Scum: Death, Destruction and Dirty Washing* (1976).
4. Diane Adderley, Chris Bowler and Mary McCusker in *Time Gentlemen Please* (1978).
5. Chris Bowler and Mary McCusker in *Teendreams* (1979).
6. Mary McCusker, Chris Bowler, Josefina Cupido and Gillian Hanna in *Shakespeare's Sister* (1980).
7. Maggie Nichols and Paola Dionisotti in *The Fourth Wall* (1983).
8. Tamsin Heatley, Celia Gore-Booth and Sally Cranfield in *Enslaved by Dreams* (1984).
9. Mary Shand in *Point of Convergence* (1985).
10. Maureen Morris and Yolanda Vazquez in *My Song is Free* (1986).
11. Pamela Lane and Pauline Jefferson in *Waving* (1988).
12. Maggie O'Neill, Tilly Vosburgh and Suzanna Hamilton in *My Sister in This House* (1987).
13. Tilly Vosburgh and Maggie Steed in *My Sister in This House* (1987).
14. Joanna Field in *Island Life* (1988).
15. Joan Hooley and Stella Tanner in *Island Life* (1988).
16. Mary McCusker in *Beatrice* (1989).
17. Gillian Hanna and Mary McCusker in *Love Story of the Century* (1990).
18. Mary McCusker in *Love Story of the Century* (1990).
19. Natasha Williams Geraldine Somerville and William Gaminara in *More Than One Antoinette* (1990).
20. Monstrous Regiment: The Company, 1991.

All efforts have been made to trace and contact photographers for permission to reproduce their work, and credit has duly been given. Apologies are offered to those who proved impossible to trace before going to press.

1. Monstrous Regiment 1976/77. *Left to right:* Meri Jenkins, Linda Broughton, Chris Bowler, Mary McCuskcr, Susan Todd, Josefina Cupido, Sue Beardon, Helen Glavin, Roger Allam, Ian Blower and Gillian Hanna.

2. Gillian Hanna in *Scum: Death, Destruction and Dirty Washing*
(1976). Photo: Roger Perry.

3. *Left to right:* Ian Blower, Roger Allam and Linda Broughton in *Scum: Death, Destruction and Dirty Washing* (1976). Photo: Roger Perry.

4. *Left to right:* Diane Adderley, Chris Bowler and Mary McCusker in *Time Gentlemen Please* (1978).

5. Chris Bowler and Mary McCusker in *Teendreams* (1979).

6. *Left to right:* Mary McCusker, Chris Bowler, Josefina Cupido
and Gillian Hanna in *Shakespeare's Sister* (1980). Photo:
Mark Rusher.

7. Maggie Nichols (front) and Paola Dionisotti (back) in *The Fourth Wall* (1983).

8. *Left to right:* Tamsin Heatley, Celia Gore-Booth and Sally
Cranfield in *Enslaved by Dreams* (1984). Photo: Roger Perry.

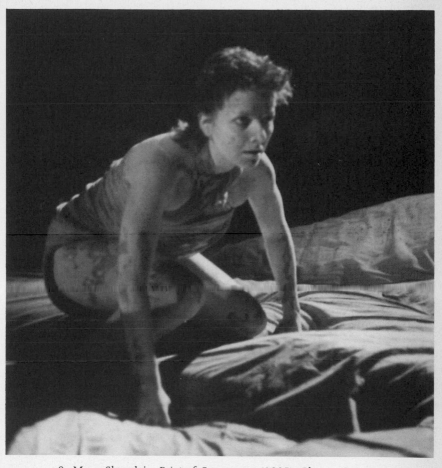

9. Mary Shand in *Point of Convergence* (1985). Photo: Greater
London Council.

10. Maureen Morris (back) and Yolanda Vazquez (front) in *My Song is Free* (1986). Photo: Willoughby Gullachsen.

11. *Left to right:* Pamela Lane and Pauline Jefferson in *Waving* (1988). Photo: Gerry Murray.

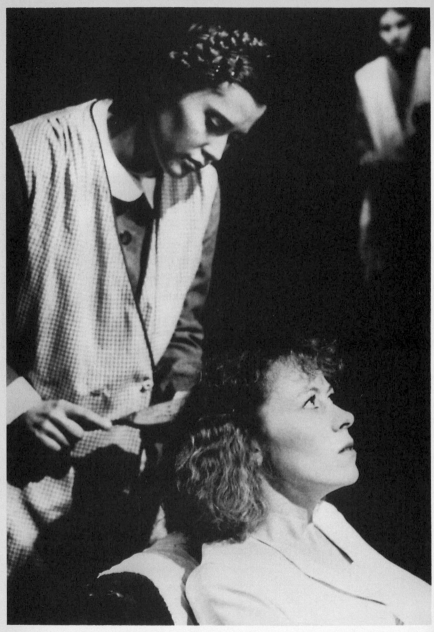

12. *Left to right:* Maggie O'Neill and Tilly Vosburgh
(background: Suzanna Hamilton) in *My Sister in This House*
(1987). Photo: Phil Cutts.

13. *Left to right:* Tilly Vosburgh and Maggie Steed in *My Sister in This House* (1987). Photo: Phil Cutts.

14. Joanna Field in *Island Life* (1988). Photo: Mary Tisserand.

15. *Left to right:* Joan Hooley and Stella Tanner in *Island Life* (1988). Photo: Sarah Ainslie.

16. Mary McCusker in *Beatrice* (1989). Photo: Sean Hudson.

17. Gillian Hanna (front) and Mary McCusker (back) in *Love Story of the Century* (1990).

18. Mary McCusker in *Love Story of the Century* (1990).

19. *Left to right:* Natasha Williams, Geraldine Somerville and William Gaminara in *More Than One Antoinette* (1990). Photo: Sarah Ainslie.

20. Monstrous Regiment 1991. *Back, left to right:* Mary McCusker, Gillian Hanna, Katrina Duncan. *Front, left to right:* Rose Sharp, Chris Bowler, Clare Venables. Photo: Dee Conway.

SCUM: DEATH, DESTRUCTION AND DIRTY WASHING

A musical celebration of the events of
the Paris Commune of 1871

by Claire Luckham and Chris Bond
with additional material
by The Monstrous Regiment
Music by Helen Glavin

CLAIRE LUCKHAM's best known play is *Trafford Tanzi* which has been seen all over the world, after starting life in 1978 in a production by the Liverpool Everyman, where several more of her plays were first staged. Her other work includes an adaptation of *Moll Flanders* and *The Dramatic Attitudes of Miss Fanny Kemble*. *Scum* was her first piece of work for the theatre.

CHRIS BOND has written over thirty shows of various shapes and sizes, as well as novels and new librettos for old operas. He has been Artistic Director of both the Everyman and Playhouse Theatres in Liverpool, and of the Half Moon Theatre in London's East End.

Scum was performed by Monstrous Regiment between April 1976 and April 1977 and later revived.

Written by Claire Luckham, Chris Bond and the company
Directed by Susan Todd
Music written by Helen Glavin
Designed by Andrea Montag
Costumes by Hilary Lewis

Performers: Chris Bowler
Helen Glavin
Gillian Hanna
Mary McCusker
Susan Todd
Roger Allam
Alan Hulse

Technician: d. Wilson
Poster/graphics: Chris Montag
Photos: Roger Perry

In subsequent versions the following also appeared:

Linda Broughton
Ann Mitchell
Ian Blower
Clive Russell

Musician: Josefina Cupido
One subsequent version was redirected by Ann Mitchell
Technician: Meri Jenkins
Administration: Sue Beardon

The scene throughout is a laundry in Paris: Things are taken off or added as necessary. The play begins in September 1871.

Lights up: a large pile of dirty washing moves: MOLE *emerges from it and addresses the audience.*

MOLE. Madames and Monsieurs bonsoir and welcome to Paris. City of light, gaiety, effervescence. The seat of reason, the home of culture, the cradle of civilisation and the biggest knocking shop in Europe. Well. Perhaps you have heard about our Parisienne women, yes? Perhaps you have heard about our laughing eyes, our twinkling toes? Perhaps you have heard of our glittering coutures of which I present to you such a beautiful example here this evening?
If you haven't heard about French women you must have heard about an extremely naughty dance that we've just invented called the can-can. Would you like me to tell you why it's so very naughty, yes? It is because we lift up our skirts and show you what we got underneath.

She does so, revealing her long ragged drawers.

Yes well, that's all very well but there is a war going on you know. Oh yes. We are fighting the Prussians. Why? Well frankly your guess is as good as mine. Death or glory, La Patrie, L'Honneur all that crap. Chasing the Prussians round the countryside takes our minds off rising prices something wonderful and here's the best bit. We've gone and lost our Emperor. Well he lost himself, that's to say he has gone and got himself captured, the horrible little whore-master. So we've told him not to bother coming back thanks very much, we can manage very well without him and we have gone and declared a Republic. Oh glorious day, oh wonderful 4th of September! No more monarchs, no more oppressors. Let the voice of the people command. Come on let's hear it for Liberty, Equality and Fraternity!
Republic of the People my arse. What have we got? A very clean, very respectable bunch of doctors, lawyers and merchants have taken over. And Adolphe Thiers – the greasy eminence of French politics he is – he has been lurking in the

wings of our little show here for the last forty years just waiting to come lamming in with the old law and order philosophy the minute we get a little bit restless. Now you can't call that a revolution can you eh? I mean, where's the blood? Where's the babies spitted on sticks, where's the heads rolling in the baskets? Where's the priests with their bollocks stuffed down their throats?

MADAME MASSON (*off*). Mole? Mole? Oh, oh what a night.

She comes in.

MOLE. This is our boss Madame Masson. She's a very religious woman. Believes in profit and the life hereafter.

MASSON. Oh my head. Good morning Madame Mole. I'm surprised to find you still here. Guarding my laundry. I expected you to be in the streets leading the rabble. Gone to join the revolution.

MOLE. I'm not hoiking me skirts up round me armpits just because we've swapped an Emperor for a bunch of half-baked bankers. That's not what I mean by a Republic and well you know it.

MASSON. Quite right Mole. You couldn't do with all that running around. Your rheumatism wouldn't stand it. You need steady work. Settling down. A home. You're safe here with me Mole. Yes, as dear Claude was saying at breakfast, the future looks bright. Where are those girls? They're late. Up half the night screaming through the streets with the mob I suppose. Yes Mole, as Claude was saying, this new government contains some of the most reliable men in France. If they can't save us from the Prussians, who can?

JOSEPHINE (*off*). Hey look, Eugenie. They're going into the bakers.

EUGENIE. They're shitting all over his doorstep.

JOSEPHINE *and* EUGENIE *tumble in.*

MASSON. You're late.

JOSEPHINE. It's the sheep. They're blocking the road.

MASSON. Sheep!

EUGENIE. They're bringing them in for the siege.

MASSON. Siege. Mother of God, what siege?

JOSEPHINE. Go and have a look, Madame.

EUGENIE. Go and have a look.

JOSEPHINE. They're everywhere. And the smell. It's worse than this place.

EUGENIE. I never want to go to the country if it smells like that.

JOSEPHINE. You're dead lucky they haven't come in here, Madame.

MASSON. There is work to be done. I'll only mark you fifteen minutes late in the circumstances. That's three centimes off your wages.

EUGENIE. Wasn't our fault –

MASSON. And it will be six if those shirts aren't in to soak quick. Josephine tackle those stains. I don't want them coming back again. A siege. If there's going to be a siege what happens next? Someone must know. I intend to find out. Keep working girls.

Exit.

EUGENIE. She's off for a few with her mate, Madame Bouquin.

MOLE. Her that owns the posh grocers. 'Purveyors of Victuals to the Quality' over the door.

EUGENIE. Makes her own sausages. Looks like one and all. Fat cow.

JOSEPHINE. I'm pissed off.

JOSEPHINE. Emile's been out all night. Went off with Marcel to celebrate the Republic. That was yesterday dinner time. Haven't had sight nor sound of him since.

MOLE. Celebrate! The Republic isn't going to make no difference to us.

EUGENIE. No. We'll be slogging here just the same.

JOSEPHINE. The Republic won't make my money go further. Emile's had no work for six weeks. He says there's no building work about now. I'm at my wits' end to feed the kids and him.

EUGENIE. Cheer up. He'll get work now the war's over. Look on the bright side eh?

JOSEPHINE. The war may be over but the siege is just beginning.

MOLE. With a siege on we'll likely all be out of a job. There's nobody going to be worrying about clean linen. At the very least Masson will have an excuse to cut our wages.

EUGENIE. Go on. You can't get lower than one franc a day.

MOLE. You want to bet on that?

JOSEPHINE. Most of Madame's customers will be packing off to their country houses. I can't see them sitting here waiting for the Prussians to blast them to smithereens.

EUGENIE. What do you say Jose? Shall we take a little trip to our country estate? Take the waters for our health?

JOSEPHINE. The only water we'll be taking is this lot of slops out the back.

EUGENIE. Food's going to be short.

JOSEPHINE. That's nothing new.

EUGENIE. Still. At least you've got your Emile to keep you warm nights. That's more than I've got.

JOSEPHINE. Men. I shit 'em. If I had my time over I'd choose careful. I'd think twice before I'd chain myself to a man and kids.

MOLE. Too late now.

EUGENIE. I was glad to see the back of my old man. He wasn't worth a light. He would have had me lumbered with a dozen by now if he'd had his way.

JOSEPHINE. We both walked the orchard and picked a crab.

EUGENIE. Too bloody true.

MOLE. In your blooming youth! I'll bet you two were as green as grass.

EUGENIE. Remember them shows Jose? Down the Vaudeville? When we was single. I had a yellow frock. Bought it with my first wages. I went up on the stage and sang.

JOSEPHINE. I remember. I tried to stop you.

EUGENIE. You was too drunk to stop me.

MOLE. You had some nerve then.

EUGENIE. I was fourteen.

JOSEPHINE. The fellers used to buzz round us like flies round a jampot. The terrible two we were.

EUGENIE. Water under the bridge.

JOSEPHINE. Blood more like. Here Eug, give us a hand with these cuffs.

EUGENIE. Christ my legs ache.

MOLE. Keep moving or you'll seize up.

The Laundry Song

Enter MASSON.

MASSON. Josephine, how much work is there?

JOSEPHINE. Three days.

EUGENIE. At least Madame, maybe four.

MASSON. Rubbish. Looks more like one to me. It's not enough. I'm in the wrong business I can tell you. Madame Bouquin was on her way to buy up stocks of sugar, tea, butter. This siege will mean shortage and that means higher prices. She'll make her fortune.

JOSEPHINE. It's not fair, is it.

EUGENIE. There's no justice is there, Madame.

MASSON. You're getting slack Eugenie, slack.

JOSEPHINE. It's her back, Madame.

EUGENIE. It's my back.

MASSON. I am not a charity, Josephine. I cannot afford to carry invalids.

MOLE. Try the brothels. Business is very good with all the troops in town. Lots of dirty sheets.

MASSON. Hang the washing, you.

Enter LUCIE.

MASSON. Ah Madame Deschamps! The camisoles are ready. Such beautiful lace. It's not often we have the pleasure of seeing such exquisite workmanship pass through our tubs. Is it girls?

MOLE.
EUGENIE.   } Beautiful Mrs/Oh it's a real joy, (*etc.*)
JOSEPHINE.

LUCIE. I've come to ask you for a job, Madame. My husband was killed three weeks ago at Sedan. I've my little girl to keep so I thought if you could possibly give me work – I'll do anything, I'm very strong, and I'm quick. I'll soon learn –

MASSON. Monsieur killed – fighting for his Emperor. You must be proud in the midst of your loss.

LUCIE. I didn't want him to go. He was a fool, he believed the lies he read in the papers. It was a pointless futile war.

JOSEPHINE. } Blimey!
EUGENIE.   } Hark at her.

MASSON. Your grief is only natural dear. Calm down.

LUCIE. Can you help me? I'll do anything, I can sew, wash, iron, anything.

MASSON. Oh Madame, look around you. What work can I offer to an educated young lady? You were a schoolteacher before you married, I remember?

LUCIE. Yes.

MASSON. A highly respectable position. Madame, I wish it were in my power to assist you but business is bad. I'm not an uncharitable woman. It's not easy for me.

JOSEPHINE. She's ever so kind-hearted.

EUGENIE. She's a real Christian.

MASSON. I'll tell you what I'll do. I could offer you perhaps two days' work. I have some quality garments for repair and my girls are not at their best in fine sewing.

LUCIE. I can sew very neatly –

MASSON. I hope so.

LUCIE. How much will I get? –

MASSON. Seventy-five centimes a day. That's all I can afford. You're lucky to get it. Now what's your name? We don't like to be too formal here do we girls?

MOLE. Oh no we're a very friendly bunch.

LUCIE. Lucie.

MASSON. Isn't that a pretty name?

MOLE.
EUGENIE. } Oh yes, lovely, sweet, (*etc.*) Like a rose.
JOSEPHINE.

MASSON. Josephine don't sit there like a sack of flour. Get Lucie working and Mole, get that sewing sorted for her. Stay awake and see she does it. I'm just off to help Madame Bouquin buy in some stores. I shan't be long.

Exit MASSON.

MOLE. They're going to go halves on a ton of sugar and sell it at treble what they paid for it.

JOSEPHINE. We won't be buying it neither.

MOLE. Here. Look at this. You'll never get anything like that on your back, eh Eug?

JOSEPHINE. Oi. Don't kill yourself. You'll be worn out by two o' clock at that rate.

EUGENIE. And you'll make us all look slow, love.

LUCIE. Oh. I see what you mean. I've never done this sort of work before. It's very – interesting – to be somewhere so different.

EUGENIE. Different from what?

LUCIE. Well – a schoolroom.

EUGENIE. What a comedown eh? Schoolteacher to laundress. Think you can stand the pace? You looks done in now.

JOSEPHINE. Get comfortable girl. Take this off.

MOLE. You better get them specs off. You're all steamed up.

LUCIE. Oh yes. I can't see very well, I'm a bit short-sighted.

EUGENIE. Never mind. You won't have to look at the low company in here. Not what you're used to I daresay?

JOSEPHINE. Leave her alone. Come with me. I'll show you where to put your things.

MOLE. I expect she's got her schoolbooks in there.

EUGENIE. You want to watch out she don't give you a black mark.

JOSEPHINE. How old's your kid?

LUCIE. She's seven. Marie. She can read, she's clever but she's not strong.

JOSEPHINE. Shame. They're a burden when they're ailing aren't they? Still she'll be off your hands in a few years.

LUCIE. She's lovely. She keeps me company at home. She's all I've got.

EUGENIE. You needn't be short of company. You don't want to stay home moping for your husband. Not at your age. I wouldn't.

LUCIE. I don't mope.

JOSEPHINE. What do you do with yourself?

LUCIE. I read a lot.

EUGENIE. Oh. What fun.

LUCIE. No I enjoy it. I'm reading this terribly interesting book at the moment, by Darwin, it's called *The Origin of Species* and do you know –

EMILE *and* MARCEL *enter*.

EMILE. Greetings citizenesses! Long live the Republic!

MARCEL. Republic for ever! Whae hae!

JOSEPHINE. Where the hell do you think you've been?

EMILE. Give us a kiss, Jose.

EUGENIE. Watch it. She'll be back any minute.

MARCEL. Don't worry doll. She's parading off downtown with her mate from the grocers.

JOSEPHINE. Have you left the kids running wild again?

EMILE. Don't start, Jose.

JOSEPHINE. You make me sick.

EMILE. Jose. We've been out on very important business.

JOSEPHINE. Very urgent drinking.

MARCEL. Clock this girls. You are looking at two soldiers of the people.

EMILE. Members of the new Citizen Army.

EMILE. ⎫
MARCEL. ⎭ We've joined up!

JOSEPHINE. I could kill him.

EUGENIE. Oh my God.

MOLE. Blimey. Those Prussians had better watch out now.

EUGENIE. What do you want joining up now? The war's over you silly farts.

EMILE. It's the National Guard we've joined.

MARCEL. Not the sodding regular army.

EMILE. We shall defend the Republic against the Prussians and the Emperor if need be.

LUCIE. Ah. Can you tell me what tactics the National Guard are going to adopt? The regular army couldn't get rid of the Prussians could they? How are you going to do it?

MARCEL. Hello. Look what the cat's brought in. You new here darling? What's your name then?

LUCIE. I'll keep it to myself thanks.

MARCEL. Oh. She's a bit classy for this dump isn't she?

JOSEPHINE. Lay off, you.

MOLE. You going to sweet talk the Prussians into laying down their guns big boy? What's turned you two into patriots all of a sudden. Going to fight for La France now are we?

EMILE. I don't give a damn for the Emperor's France. But I'll fight for our France, our Paris. My kids, my Josie. We're the citizen's militia – to defend the people of Paris.

MARCEL. A couple of weeks of this siege and we'll have those Prussians on the run.

EMILE. The Republic's got no fight with the Prussians.

MOLE. That's your bloody trouble. You can't see a fight when it's right under your noses. All you ever eat is bread. Right? Well a

Prussian general, he likes a nice piece of sausage and a five-course meal.

MARCEL. Nothing wrong with sausage, eh?

MOLE. A sausage is a terrible thing. It's a great corrupter, a sausage is. You don't have much respect for bread eaters, not after you've stuffed a yard or two of pork down your gullet.

EMILE. Always look on the black side, that's you. Today's supposed to be a celebration. Have a drink, Mole.

MARCEL. Yeah. Wet your whistle, girls. Do you want a drink?

LUCIE. No thanks.

MARCEL. Too rough for your delicate palate, is it?

LUCIE. I don't feel like it.

MARCEL. I always feel like it.

EMILE. You make me laugh. Innocents. Do you think Thiers is going to let a bunch of armed workers stroll around Paris ready to shoot down the government if they don't like it? Not old Adolphe.

MOLE. Adolphe Thiers the Villain of our show! Aged seventy. He's one of these politicians who swears to save us from all our troubles. But when it comes down to it of course he'll drop us in it deeper than we were before.

MOLE *takes out Thiers' puppet.*

JOSEPHINE. You can't wipe your arse on a piece of newspaper without finding his name all over it.

The Thiers' song.

MOLE. The pity of it is, it's the people that's the puppet; not M'sieur Thiers.

Enter MASSON.

MASSON. Tired, girls? I could arrange a holiday. Permanently. Visitors, I see. Can I help you gentlemen or was this just a social call?

JOSEPHINE. They were just going, Madame.

MARCEL. Ah Madame. Radiant as ever I see. Me and my friend here were wondering if you could make up some uniforms for us. We just joined up, see, and we thought a nice establishment

like this, you could turn out something really smart, you know
well-tailored.

MASSON. Uniforms. Who's paying exactly?

EMILE. The Municipality of Paris.

MARCEL. Four francs the jacket, three-fifty the trousers.

MASSON. They supply the cloth?

MARCEL. Yes.

MASSON. We'll see what we can do. If you'd care to go through
to my salon at the back I shall come and measure you directly.

Exit EMILE *and* MARCEL.

MOLE. She'll be making rifles next, you mark my word.

MASSON. We must all do our duty. Well, Lucie; it appears I may
be able to keep you after all. I am sure everything turns out for
the best in the end. I had a most satisfactory time at the
warehouse with Madame Bouquin. Most rewarding. Right
Josephine, Eugenie, get those slops out the back. Get shifting
Mole.

Groans and complaints.

Backs into it, girls!

Blackout: all exit. Drums.

Enter MASSON *reading a newspaper.* MOLE, JOSEPHINE,
LUCIE, EUGENIE *sewing uniforms.*

MASSON. Would you credit it. My potatoes arrived this morning
wrapped in this red publication. It has the effrontery to say:
'Since the 4th September our government have had no
thoughts but making a peace treaty'. What do you think of that?

JOSEPHINE. Shocking.

EUGENIE. Scandalous.

MASSON. It's enough to make you change your greengrocer.

Enter EMILE *and* MARCEL.

MASSON. Ah gentlemen. Get the sheet for the gentlemen to
change behind.

MARCEL. My, my, that's a high-class piece of tailoring.

LUCIE. She's a very high class of slave driver.

MARCEL. Feeling the strain?

LUCIE. I can stand it.

MASSON. Messieurs, your uniforms. Eyes front girls.

A sheet is held up with the men in front of it and the women behind. They try on the uniforms.

EUGENIE. Perhaps the two gentlemen would like to let us know how they find the front?

MARCEL. It's very smart.

EUGENIE. The battlefront.

JOSEPHINE. What action have you seen?

EMILE. Well. We've repaired the fortifications and now we're manning them.

LUCIE. Can you see the enemy?

MARCEL. Oh yes. We can see them.

MOLE. Are they dead or alive?

EMILE. They spend all day carrying out manoeuvres.

MARCEL. Prancing up and down.

EMILE. Watching us.

LUCIE. What do you do?

MARCEL. We man the fortifications.

EMILE. We post sentries.

MARCEL. We report all enemy movements to H.Q.

EUGENIE. Where's the fighting?

EMILE. There isn't any. We're waiting for orders.

MARCEL. And when we get them we'll break out.

MOLE. Ah! Break out! This is the Great Attack we've been hearing so much about.

MARCEL. Oh yes. We'll go over the top, charge, break through their defences and totally annihilate them.

EMILE. Well let's wait until we get some guns, eh? They're big fellers some of these Prussians.

MARCEL. We'll get guns.

EMILE. When? Have you seen anyone with a good gun? The only ones I've seen you couldn't hit the Empress's arse at five yards.

JOSEPHINE. What you going to do if the Prussians attack you?

EMILE. They're not going to attack us when they can just sit round the walls and starve us out. We've been watching them for three weeks digging themselves in. They've surrounded the city.

MARCEL. Well, I'll fight them with my bare hands.

EMILE. You might have to.

MASSON. Finished, gentlemen? Oh yes, splendid. Brush, Lucie. Doesn't he look handsome?

LUCIE. He looks a real hero.

MARCEL. Thanks

MASSON. If I were ten years younger! I shall just fetch my receipt book for you to sign.

Exit.

JOSEPHINE. You want to watch it Marcel. She'll have your trousers off for a little alteration if you give her half a chance.

MOLE. Yeah. Is the crutch a bit tight?

MARCEL. Get Off !

EUGENIE. I know who Marcel fancies. And it's not you Mole. What you waiting for, Lucie? Prince Charming? You want to grab him while he's going.

LUCIE. I can get by without a man thanks.

EMILE. She's playing hard to get.

LUCIE. And I can certainly do without a loudmouth like that one.

MARCEL. What have I done? What have I done?

Enter MASSON.

MASSON. No work to do? If you'll just sign the book M'sieur. Keep it official.

EMILE. I feel like a real soldier now.

EUGENIE. So do I.

EMILE. Think we'll beat those Prussians now, Mole?

MOLE. No trouble darling.

The song of the National Guard.

Exit EMILE *and* MARCEL.

MOLE. Aren't they wonderful? That's our citizen militia that is. They're going to save us from the Prussians. 'Be terrible Oh Patriots! Pause only when you pass by some simple peasant hut to imprint a kiss upon the brow of a sleeping child'. Lot of crap like that about, you know. Victor Hugo wrote that. Well. All they need now is a gun. They won't be getting one of course. They don't give guns to scum like Emile and Marcel. Because a gun has one great big disadvantage. It fires in whichever direction you point it. So they'll be saving the guns for the flashy dressers with the waxed mustachios, the old established regiments. The old established cowards who couldn't fight a fly with its wings nailed together.

MASSON *rings the bell*.

MASSON. I shall now go and share my husband's lunch. You may have the time – fifteen minutes mind – to yourselves. Bon appetit girls. And you Mole.

ALL. Thank you Madame.

Exit MASSON.

JOSEPHINE. I'm off.

EUGENIE. Dining at the Ritz today, Jose?

JOSEPHINE. I'll cast my eye over the menu; see what takes my fancy.

Exit JOSEPHINE.

EUGENIE. Good book, is it?

LUCIE. Mmm. Where does she go?

EUGENIE. You heard her. To the Ritz.

LUCIE. Oh come on. Where?

EUGENIE. You're so green. Where do you think? She goes out looking for scraps. In the bins.

LUCIE. That's awful.

EUGENIE. Where did you get that cheese?

LUCIE. My aunt sent it from Brittany.

EUGENIE. Before the siege started?

LUCIE. Yes.

EUGENIE. A piece of cheese that size costs two francs now. Eggs four francs each. How can Jose and Emile afford that? They've got kids. Kids don't understand about not eating. How do you get by with your little girl to feed?

LUCIE. I get by, just about. I'm lucky. I saved a bit while I was married.

EUGENIE. What you going to do when that runs out?

LUCIE. I try not to think about it. Would you like some?

EUGENIE. It's nice. Here. When your kid's better she'll be able to help you out. They always want girls for doll-dressing. She could get fifty centimes a day.

LUCIE. I can't let her go out to work. She's only a child. I want her to go to school.

EUGENIE. Sorry I spoke.

EUGENIE *looks for her bread which* MOLE *has pinched*.

Where's my bread? I had it here. I swear I did. Mole! You cow. You poxy old arse-licker. I'll do for you this time.

EUGENIE *and* MOLE *fight*.

LUCIE. Stop it Eugenie. Stop it. Have mine.

EUGENIE. You keep out of this. Stuck up bitch. You come in here with your cheese, chucking your bread around. Treating us like dirt. Saved a bit, have you? What do you know? You don't want for a good dress or a place to sleep. You don't know you're born. Wait till you've been slaving here on one franc a day for ten years. Then we'll see.

MOLE. She's right. Getting a bit of sense in her head at last. Clear off. Piss off out of it.

Enter JOSEPHINE.

JOSEPHINE. What's going on? Look at your faces, you're enough to turn the milk sour. Listen if anyone should be bellyaching I should. I'm getting so thin I'll be able to crack nuts with my knees soon. Look at 'em. I watched the fat men in the cafés. You should see the menu at Maxim's – 'Cat au Vin' – 'Dog's Leg à l'Orange'. It's bad enough without us fighting each other.

LUCIE. I hear they're eating the elephants out of the zoo.

JOSEPHINE. Some people are doing all right out of this siege. How are we supposed to live?

MOLE. We're not. That's the whole point.

Enter MASSON.

MASSON. Well. And what have we been plotting? Come along girls, look lively. Time is money. Mole? I'm giving you permission to go.

MOLE. Go?

MASSON. Yes. Monsieur tells me they are forming a women's batallion. You're always going on about the army and how you could do it better if you were a man. Now's your chance.

MOLE. Oh very nice. I'd look a treat goose-stepping along the street with my rags flapping around me ankles.

MASSON. I thought you'd jump at the chance. Mind you, with those legs you can't jump at much any more can you?

MOLE. A women's batallion indeed. Ha. Attached to the cavalry no doubt so they can ride us into battle. Charge!

MASSON. You're disgusting.

MOLE. Oh dear me no. What am I thinking of? They wouldn't let us within a mile of the Prussians. We might beat the bastards, then what? No more secret deals, no more seven course suppers for Thiers and Bismarck. Hey Josephine, now she'd make a good soldier.

JOSEPHINE. A women's army? I might join that. But not to fight the Prussians.

MOLE. Quite. Why worry about lice when you've got cancer? That's it. We're stuck. Stuck and starving. Paris is surrounded. The last train left a week ago. And guess who was on it. The mighty midget, gone to negotiate, so we're told. There's nothing to eat. You can only get rat in high class restaurants. What I wouldn't give for a nice piece of rat. Our only link with the outside world is balloons. I ask you, balloons. There's one. There's one now. That is vital. That's got a very important message in it. It names the date of the great break out, the great attack when we're going to smash through the Prussian lines. Now that is going to rally support for us throughout the world. Good luck, good luck, oh good luck! It came down in Sweden and the pilot broke his leg.

Exit MOLE.

Blackout. Sound of gunfire. Drums.

Enter JOSEPHINE *and* EUGENIE *with logs. They are wet and tired.*

JOSEPHINE. Oh no. This bloody stove's gone out.

EUGENIE *sinks down.*

Don't sit down Eugenie. I keep telling you, she's only waiting for an excuse to get rid of one of us.

Enter LUCIE: *with a branch.*

LUCIE. That's the last of the last trees of Paris. It's tragic.

JOSEPHINE. Never mind that. Let's get this stove lit.

LUCIE. The wood's wet.

JOSEPHINE *takes papers from* MASSON's *desk.*

JOSEPHINE. We'll use this.

LUCIE. You can't use that.

EUGENIE. That's her paperwork.

JOSEPHINE. So what.

LUCIE. Come on, quick.

They begin screwing up the paper to light the fire.

Enter MASSON.

MASSON. Josephine! How dare you. That is sacred, that is my paperwork.

JOSEPHINE. When we get the Commune everyone will do their own washing.

MASSON. Don't blaspheme Josephine! I will, I must have order. In my own house, in my own business. Everything in order. Everything accounted for. I shall go to heaven with the correct papers, my balance carried forward, and throw myself upon the mercy of the celestial auditor confident of double entry into the book of eternal life.

Enter MOLE: *Drops logs.*

MASSON. Mole, have you no feelings? My head. You've no idea what those guns sound like close to.

MOLE. We will have. Soon.

JOSEPHINE. What do you mean?

MOLE. The great break out. The great attack. The Prussians wiped us out.

MASSON. This is just a minor defeat, minor. I was with M'sieur watching the last batallions leave. You should have seen them Mole, their buttons gleaming, guns glistening in the sun, they were magnificent. If it weren't for that noise.

MOLE. Perhaps Madame would prefer it if the guns were to play a waltz?

MASSON. I want this war to finish just as much as everyone else does. I'm suffering, we're all suffering. Doesn't it move you to see my business grinding to a halt and nothing to heat the boilers with?

MOLE. Doesn't it move you to see us starving?

MASSON. I'm sick of you and your remarks. Keep them to yourself or out you go. I must lie down. There are some problems which can only be solved with a little silence.

Exit MASSON.

EUGENIE. They can't all be dead, Josie. Emile can look after himself.

JOSEPHINE. I haven't seen him for days. I'm worried sick.

LUCIE. This defeat means the siege goes on.

EUGENIE. And we're defenceless.

MOLE. All the Prussians have to do is start knocking down the walls of Paris and we've had it.

Enter EMILE *and* MARCEL.

MARCEL. Hello girls. Have you missed us?

EMILE. Look Josie. We've got guns. Well one between us anyway.

JOSEPHINE. Where the hell have you been? Not a word for four days. For all I knew you could have been dead. Not that I'd care.

EMILE. Give it a rest, Josie. Just once.

LUCIE. I must get back to Marie. Cover for me will you?

MARCEL. Don't let me drive you away.

LUCIE. I have to go. My girl's sick. If I don't look after her no one else will. She'll die.

MARCEL. What can I do?

LUCIE. You wouldn't know where to start.

Exit LUCIE.

MARCEL. What did I do this time? Here look Mole we got a gun at last. Yes well it's a bit old, it's a blunderbuss; what you do is you get the powder and you stuff it down the barrel like this . . . then you get the lead and you stuff that in afterwards . . .

EMILE. They don't want to know. We'll not stay where we're not wanted. Let's take our jug of wine elsewhere.

JOSEPHINE. On the piss again. No wonder you got defeated.

EMILE. Oh, you've heard. The great break out. What a bloody fiasco. Well don't blame us. We weren't there.

MARCEL. Wouldn't use the National Guard. Used the bleeding regulars.

EMILE. You should have seen them. Our lads.

MARCEL. You've got to admit they were smart.

EMILE. Magnificent sight. Trumpets and drums, hair parted down the middle, boots shining.

MARCEL. Teeth bared, nostrils flared – and that was just the horses. And the officers – left, left, left. Chaps right.

EMILE. We sat there watching them go. Three days later they marched back in –

MARCEL. Covered in glory.

EMILE. Covered in shit.

MARCEL. The Prussians had laid them out flat.

EMILE. Arses hanging out of their trousers.

MARCEL. A drunken newt could've pissed all over them.

EMILE. Funniest thing I've seen since my Josie got the measles.

General laughter and merriment.

Enter MASSON.

MASSON. You're disgusting. You're no better than animals. Have you no respect? I've had enough. Get out. Go on get out. All of you. Get out.

EUGENIE. We've worked here ten years –

JOSEPHINE. You can't just sack us –

MASSON. This is my laundry. I can do what I like. Get out. And don't come back.

Exit JOSEPHINE, EMILE, MARCEL, EUGENIE.

MASSON. Don't think I can't see you under there Mole, come out!

MOLE. Not Mole, Not your old friend Mole. You wouldn't. You couldn't have it on your conscience. A Christian woman like you . . .

MASSON. All right, all right. Shut up Mole. We can't work without fuel anyway. And if this siege goes on much longer there won't be any customers left.

Masson's Song.

EUGENIE (*off*). Mole? Mole? Thank God you're here. I've run all the way from Josie's. Lucie's there with her kid. She's in pain, she's really bad. Josie says can you get any laudanum?

MASSON. Lucie's girl? Poor little mite. Has she got clean sheets? Has the Doctor called yet?

MOLE. Where would they get the money for a quack?

MASSON. I'll pay. Eugenie, fetch Dr Gollet. If there's any query tell him Madame is paying. Run! I'll follow. Oh poor little mite.

MASSON *and* EUGENIE *exit.*

MOLE. You've got to admit it, she's all heart. You can always fool a woman with a sick kid. Even a mean old skinflint like Masson.

A howl from LUCIE, *off: lights dim.*

Re-enter MASSON.

MASSON. Dead. Cost me ten francs. That hole Josephine lives in. I was ashamed when Dr Gollet came, ashamed. Dr Gollet I said, please forgive these dreadful conditions. I can supervise my girls at work – but at home. Oh the smell. You really are like vermin aren't you? One thing I've learnt, there are things more important than money. Cleanliness for one. I can't wait to get home and have a bath. Then I shall prepare M'sieur's supper. There are still a few morsels left in the store cupboard. A few slices of smoked ham and the last of the brandied cherries. Yes. There are some things more important than money.

Blackout.

Drums. Night: a small area of stage is lit. Enter MARCEL *shaking a collecting tin mug.*

MARCEL. Guns for Paris! Guns for Paris! Give what you can brothers and sisters. Guns for Paris! Guns for the people! Give what you can for guns for the people.

VOICE OFF. Slut! You filthy little whore! Fornicating on my doorstep like an animal. I'll throw a bucket of cold water over you if I catch you here again. You whore! You're scum. Get back to the gutter where you belong. Scum.

Enter LUCIE.

MARCEL *recognises her.*

LUCIE. Don't touch me, don't. I'm so sick of being hungry. That was the first time. You've no idea, men. You go off, leave us, leave your children. All you can think about is beating the Prussians, tactics, manoeuvres, the excitement. You don't have to listen to your child crying for its father. I used to give her pebbles to suck. We pretended they were sweets. I made a game of it. But it wasn't a game. She's dead because I couldn't feed her, house her, give her medicine. That's real. And it's real when I stand in an alley and lift my skirts for a bit of bread.

MARCEL. I didn't know.

LUCIE. Well you know now.

MARCEL. I'm collecting for guns to defend Paris. So far I've got a hundred and fifty-three francs, and a tin button.

Exit MARCEL *and* LUCIE.

Drums.

Enter MOLE.

MOLE. The Prussians started to bombard Paris on the 23rd of January. Our so-called leaders wanted to throw in the towel straight away. We said no. We were the ones who'd been starving, we weren't going to give in now. With us it was death or victory, there will be no surrender!

JOSEPHINE. Thiers has surrendered! (*Enter.*)

EMILE. They've chucked it in! (*Enter.*)

EUGENIE. Sold us out! (*Enter.*)

Enter MARCEL *and* LUCIE.

EMILE. A hundred and thirty-four days we've held out and the bastards have chucked it in.

LUCIE. What have we been starving for?

JOSEPHINE. They've given in.

MARCEL. Without a fight.

EUGENIE. Tomorrow thirty thousand Prussians will march down the Champs Elysées.

LUCIE. Just to rub our noses in it.

MARCEL. We didn't sign any armistice.

JOSE. And Thiers has handed over Alsace, Lorraine and twenty million francs.

MOLE. How much?

They stand facing each other on either side of the stage.

Enter MASSON *down the middle.*

MASSON. It is rather a lot of money isn't it? As the Governor of the Bank of France wrote to M'sieur Thiers: 'Where is the guiding hand, the rallying influence, the decision that sets uncertainty at rest?' Yes. Well I don't always understand what my bank manager says either. But I think this makes it slightly clearer. It's from the financiers, and it says 'You, Monsieur Thiers, will never get any financial business done until you put an end to those scoundrels, and take their guns away from them.'

Exeunt.

Enter MOLE *with bucket and brush: scrubs.* LUCIE *and* EUGENIE *appear above the washing lines.*

LUCIE. Eugenie! Eugenie look.

EUGENIE. What?

LUCIE. Look at Mole. She's scrubbing.

EUGENIE. So?

LUCIE. She's outside. She's scrubbing the street.

EUGENIE. Let's go down and help her then.

LUCIE. What's she doing it for?

EUGENIE. She's scrubbing out the smell of Prussians.

A black sheet is hung on the front line.

EUGENIE *and* LUCIE *join* MOLE *scrubbing.*

Song: The Lament of Louise Michel

Exit LUCIE.

Enter MASSON.

MASSON. That's right, put your backs into it. Clean floor, clean start. Everything back to normal. Or soon will be, so M'sieur tells me. Ah. The aroma of good food drifting through the streets. Crisp white napkins, clean tablecloths. My sister in Dijon sent me a pot of mustard today. I haven't seen a pot of mustard in months.

Enter LUCIE.

LUCIE. They're taking the guns, our guns.

MASSON. You're late.

LUCIE. Have you heard anything?

EUGENIE. Heard what?

LUCIE. About the guns.

JOSEPHINE. What guns?

LUCIE. Our guns.

EUGENIE. What about them?

LUCIE. They're taking them.

JOSEPHINE. Who's taking them?

LUCIE. The government.

JOSEPHINE. Do you mean Thiers?

LUCIE. Yes. Thiers and the Government. Taking our guns.

EUGENIE. The ones we paid for?

LUCIE. Yes. Our cannons.

JOSEPHINE. The bastards.

EUGENIE. Why?

LUCIE. So we can't use them against them, that's why.

JOSEPHINE. Bastards.

MASSON. What is that whispering?

EUGENIE. They're taking our guns.

JOSEPHINE. Stealing them.

MASSON. Guns? What guns?

LUCIE. Thiers and the government. Taking our guns that we paid for by public subscription.

JOSEPHINE. They're stealing them.

MASSON. Stealing? Who's stealing?

JOSEPHINE. Are they taking them from Montmartre?

LUCIE. Montmartre, Belleville, La Villette, everywhere.

EUGENIE. Where have they taken them *to*?

LUCIE. They haven't. Yet.

EUGENIE. What's going on?

JOSEPHINE. What are they doing?

LUCIE. I don't know but the guns are still there. They haven't moved them.

JOSEPHINE. ⎫
EUGENIE.　⎬ Why not?

LUCIE. I don't know.

Enter MOLE *followed by* EMILE *and* MARCEL.

MOLE. Get your red flag out, Masson. You'll be needing it. Come on you lot, there's work to be done.

LUCIE. Have they taken them?

MOLE. Oh yes we're taking them.

JOSEPHINE. Thiers?

MOLE. No. Us.

EUGENIE. Who?

MOLE. The people.

MASSON. What people?

MOLE. What people do you think Masson?

LUCIE. I thought Thiers was taking them.

MARCEL. He was. He sent in the 88th under Lecompte.

EMILE. The troops got the guns.

MARCEL. But they couldn't move them.

ALL. Why?

EMILE. Because they forgot the bloody horses, didn't they!

MARCEL. To move the gun carriages away.

EUGENIE. So they're still there?

MARCEL. Yes. All around them people are –

EMILE. There's a crowd gathering.

MARCEL. And some of the troops have deserted already.

MOLE. Hail Mary, kiss my arse! Masson this is it.

Loud bang off.

MASSON. I'm going to faint.

MARCEL. It's Belleville.

MOLE. I'm going to miss it.

MARCEL. It's a signal. They're rising.

LUCIE. Come on.

MASSON. Where are we going?

ALL. Forward!

Exeunt. MASSON *is hustled out with the others.*

Shouts off: 'Give us those guns'/'They're ours'/'Hand them over,' *etc.*

Re-enter MASSON *running. Kneels as at confession. Stamping and shouting continue.*

MASSON. Bless me Father, for I have sinned. Oh Father I don't know how, or why, or where or when, but there I was in the street. Hundreds of people were swarming up the hill in a crowd, in a bunch. Artillery men, soldiers, trying to get through but they couldn't. And the people swarmed up, over the ammunition wagons, under the wheels, under the horses. Oh, and the females, of whom I was one Father – under duress, Father – the females were at the front screaming in fury. And I'm sure Mole was there.

MOLE (*off*). Give us those fucking guns!

Exit MASSON.

Enter MOLE, MARCEL, EMILE, EUGENIE, JOSEPHINE, LUCIE, *in line as if facing troops. All shout together until* JOSEPHINE *steps to the front.*

JOSEPHINE. Well if that was a riot I reckon we ought to have them more often. I mean it was great. We were shouting and screaming. And then I found myself hanging on to the wheel of a cannon.
JOSEPHINE, MOLE, EUGENIE, *and* LUCIE *mime holding the cannon.*

MOLE. Hang on, Josie.

EUGENIE. Keep hold.

LUCIE. Don't let go.

EMILE.
MARCEL. } Cut the traces.

EUGENIE. What with?

LUCIE. Give us a knife.

EUGENIE. They passed these little knives up the front. The one I had was little with a white handle. I was hacking away at the traces. We was all pressed up tight round the cannon. Mostly women, it was. All laughing and shouting and that. Anyway I managed to cut through – and the horses were off!

They fall as if suddenly releasing the cannon. JOSEPHINE *scrambles up.*

JOSEPHINE. We were all squashed together. It was a bit frightening, but everyone was happy and good-natured. Then we went up to the troops and started talking to them face to face.

The women speak as to troops on the other side persuading them to join them.

EUGENIE. Anyway after that the troops just sort of gave up and joined us.

MARCEL. Then we saw the 79th coming to a halt at Solferino Tower. Two officers were coming for a parley. Suddenly General Lecomte was there. There was a crowd of women and children at the top of the Rue Muller. Lecomte was giving orders to fire.

EMILE. The women and children stood their ground and began to shout 'don't shoot, don't shoot'. And then we heard the General say:

MARCEL. Make ready to fire!

EMILE. Nobody moved.

MARCEL. Take aim!

EMILE. Still nobody moved.

MARCEL. Fire!

EMILE. Nothing happened. One by one, the rifles went up in the air. The soldiers had refused to fire on their own people.

MARCEL. The General he kept shouting 'Fire! Fire!' But no one took any notice. And then he said 'Are you going to surrender to this scum?'

EMILE. And one soldier turned round and said 'Yes.' 'That's exactly what we're going to do.' And he threw down his rifle. And everyone else ran off.

MARCEL. The General was bloody livid. Puce he went. He kept shouting to the police 'Defend me. Fire! Fire!'

EMILE. Then we arrested the police. It was great.

EUGENIE. We found out afterwards it was the same everywhere. You know, when the word went round. It wasn't planned out or anything. Well I don't think it was. It was really nice, wasn't it Lucie?

LUCIE. Yes.

JOSEPHINE. And we did it.

MOLE. The scum did it.

EUGENIE. It was the nicest day I can remember anyway.

MOLE. And then Thiers and the government, they were so scared they packed up their little toothbrushes into their little bags and they all ran off to Versailles so they could ask Bismarck what to do next.

MARCEL. They left. The whole lot. The whole shower. Without fighting or negotiating or anything. Cowards.

EMILE. Three days ago I was elected to the Central Committee of the National Guard.

MARCEL. I voted for him. We're in the same batallion.

EMILE. When they left there was no one in the city to run it, you see. So we did. We did it. The Central Committee. I was put in charge of distributing the Manifesto.

MARCEL. We discussed all that and wrote it down. And this is what it is. 'We are an irresistible barrier against all attempts to overthrow the Republic. Ours is the perilous honour of defending it. We will not fail in our mission. Let them call us troublemakers, creators of dissension and disorder. Our behaviour proves beyond all doubt that these accusations are false. We are obdurate conservatives. Our aim is to conserve all forms of Liberty for which the Republic stands. Nothing could be further from our intentions than to create violent and damaging conflict between citizens. We reach out a fraternal hand to all our fellow citizens, and to all the peoples of the world. But now that we have won back the right to control our lives we will not part with it. We will no longer put up with alienation, with monarchs, oppressors and exploiters of all kinds who have come to regard people as property, and who use them for the satisfaction of their criminal instincts. To each the rights and duties befitting the conditions of a free man. This is our programme which we loudly proclaim for all to hear.'

ALL. Long Live the Commune!

ACT TWO

EUGENIE *and* JOSEPHINE *watch* EMILE *putting up a poster. They stare at it.*

JOSEPHINE. What does it say Eugenie?

EUGENIE. It's about the elections. It's a message.

JOSEPHINE. What does it say?

EUGENIE. It's an address to the Citizens. To us.

JOSEPHINE. I can see that. It's on the wall for us to read. What does it say?

EUGENIE. I can't bloody read, can I.

JOSEPHINE. Oh Christ, no wonder we're so bloody helpless. How are we going to have anything to do with running this fine city when we can't even read? Try Eugenie. Surely you can read a bit. Try. Try. Go on.

Drags EUGENIE *to the poster. Both try to spell out some of it. Enter* LUCIE.

LUCIE. There's a big meeting in the square! There's a band and a singer.

JOSEPHINE. You can read. Here. Read that.

LUCIE *starts to read. Silently.*

JOSEPHINE. Out loud!

LUCIE. Oh I see. 'Citizens, our mission is at an end. We will now hand over your town hall to new and rightful representatives. Citizens, remember that the men who still serve you best are those whom you will choose from among your own ranks, who lead the same lives as yourselves and suffer the same hardships. Beware of the ambitious and the newly rich. Beware too of windbags who prefer words to deeds. And avoid those whom fortune has favoured excessively. The wealthy are rarely disposed to considering the working classes as their brothers. We are confident that if you follow these suggestions you will at last have achieved an authentic people's representation and found representatives who will never see themselves as your masters.

Town Hall. Signed Central Committee of the National Guard.'

JOSEPHINE. That's right. Good.

EUGENIE. Except we won't be voting will we? In the baggage wagon as usual. Propping up the menfolk so they can make decisions for us.

JOSEPHINE. I'm not having that. Not now.

EUGENIE. How are you going to vote? How are you going to let your dulcet voice be heard?

JOSEPHINE. Loud and clear. I'll be down that town hall when the Commune's meeting in there. I'll be listening and I'll be asking questions too. For a start, I want to know when my daughter's going to learn to read and write. So she won't be an ignorant cow like me.

LUCIE. You're not ignorant. You've taught me how to survive.

JOSEPHINE. That's what women are good at. It's not enough. You see. I'll be standing on the town hall steps waiting to get in on the day they start.

EUGENIE. They might not let you in.

JOSEPHINE. Just let them try and keep me out. And you. Let's go and hear this band.

Exeunt.

Enter MASSON. *She fills a basket with as much that is movable as she can.*

Enter MOLE, *with a knife.*

MOLE. Going for a stroll are we?

MASSON. Mole! Oh I've had the most dreadful day, Mole, dreadful. Deserted by everything, everyone I hold dear.

MOLE. Oh dear, oh dear.

MASSON. Soften your heart, Mole. You see before you a woman alone. Monsieur has gone to Versailles with the government naturally –

MOLE. Naturally.

MASSON. And the most crushing blow. The priest – gone!

MOLE. That's just as it should be. The church following the state, bosses sticking together. Never mind. I'll stick my knife up him for you if you like?

MASSON. Mole, that knife! You have never understood, Mole, the support I get from the Church.

MOLE. Oh I do.

MASSON. The exhilaration I feel after a good confession.

MOLE. Is it like the other day? When we got the guns? That was exhilarating wasn't it?

MASSON. I am grateful for the experience of course. But if Claude should ever find out –

MOLE. You needn't worry about Claude. He's buggered off to Versailles hasn't he? You're one of us now aren't you, Margot? You're one of the workers; what you did the other day proves it. And the workers are going to take control, aren't we? Make sure the bourgeois don't drop us in it like they did the last time.

MASSON. The workers, yes, Eugenie, Josephine. And you, Mole. You must learn to govern, to take control. How wonderful, Mole. You must build yourself up for the great struggle ahead. There's some fresh bread in the kitchen, Mole. And a bottle of brandy. Will you fetch it Mole? I feel quite weak.

MOLE. I'll go. And when I come back we'll have a nice little chat about Forty-Eight and what went wrong. Shan't be long, Margot.

Exit MOLE – *taking* MASSON's *account book from her basket.*

MASSON *gathers up her basket, throws in some of the good laundry.*

MASSON. Who's going to miss a few pieces of lace now the world's gone mad? To Versailles! To Versailles!

Exit MASSON.

Re-enter MOLE.

MOLE. Margot! Oi, Margot? I knew she'd go the minute my back was turned. I'm just too kind-hearted, that's my trouble. What I should have done is I should have stuck my knife right up her.

I shall live to regret that. I'm like the barber's cat. All wind and piss.

Exit MOLE.

EUGENIE *starts to hang up red pillowcases on the line.* LUCIE *and* JOSEPHINE *enter: they play cards.*

EUGENIE. Do you like them? I think they're lovely. It's a treat to see a spot of colour. Had a bit of trouble getting the dye. It's so popular nowadays. Mole let me in here to do the dirty work. Gay as a lark she is. It's all legal now. The Commune has been elected by two hundred and twenty-nine thousand, one hundred and sixty-seven votes. We, the men, that is, made the big decision last Sunday. March 26th. I was worried you know, in case it went the wrong way. I'm all for people voting but it's hard when you have to stand by and watch. It's not like taking the guns. Is it? Mind you, there's no law against celebrating. I've got such a hangover. The celebrations that went on yesterday. They were something. I got the idea for these then. They had red drapes, everywhere. On the platform, round the statue of the Republic, on the bayonets. The jingling was lovely. Made me feel like a girl. And that's saying something.

She joins LUCIE *and* JOSEPHINE.

LUCIE. There's no more soup. I don't know what we're going to do tomorrow.

EUGENIE. Sing for our supper.

Enter MOLE. *She wears a red bonnet.*

MOLE. What do you lot think you're doing in here, eh?

EUGENIE. Oh Mole, you do look Smart!

MOLE. Mop that lot up you bitches. Masson's gone now and she's left me in charge. Let's see some work round here for a change.

MOLE *chases them.*

JOSEPHINE. Come off it, Mole!

LUCIE. Will you pay us then, Mole? Will you give us a rise?

MOLE. Who's a clever girlie then. Knocked it on the head. Where would I get the money to pay you lot? I was only trying to give you a bit of a thrill. How do you like my bonnet?

LUCIE. Lovely.

EUGENIE. Matches my pillowcases.

MOLE. When you get to my age best put your head where your mouth is. If you see what I mean.

JOSEPHINE. She's got a point. We can't just sit about doing nothing for ever.

LUCIE. I've been looking round the bins.

EUGENIE. No luck?

JOSEPHINE. Half the shops are empty. There's a grocer down the hill, the one that made a packet in the siege. He's gone off to Versailles and left his assistants guarding the shop.

EUGENIE. With pickhandles.

LUCIE. Surely someone will do something?

MOLE. Don't expect the Commune to do more for you than you can do for yourselves.

JOSEPHINE. We're wasting time arguing. Why don't we go down the grocers and take the food? They're only lads. It should be shared out. We took the guns. Think of those bastards sitting on all that food. All through the siege when people were starving.

LUCIE. And children dying.

JOSEPHINE. Let's go.

EUGENIE. He won't be there will he?

JOSEPHINE. Who?

EUGENIE. The boss.

JOSEPHINE. }
LUCIE.   } No.

JOSEPHINE. He's lounging about in some posh hotel in Versailles drinking champagne with Masson.

MOLE. Now Masson's gone we can do what we like with this place. What do you fancy? We could smash the place up?

She kicks a basket to EUGENIE.

EUGENIE. Give us a lift wouldn't it? All the years we've slogged here.

EUGENIE *kicks the basket back.*

JOSEPHINE. Not food though, is it?

MOLE. All right. Flog the sheets.

EUGENIE. We could get a bit for some of this stuff. There's some good lace here.

JOSEPHINE. We could buy food if we sold these sheets.

LUCIE. What do we say to the people this stuff belongs to? They're not all like Masson, up and gone.

MOLE. Property is theft.

LUCIE. We've got to find work.

EUGENIE. The only work we know is laundering. There's no laundries open to employ us so that's that.

LUCIE. We could start this one going again.

EUGENIE. It isn't ours, stupid. It belongs to –

ALL. Masson!

LUCIE. Yes but she's not here is she?

EUGENIE. So?

LUCIE. All I'm saying is why don't we work it? Make our living from it?

EUGENIE. She'd have the police on us.

JOSEPHINE. She'd have fifty fits.

LUCIE. She's gone. Why keep going on as if she's coming back? We've got the Commune now. Could you see Masson living under a worker's government? Besides there are no police.

EUGENIE. It's stealing.

LUCIE. You don't mind pinching the lace but you won't take over this place.

EUGENIE. That's different.

LUCIE. How?

EUGENIE. I could say it got lost. Stolen. Fell off the back of a cart. But people would see us working here.

MOLE. How much would you get if you flogged that lot?

EUGENIE. A few francs.

MOLE. How long would that last?

EUGENIE. A couple of weeks.

MOLE. Then what?

EUGENIE. Short life and a gay one, eh?

JOSEPHINE. That's our trouble. No foresight. Masson, she thinks ahead.

LUCIE. What else does she do?

EUGENIE. Watches us working.

JOSEPHINE. She makes sure we work.

EUGENIE. That's her job. If you can call it a job.

JOSEPHINE. We do the real work. Washing, ironing, humping tubs.

EUGENIE. All for six francs a week. Cheap at the price.

JOSEPHINE. How much do you reckon she took home?

LUCIE. We could find out. From the account books.

EUGENIE. Her paperwork.

LUCIE. She's taken them . . .

MOLE. If a job's worth doing, it's worth doing well . . .

She rummages in her drawers and fetches out the book.

Citizeness! Madame's work book. Come on then, sit down at her desk. See what she had to say about all her customers . . .

LUCIE. Shall I have a look?

JOSEPHINE. ⎫
EUGENIE. ⎭ Yes.

LUCIE. Let's take an average week shall we? June 13th last year.

JOSEPHINE. Lots of soldiers and tourists about then.

LUCIE. Income. Eighty francs.

EUGENIE. Fifty centimes a bundle, that's a hundred and sixty – about twenty-six a day.

JOSEPHINE. Sounds right.

LUCIE. Expenditure. Wages eighteen francs.

JOSEPHINE. That was before you came.

EUGENIE. Three of us at six francs each.

LUCIE. Wood fifteen francs.

JOSEPHINE. She swore she spent thirty on wood.

LUCIE. Soap five, oil two.

JOSEPHINE. How much does that add up to?

LUCIE. Forty francs.

EUGENIE. But you said she was taking in eighty.

LUCIE. That's right.

JOSEPHINE. The greedy cow. I knew she was bleeding us but I didn't know it was that much.

EUGENIE. I'd bleed her sodding throat if I could get my hands on her. I'd stuff a bit of Bouquin's sausage right down her windpipe.

LUCIE. For every franc she gave you lot she made two.

JOSEPHINE. Forty francs a week clear profit. How much is that a year?

EUGENIE. It's a hundred and sixty a month.

LUCIE. Twelve months – it's almost two thousand francs.

EUGENIE. Where did it go?

JOSEPHINE. Down her throat and on her back.

LUCIE. How long have you worked here?

EUGENIE. Ten years.

LUCIE. That's twenty thousand francs-worth of your labour. One could say that you've invested twenty thousand in this business. Good heavens. You could have bought your own laundry by now.

MOLE. Still think it's stealing to take over this place?

JOSEPHINE. We've paid for this stuff ten times over with our labour. All the time we've been here she's never replaced a thing.

EUGENIE. Twenty thousand francs just for one person. I don't know whether to laugh or cry.

JOSEPHINE. I think we should give it a try. Eugenie?

EUGENIE. Count me in.

MOLE. We'll have to work hard you know, harder than before.

LUCIE. But we'll be working for ourselves and each other.

EUGENIE. Will we get wages? We haven't got any soap, we can't start.

JOSEPHINE. I've seen a bit of soap left somewhere.

LUCIE. That's all we need. Enough to get us through the first week.

EUGENIE. Then we'll have money coming in.

LUCIE. We take out what we need for supplies each week, and divide the rest equally between us.

JOSEPHINE. What about wood?

EUGENIE. We've got no wood.

JOSEPHINE. I've got a table. We'll chop it up.

MOLE. I can nip down the Bleeding Heart of Jesus and borrow a couple of pews.

LUCIE. Are we all agreed?

ALL. Yes.

They begin putting the laundry to rights.

JOSEPHINE. We'd better get some work in.

EUGENIE. Start with tidying this place up.

JOSEPHINE. There's a lot of filthy National Guards about.

EUGENIE. We want to get the drawers off them.

LUCIE. I think I'll write to the Commune. Ask for a contract.

JOSEPHINE. Write to the Central Committee as well. Ask Emile for a contract for his batallion. They're a dirty lot.

LUCIE. I'll do both.

Enter EMILE with a newspaper.

EMILE. Here. This is interesting. The Commune has decreed that workshops abandoned by their owners should be taken over by the workers and run co-operatively. What do you think?

MOLE. Never work sunshine, never work.

Blackout.

Birdsong noises. Enter MASSON *with parasol and picnic. She spreads a cloth in the spotlight.*

MASSON. How pleasant to be out of Paris. The formal gardens here at Versailles are quite remarkable. I am meeting such nice people too. I saw the Marquis de Gallifet. Such a gallant man. Only in the distance of course. And the gowns! The one worn yesterday by Blanche d'Antigny – she is not quite respectable but she is intimate with some of France's most distinguished persons – the gown she wore had two hundred and fifty yards of material and she wore it with white camellias. Madame Bouquin said it cost ten thousand francs. Mind you, everyone here is deeply moved, profoundly concerned with what is happening in our beloved Paris. Why, only yesterday a friend told Claude, who told me, that M'sieur Thiers was preparing to take the necessary steps in the national interest. My friend heard M'sieur Thiers say 'The extremists have taken over! Have I not warned you? These brigands and criminals have shed the blood of two of my loyal supporters, Clement Thomas and General Lecomte.' M'sieur Thiers was, so the friend said, almost in tears. He's not a man who cries easily either. Then he said 'This Parisian conspiracy against the Republic compels me to shed French blood.' I fear Monsieur Thiers is far too moderate. One can expect no moderation from those thieving murdering scum. But dear Claude assures me that Herr Bismarck will send his brave Prussian troops to aid our noble French soldiers, to save Paris. Most reassuring. Claude! Wait for me Claude! I said wait!

Exit.

Blackout.

Lights come up on MOLE, JOSEPHINE, LUCIE, MARCEL, EUGENIE, EMILE, *deep in thought. They wear red sashes.*

JOSEPHINE. Your trouble is you think they're as soft as you are. You mark my words that little bleeder Thiers is just waiting to get his forces marshalled. They'll be on us like wolves.

EMILE. I'm not disagreeing with you Josie. But you're talking about civil war. Just be clear about that, it's civil war.

MARCEL. As far as I'm concerned they're the bloody enemy now. That lot at Versailles. Let's get that straight once and for all.

LUCIE. Just because they're savages doesn't mean we have to be. We have to be careful. We know here in Paris we know we're right but we've got to show the rest of France. We shan't do that with guns. With words and actions we show them.

MARCEL. Well I know what action I'd take. And I won't be talking.

JOSEPHINE. Where have you been? Cloud cuckoo land? The regulars are creeping back to Versailles. Bismarck is handing over the prisoners of war he took last September. Know why? So Thiers will have the muscle to defeat us, that's why.

MARCEL. We should smash him and his crew first.

MOLE. Yes. Attack. That's what we want. We should form our battallions and attack. Bombard them, shell them, attack, attack.

EMILE. You're just bloodthirsty. Let it never be said that we of the Commune fired the first shot in a civil war.

JOSEPHINE. Emile, you're a good man. They won't be so good. I say we should attack now.

MARCEL. Now while we're strong.

LUCIE. You make me sick. There's so much to be done.

EUGENIE. How can you talk about fighting when there's so much to be done?

LUCIE. The Commune has only just begun. They've decreed for a start, just a beginning, the separation of Church and State.

MOLE. Oh goody goody. No more priests to tell us what's right.

LUCIE. Do you know what that means, Mole? It means new

kinds of education, not the old schools run by nuns and priests where the only thing you learn is the catechism. It all has to be thought out and made to work. How can we put our energies into fighting? That would kill the Commune.

EUGENIE. You can't build anything good out of killing.

EMILE. Socialism goes forward without bayonets.

MOLE.
JOSEPHINE. } It's got bayonets against it!

MARCEL. I'll fight to keep the Commune. I'll use a bayonet, catapult and stone, anything handy, mate.

LUCIE. We cannot place our energies in defence. We must build. No good talking about a new life. We've got to construct it brick by brick.

EUGENIE. I'm happy. For the first time in my life. Work makes me happy. I couldn't abide to lose that. Talk of fighting, that's blood in the gutters and death every day. We'll lose it all. We couldn't go back as it was.

EMILE. In time they'll see our ideas are just and our procedure democratic.

MOLE. You haven't half learnt to put the talk on.

EMILE. Well I've had to. A communal way of organising life is the only way we shall achieve liberty. It places liberty within the people's grasp. It is in the Commune that the strength of free people resides. They must see the Commune is right, in time.

MARCEL. Who? Who must see?

LUCIE. All right-thinking people.

MOLE.
JOSEPHINE. } TIME?

JOSEPHINE. Time! That's just what they're not going to give us. Thiers and his parasites.

MOLE. I had a dream last night. Horrible nightmare it was. I dreamt that old Bismarck said to Thiers, 'My friend, you must provoke the insurrection while you still have the power to crush it. For good.' And do you know what Thiers replied? He said 'But of course Monsieur Bismarck. That is my plan. That is precisely what I mean to do.'

JOSEPHINE. We've got the strength to crush them now, if we organise.

MARCEL. See? That bastard will even deal with the Prussians. To smash us. We fought, week in, week out; we stood against the Prussians. Now he's dealing with them. We should attack.

JOSEPHINE. Now.

EUGENIE. Blood and death, that's you. Women's sons slaughtered, all you care.

MOLE. Not so. But they're weak now. We have strength of numbers. Know what that gives us? Elbow. Strike a little terror to get and keep some, just some of our demands. It's known as a strong negotiating position.

EMILE. They will see in time that what we are doing is just.

LUCIE. And humane. And rational.

MOLE. Humane?

JOSEPHINE. Just? Them?

MOLE. Do you think they're as decent as you are? That's your trouble, too much respect for property. Look at the bank. We should be out there taking it over. Getting our hands on the money. How are we going to get on without money? Governor of the Bank of France going to give the Commune an overdraft is he?

LUCIE. Mole. I've explained all this. Money is only paper. It's only worth anything if everyone agrees to take it in exchange for goods. Do you think the business people will take money stolen from the bank?

MOLE. That's why we've got to take over the lot, businesses and all.

Everyone shouts at once.

EMILE. Stop. Everyone. Stop rowing. Jesus! We don't have to fight today. Do we? Maybe tomorrow. The sun's out, the cherry trees are all hung about with white blossom, it's May time. Birdies singing. People in the streets promenading in their Sunday best. Be happy all. Drink. Beloved Jose I respect you. I kiss you Josie.

JOSEPHINE. You're a good man, Emile.

EMILE. I kiss you all. (*Kisses all round.*)

MARCEL. You're a clever woman, Lucie. I wish I could talk like you.

LUCIE. Talking's not everything.

MOLE. 'Ere Eug. Think they'll be walking up the aisle soon? You and me can be the bridesmaids. What shall we wear? Myself I fancy the chantilly lace with pale yellow ribbons and a bouquet of camellias.

Blackout.

Lights up on JOSEPHINE, EUGENIE, LUCIE *and* MOLE, *at a public meeting. They speak as if to a large assembly, nervously at first.* JOSEPHINE *bangs a gavel.*

JOSEPHINE. Marriage is slavery. A woman who enters legal marriage sells herself, body, soul and property! If she's got any!

EUGENIE. It should be a crime to sell your liberty. It's a base bargain no free woman should accept – and no free city should tolerate!

MOLE. Abolish it! The women of Paris should let the Commune know their views on this!

JOSEPHINE. I earn my living. I depend on no man for my bread. I choose to live with a man because I fancy him and because we think alike.

LUCIE. Marriage makes you part of a man's possessions. He is put above you, he is your owner.

EUGENIE. If you're at the top of the dungheap, marriage makes sense. Warm bed, silk nightdress, plenty to eat – everything taken care of.

MOLE. Same as the nuns. Not a worry in the world. The Church sees you all right if you sell your daughter to be a bride of Christ.

LUCIE. That's another thing. Look at how cheap nuns sell their work, fine needlework. They can undercut any seamstress in France.

EUGENIE. Women's work is the worst paid. Maybe the employers think our husbands keep us.

JOSEPHINE. They know well enough we have to work. But they know they can get our labour cheap because we're too scared to ask for more.

LUCIE. Sisters! We should propose to the Commune that the question of female labour be discussed.

EUGENIE. This is a very important thing. We should let them know how poor the working women of the city are.

LUCIE. They're losing what little work they have with everything at a standstill.

JOSEPHINE. Hunger will soon take away their fighting spirit. The women's manufactures must be shielded. I propose the Commune should distribute work for women in all their trades. Embroidery, hat making, buttons, umbrellas, tie making –

EUGENIE. Flower making, fans, banners, beads and pearls, typography –

LUCIE. Type-setting, bookbinding, glass-blowing, painting porcelain, all the things women do.

MOLE. What about laundries!

JOSEPHINE. We work as long hours as any man.

MOLE. And get paid half the rate.

EUGENIE. We should be paid the same.

LUCIE. Thousands of women have no skill.

EUGENIE. They work for as little as fifty centimes a day.

LUCIE. They haven't enough learning to master a trade – to earn enough to keep themselves.

JOSEPHINE. We are denied education, the means to understanding. But it's beginning. Citizeness Maniere has set up an industrial school to train women and to give them a scientific education.

LUCIE. Education starts from the very first day of life. The *Journal Officiel* has published a proposal for the establishment of day nurseries for the children of women workers.

JOSEPHINE. It says we must have healthy children to build the future. It says that children will be happy there.

LUCIE. They'll have toys, carts, an aviary full of birds, painting and sculptures –

MOLE. Not religious ones either!

LUCIE. The premises to be light and airy.

EUGENIE. And the gardens used as the weather permits!

JOSEPHINE. With such a good beginning we'll see a new race of women.

EUGENIE. I daresay there'll still be plenty of men to sneer at us as incapable weaklings.

JOSEPHINE. Some of them say our minds are dull.

LUCIE. Some say that our bodies are less perfect than a man's.

EUGENIE. Men are cowards. They call themselves the masters of creation and are a set of dolts.

LUCIE. The interests of working men and women are the same. We all suffer the same privations under the same masters.

MOLE. We have petroleum, we have hatchets and strong arms to fight those masters.

JOSEPHINE. We may be simple women but we're not made of weaker stuff than our grandmothers of 1793. We should be up and doing, as they would if they were living now!

Exeunt.
Blackout.

Enter MASSON *with binoculars and parasol in spotlight. She is watching something.*

MASSON. Claude, beloved. What are all those people doing round the Vendome Column? They have affixed red flags to it. Red flags on our national monument to Napoleon! The symbol of France's military glory desecrated by the foul insignia of the scum insurrection! Claude, what are those curious strings descending from the Column? I see, cables. They appear to be

moving. By a what? I see. A capstan is turning and thus
tightening, pulling the cables. Claude. It moved. The column.
It's moving – it's gone! They have pulled down the column!
Claude, imagine it. The bust of Caesar which adorned the top
of the Column lying headless in the gutter! Who was
responsible for this outrage? A painter? Do you mean a house
painter Claude, an interior decorator? Oh. An artist. Gustave
Courbet? One of those depraved depicters of modern scenes I
suppose. I am too ashamed to watch any more Claude. Take
me away, take me away. They shall pay for this. I'm sure Mole
was there.

Exit.
Blackout.

Lights up on LUCIE *and* MARCEL. LUCIE *is preparing a speech.*

MARCEL. Go on then.

LUCIE. Well, listen then.

MARCEL. I am listening.

LUCIE. 'Today it is the duty of the Commune to the workers
who created it, to take all necessary steps to achieve constructive
results. Action must be taken.'

MARCEL. Fast.

LUCIE. 'And it must be taken fast. The Commune must abandon
the mistaken ideas of old, and get its inspiration from the very
difficulties of the situation. It must apply methods that will
survive the circumstances that first led to their use.'

MARCEL. What mistakes?

LUCIE. What?

MARCEL. 'Mistaken ideas of old' you said.

LUCIE. I meant the workers of 1848 didn't think in the long
term. They adopted quick solutions.

MARCEL. Go on then.

LUCIE. 'We shall achieve this through the creation of special
workshops and training centres where finished products are
stored and sold' –

MARCEL. How are you going to organise it?

LUCIE. I'm just coming to that bit. 'The necessary organisation for this scheme will be under the control of a committee of women appointed in each district' –

MARCEL. What about money?

LUCIE. 'The Finance Delegate will make a weekly credit available so the work of the women can be organised immediately.'

MARCEL. Is that it?

LUCIE. Yes. What's wrong with it?

MARCEL. Nothing.

LUCIE. Say if you don't like it. It's not just my ideas you know, we all discussed it –

MARCEL. You're nervous aren't you?

LUCIE. Yes. I've got to speak before the whole Commission of Labour.

MARCEL. You'll handle them, no trouble.

They kiss. Enter MOLE, JOSEPHINE, EMILE *and* EUGENIE.

MOLE. Roll up, roll up! The first person to guess how old I am wins a night with me! Consolation prize two nights.

EMILE. I'd say you were a fine figure of a woman when you were young, eh Mole?

JOSEPHINE. She was.

MOLE. A raving beauty I was. Raving. I could knock spots off that La Bordas any day of the week. You should have seen her, strutting about up there like a cockatoo.

EMILE. Anyway she got you singing – more's the pity!

EUGENIE. Here, you two. We've been to the Tuileries Palace.

JOSEPHINE. Seeing how the other half used to live.

EUGENIE. You should have seen it, Lucie. The chandeliers, the gold – even the walls have carpets on them.

EMILE. La Bordas sang. She was magnificent.

EUGENIE. We waited all evening for her. Then suddenly she

appeared in a long white dress with a scarlet sash. She stood there still as a statue. Then she began to move very slow, and started to sing The Song of the People. It gave me shivers down my spine.

MOLE. Come on, Eug, show them how she did it.

EUGENIE. No, no I couldn't.

ALL. Go on Eugenie.

EUGENIE. If you insist.

EUGENIE *and* MOLE *go behind the sheets.*

JOSEPHINE. Mole what did that poster say? The one on the walls of the Palace?

MOLE. 'The gold that glitters on these walls is the product of your toil.'

JOSEPHINE. 'Today the revolution has made you free. At last you claim your rightful property.'

EMILE. 'This land is yours. But retain your dignity for you are strong. And be watchful, for the tyrants must never return.'

MOLE. Ta ra! Ladies and Gentlemen, I give you, and you can keep her – straight from the sewers of Paris – Madame Eugenie!

EUGENIE *re-enters and gives her impression of La Bordas singing 'La Cannaille'. She has on a long white gown and red feathers.*

MOLE. No no, it wasn't like that. She had a shaky sort of voice.

MOLE *gets up and gives her impression of La Bordas.* EUGENIE *continues.*

JOSEPHINE. Oh no Mole, she sang much higher than that . . .

JOSEPHINE *gets up and does her impression of La Bordas. All three sing at once.*

EMILE. Girls! Have you no respect? Get out! Get out of my laundry! Get out!

Laughter and merriment.

The Scum Song.

In the last chorus of the song loud rumblings are heard of distant guns. (Drums).

EMILE. It's them.

MOLE. I told you. I told you we should have attacked.

EMILE. Let's go.

Exeunt.

Drums.

Enter EMILE.

EMILE. Soldiers of the Versailles army. We are family men. We
are fighting so that our children will never have to bend, as you
must, under military despotism. One day, you will have
children too. If you fire on the people your sons will condemn
you, as we condemn the soldiers who massacred the people in
June 1848 and December 1851. Two months ago, on the 18th
March, your brothers of the Paris army, bitterly resentful of the
cowards who had betrayed France, fraternised with the people.
We urge you to follow their example. Soldiers, our sons and
our brothers, listen to these words and let your conscience
decide. When the orders are immoral, disobedience is a duty.
Signed: the Central Committee.

Exit EMILE.

Enter LUCIE.

LUCIE. Workers! Enough of militarism! Away with Staff Officers
bespangled and gilded! Make way for the people, the bare
armed fighters. The hour of revolutionary warfare has struck!

MOLE *has entered and is listening to this.*

The people know nothing of manoeuvres. But with a rifle in
their hands and cobblestones under their feet they have no fear
of all the monarchist strategists! To arms, citizens! To arms! If
you wish that the generous blood which will flow like water be
not infertile – if . . .

MOLE. He can't be as old as me. Whoever wrote that ought to be
writing romantic novels.

LUCIE. It may be romantic. But it's true.

MOLE. It's daft to fight when you can't win.

LUCIE. You don't know that till you've fought.

MOLE. You may not. I do.

LUCIE. You're frightened.

MOLE. Too right I am. But what do you think I'm frightened of?

LUCIE. Dying.

MOLE. No. Failing.

LUCIE. Fight then. And if we all fight –

MOLE. I will. But not here. And not today.

LUCIE. I'm not giving up without a fight.

MOLE. Who said anything about giving up? Dying is giving up. If you don't have to.

LUCIE. I must go.

MOLE. Here you are then. Take me hat. It'll look a treat on you. Besides, it'll attract the bullets. Get it over quick. Before it crumbles.

Gives LUCIE *her red bonnet.*

LUCIE. Where will you go?.

MOLE. You know me. Everywhere and nowhere. Down a sewer. On a roof, under the ground. I'll find a place. Don't let me keep you.

They exit.

Enter EMILE, EUGENIE, JOSEPHINE, LUCIE *and* MARCEL. *They construct a barricade from all the movable objects on the stage, very swiftly.*

EMILE. First the barricade. The barricade is not designed for shelter. Its main purpose is not for you to crouch behind it.

EUGENIE. Aren't we going to fight them from behind it?

EMILE. You'll only get massacred that way.

LUCIE. If we're not to be behind it, what's it for?

EMILE. The purpose of the barricade is to prevent the enemy from moving freely.

EMILE. It doesn't need to be perfectly built.

MARCEL. It acts as an obstacle.

EMILE. Use anything. Cupboards, doors, cobblestones from the street, beams, barrels, anything.

EUGENIE. Where will we fight?

JOSEPHINE. How?

LUCIE. Where will we go?

EMILE. We'll fight from inside those houses. There and there. Then we can pelt them from above with anything and everything we can find.

JOSEPHINE. Bits of wood, furniture, stones.

EMILE. In order to bring the enemy to a halt we'll cover the street here with broken bottles, nails, stones, anything sharp.

EMILE. We'll reserve the bombs for throwing down from up there.

JOSEPHINE. Look they've been ordered to give no quarter. We can't either, we haven't any choice.

LUCIE. They've brought us to this. Victory or death.

EMILE. Now is that quite clear? No one is to remain behind that barricade.

MARCEL. I wish we had more to fight with. They've got every weapon money can buy.

EMILE. Listen. They're fighting for their officers' pay. We're fighting for the Commune and in that we are the stronger. In street fighting the important thing is the value of the individual fighter, not strength of numbers.

MARCEL. How could we get more guns?

JOSEPHINE. We can't, we've tried.

LUCIE. We've got everything here we can lay our hands on.

EMILE. Our aim must be to prevent them from using their guns.

LUCIE. How?

EMILE. Offer them no targets. If they can't see you they can't shoot you.

EMILE. Never fight in the open, always under cover. Not in the streets. In the houses.

JOSEPHINE. What if we get driven out of the houses by fire?

EMILE. Always find cover. When the enemy is approaching it's better to set fire to buildings rather than occupy.

MARCEL. If I go I'll take a few with me.

EMILE. Our aim should be to destroy property rather than people. War on material. We must not hesitate to destroy what we cannot defend.

JOSEPHINE. Even if it means the whole city?.

EMILE. Yes.

LUCIE. That's hard counsel.

EMILE. It's only the opposite of their kind of warfare. For them men are cheap and are destroyed without counting the cost. But property which costs a great deal is respected.

LUCIE. There is another type of action which succeeds. Like when the women and children spoke to the soldiers.

EMILE. There's not one soldier doesn't dread that moment. He's told to avoid it at all costs. His leaders know that once contact is made the fight is at an end. The main difficulty with this tactic is knowing how to bypass the officers.

JOSEPHINE. We did it once. We can do it again.

EMILE. Thiers knows that. That's why the front line soldiers are Bretons. They don't even speak French.

LUCIE. We didn't make a choice.

MARCEL. The Versailles Army are just as much our enemy as ever the Prussians were.

Characters guard the barricade/wait for attack. Strong light. Wine is passed round.

Song: Cherry Time

End of song: Drums.

EMILE. Take cover!

All scatter as the lights quickly fade to blackout.

MASSON *appears in a spotlight above the lines of washing. With binoculars.*

MASSON. Oh good shot! Our guns are doing excellent service. That scum. They have set Paris alight, they are destroying it. Everywhere on fire! What does it matter as long as the vermin are burnt out of their hovels. Burn them, burn them out! Those

women. I've heard of those women slipping into the cellars of our houses with their petrol bombs to blow them up. They must be denounced and shot. Stamp them out.
What sewers, what jails could have spewed out such brutes? The heart delights to see them lying in the streets riddled with bullets, rotting! The stink of their corpses is the odour of peace. The nostrils may revolt but the soul rejoices. Monsters. They recoiled before no atrocity, killing, plundering. We too have become pitiless. Cruel and pitiless. It is a pleasure to wash our hands in their blood.

Blackout.

Dim light up on EMILE, JOSEPHINE *and* EUGENIE, *entering one by one.*

EMILE. Where's Lucie?

JOSEPHINE. She'll be here.

EMILE. One, two, three, four, five, six.

JOSEPHINE. What you counting them for?

EMILE. To see how many I've got. Seven, seven bullets left.

JOSEPHINE. That's seven more than I've got.

EMILE. It'll be enough.

EUGENIE. Look at the colour of the sky. All red and purple.

JOSEPHINE. Like Masson's face on a bad day.

EMILE. Tell you one thing, I wouldn't want to do this for a living.

JOSEPHINE. Going to die doing it. Where you going, Emile?

EMILE. Thought I'd go and see if Lucie's near.

JOSEPHINE. We agreed to wait here so she'd know where to find us.

EUGENIE. I saw this young fellow today. Spitting image of my old man. Dead he was. Looked just like my Jean lying there asleep with his mouth open. Wasn't of course. My Jean must be all of forty by now. Turned my heart though. He looked so young. God, how long's this going on?

JOSEPHINE. Don't ask God for anything. You need something you'll get it here or not at all. Won't be much longer girl. God would tell you. It took him six days to make the world. It can't take Thiers any longer than that to destroy Paris.

Enter MARCEL *dragging* LUCIE's *body.*

MARCEL. I was on a roof. I saw her looking for guns. There was a platoon of soldiers coming round the corner. She had a trial. There was powder on her hands. That was it. Guilty. Up against the wall. Bang. Do you want to hear another lovely story? You remember Eugene Varlin the Bookbinders' leader? Quiet man. Busy. Self-educated, polite. They found him in the Rue Lafayette. He was recognised by a priest in plain clothes. The soldiers tied his hands behind his back and dragged him off to Montmartre. They made him run the gauntlet of a crowd that was stoning him for over an hour. Then they took him off to the house in the Rue des Rosiers where Lecomte and Thomas were shot. They've been butchering people there all week in revenge. They were going to shoot him in the garden but the Commanding Officer was there. He doesn't like to see the victims. So they took him out again. They paraded him up and down until the crowd had beaten his face to a jelly. Then they shot him at the corner of the street. An Officer stole the watch that the Bookbinders' Union had presented him with.

EUGENIE. They really hate us, don't they?

JOSEPHINE. Once you lift your head out the sand you can't miss it. We're being shot at by men who could be our brothers, sons, lovers. They've had the same struggle to eat to live we've had. How can they?

EMILE. They've been fed a lot of lies. The rest of France thinks the Commune is an excuse for the rabble to kill and loot.

MARCEL. There'll be no tears on my face when they come at me. If I give them the chance.

JOSEPHINE. Them at Versailles. I want them to know. I want them to remember every Spring when they look at the buds coming through. The lice can desert the trees but the leaves can't. We are the leaves of the tree. I want them to remember. And be afraid.

They stand facing the front with their weapons.

Lights fade.

Song: The Boulevards of Paris.

During the song a sheet is placed on the line with the number of the communard dead on it in red. The cast sit at the side of the stage as MASSON *enters and begins to try and tidy the mess. She carries her parasol.*

MASSON. Plenty of clearing up to do. New girls to find. Here's hoping they're better than the last lot. One must look on the bright side and hope that people learn from their mistakes. As Monsieur Thiers himself says 'The ground is littered with corpses. Let this terrible spectacle be a lesson to workers everywhere.' I asked about Mole but nobody seems to know anything. At all. Surely she must be dead. Mustn't she? I mean that's why I asked, I'd like to see her decently buried. They say most of the – corpses – are barefoot. And I can't imagine Mole ever taking – those things – off her feet. Or anyone else ever trying to. You'd have to chop – what am I saying?
To tell you the truth I haven't been sleeping too well these past few nights and . . . I realise that when you are dealing with avengers like Josephine and the rest you have to take a course of action that is – unpleasant. To say the least. But I can't help wondering if one or two of our people – on the fringes – became a little over-excited. There are so many bodies. And they seem to be taking such a long time to get rid of them. It's not that I don't understand the practical problems involved. But they smell. I'm afraid. They do smell. And then there are these flies and . . . it's hot. Has been hot. I've never seen flies quite . . . Everywhere seems somehow –
Now here's a funny story. A bird fell into my parasol yesterday when I was walking. It was in the furled position you see. And I looked down and there were – a lot – of these birds. On the ground. Lying. Dead. And I shook and tried to get it out. The one in my parasol. I shook. And I shook. It wouldn't come. I stood there for quite some time. Shaking and shaking. Then Monsieur tipped it up and out it dropped. But I didn't seem able to. Silly really.
Yes. These – over-excited minority. They have shot at and succeeded in hitting, killing if you like, quite a lot. Hundreds in fact. And in some cases it would appear they haven't shot at quite the right people. And then – and then – It's entirely understandable, yes, and reprehensible too, they have tried to hide. To cover up. Out of sight. And it's simply that as Monsieur says the heat makes them swell. Grow bigger. The

bodies you see. In the Place St Jacques you can hear noises.
From under the ground. They're not buried deep enough. It's
as if they're trying to force their way up. And you can – I'm not
making it up you can – see things. Hands and arms and limbs
and things coming up. They're in the river. In the lake. One
minute they're not there and then there's this terrible noise.
Gas, Monsieur says. And then there they are. And there they
stay. And they're big. So big. Mole – Mole must be amongst
them. If I could be sure. If I could be sure she was never, ever
coming back – oh, I could sleep easier then.

Song: Week of Blood.

1. Laundry Song

(Unaccompanied; for three or four voices)

Working working working working
Working working working working

Working in a laundry every day
Steam and sweat and hardly any pay
Working in a pool of rich men's grime and dirt
Washing and ironing till my body hurts.
Look at my hands they're red and raw.
My head is aching and my feet are sore.
My life is spent in dirt and grime
Will it ever change to a better time?

Working in a laundry every day
Steam and sweat and hardly any pay
Working in a pool of rich men's grime and dirt
Washing and ironing till my body hurts.
At any minute we could get the sack
Then we'd have to make a living by lying on our backs
Scrubbing all day or scrubbing all night
Is this called justice? Is this what's right?

Working in a laundry every day
Working in a laundry every day
Working in a laundry every day

Music and lyrics for all the songs by Helen Glavin ©1976, except
where stated otherwise.

2. Adolphe Thiers

(*Sung by* MOLE. *Guitar or banjo accompaniment.*)

From the Place Pigalle to Rue Genais
And the fields of Saint Jerome
You can hear the people talking
About Thiers that naughty gnome.

'Well I may be small in stature
But Napoleon he was too
And if you've got the time to spare my friends
I've a few words to say to you.

I'm a brilliant politician
My weapon is my brain
I know every trick there is to know
About the power game.

You can put your faith and trust in me
I'm a man who's firm but fair
If you believe in law and order
Then you'll vote for Adolphe Thiers.

I'm a devil when in power
I'm a challenge in defeat.'
Don't listen to a word he says
He's a stinking little cheat.

With words he's like a twisting snake
As an historian he lies
His face it's just a painted mask
With squinty little eyes.

But the bourgeoisie they love him
He's got the trappings of their class
Are you impressed by his cavortings?
'No'? Well boot him up the arse.

'I'll sell you down the river
To that autocratic kraut
Who knows what I'll get up to next
If you don't boot me out.

Don't think that you can move me
With reason or with tears
I'm a rogue with no compassion
Despite my seventy years.'

So –
Don't trust that little bugger
'Cos he thinks that we are vile
And he's plotting our destruction
Behind his painted smile.

So remember everybody
You'd better all beware
Of Adolphe the Mighty Midget
That scheming Monsieur Thiers.

(*Repeat last verse faster.*)

3. The Song of the National Guard

Some men fight for money, some for glory die
Some men fight for Jesus some for wine.

CHORUS:

But when you've come up from the gutter you've been fighting to
    survive
Each day is a battle just to stay alive.
They can kill us with a bullet and not listen to our pleas
So we'll use any tactics to keep the people free.

We'll save you from the Prussians, on us you can rely
'He's got the guts', 'He's got the brains', and we're not afraid to
    die.

CHORUS:

'Cos when you've come up . . .

We're not the Emperor's warriors or knights of chivalry
We're the soldiers of the people, we control our destiny.

CHORUS:

Cos we've come up from the gutter . . .

(*Repeat second half of Chorus.*)

4. Masson's Song

Verse 1.

Single sheets, double sheets
Had a spot of trouble sheets
Coarse sheets, silk sheets
Whiter than milk sheets
Heavy sheets, light sheets
Covered in shite sheets
I'll take them all
I'll take them all
'Cos this is the tightest spot I've been in
Don't give me speeches, give me dirty linen.

CHORUS:

Why can't we all
Sit down and talk together
Oh why can't we be one happy family?
Why can't we all agree upon a plan
That's fair to all and ends up helping me?

Verse 2.

Frilly shirts, lace shirts
Button out of place shirts
Blue shirts, red shirts
Stripped off from the dead shirts
I'll take socialist chemises
Who cares about diseases
I'll take them all
I'll take them all
But if you want to talk politics I must insist
That you write them at the bottom of your laundry list.

CHORUS:

Why can't we all etc . . .

Verse 3.

Woollen socks, cotton socks,
Decomposing rotten socks
Small socks, big socks
Stinking like a pig socks
Darned socks, holey socks
I'd even take 'La Mole's' socks
As it is now and was in the beginning
I put my trust in God and dirty linen.

Music by Helen Glavin, lyrics by Chris Bond copyright 1976.

5. Blow Winter Winds

(*Unaccompanied song for solo voice.*)

Blow O winter winds
And fall more, O snow.
Beneath your icy veil
We're closer to the dead
Endless be the night
And shortened will be the day
In winter we are as one with
The cold friends we mourn.

Music by Helen Glavin – copyright 1976. Lyrics, a poem by
Louise Michel, a Communard

6. Scum

In the old French city
There lives a race of people
With iron in their souls
And fiery hearts
They have no palace
Their sons are born on straw

They are the scum
And I'm one of them
They are the scum
Well I'm one of them.

Workers of the city
Dressed in rags and clogs
Strong arms with nervous hands
Toiling night and day
They do not ask for pity
Just listen to their cry

They are the scum
And I'm one of them
They are the scum
And I'm one of them.

Music by Helen Glavin – copyright 1976. Lyrics from an original
song of the Commune translated by Gillian Hanna, adapted by
Helen Glavin

7. Cherry Time

When it's cherry time
And the gay nightingale and the mocking blackbird
Are having a good time, are having a good time.
Pretty ladies have sadness in their heads
And lovers have sun in their hearts
When it's cherry time
The mocking blackbird will sing more sweetly.

When it's cherry time
If you fear the griefs of love
Avoid beautiful women, avoid beautiful women.
But I don't fear the cruel pain
So I live each day in sorrow
When it's cherry time
You too will fear the griefs of love.

But cherry time is very short
We stroll along in dreaming pairs
Gathering earrings, cherries of love
Dressed all the same
Hanging under the leaves like drops of blood
O cherry time is the time to dream.

I will always love cherry time
Though it's made an open wound in my heart
And Lady Fortune having caused me such pain
Can never soothe me.
I will always love cherry time
And the memory that I keep in my heart.

Music by Helen Glavin – copyright 1976. Lyrics: an original
popular song sung by the Communards on the barricades.
Translated by Gillian Hanna and adapted by Helen Glavin.

8. The Boulevards of Paris

1.
On the boulevards of Paris in 1871
Pink and white cherry blossoms come out in the sun
The ashes of the fire are cooled by the rain
But the blood of the people
    the blood of the people
    the blood of the people
Flows down to the Seine.

2.
All the barricades of Paris are smashed to the ground
Let's sing a sad lamentation for the death all around
O sisters and brothers, please do not dismay
For the Commune of Paris
    the Commune of Paris
    the Commune of Paris
Has shown us the way.

3.

On the boulevards of Paris in 1871
The Versailles soldiers have made the blood run
But the streets where the blood flows will never be the same
For the scum of the earth
    the scum of the earth
    the scum of the earth
Will rise up again.

La la la la la/la la la la la/la la la la . . .
The scum of the earth!

9. The Week of Blood

Verse 1.

Apart from informers and the police
All you see on the streets now are old men in tears
Widows and orphans crying in misery
Left all alone, they weep in despair
The Commune is in for a slaughter
Is there no way to stop the flood?
The talk is of war and everyone's shaking
And the streets are running with blood.

CHORUS:

But we are ready and waiting
This terrible time must come to an end
And then you'd better beware
When we the poor take revenge
When we the poor rise again.

Verse 2.

They're tracking us down now and chasing us up
They're stabbing and shooting just anyone
The mother that's shielding her little daughter
Or the baby in the old man's arms
The hardships we knew in the Commune
Have given way to massacre
Must we be hunted by these bastards
These lackeys of kings and emperors.

CHORUS:

But we are ready and waiting . . . etc

Verse 3.

Tomorrow informers will still walk our streets
Proud of their record, they don't want to be missed
Wearing their pistols slung on their shoulders
Services given with a Judas kiss.
But we have nothing to eat
No work, no weapons to fight
We're going to be ruled by police and informers
Killers and priests to tell us what's right.

CHORUS:

But we are ready and waiting etc . . .

Verse 4.

O when will the people break free from their chains
Will we be always in misery
The masters of war have the upper hand
Till the time comes we take it away.
Till then that pack of wolves
Can think that we are scum.
O when will we have a people's republic,
We can't wait for that day to come.

CHORUS:

But we are ready and waiting etc . . .

Music and lyrics are from an original song of the Commune.
Lyrics translated by Gillian Hanna. Music and lyrics adapted by
Helen Glavin.

1. Laundry Song

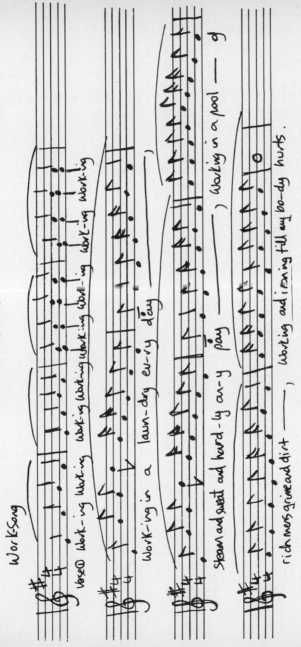

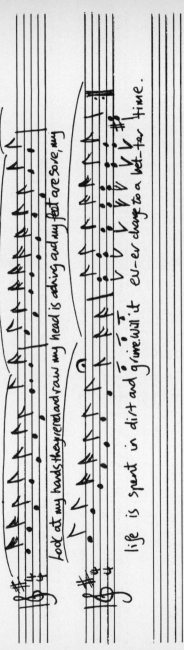

look at my hands they're red and raw my head is aching and my feet are sore, my

life is spent in dirt and grime will it ev-er change to a bet-ter time.

© John Glavin -

2. Adolphe Thiers.

Spoke Sung in
Music Hall style
con gusto

Verse ①
Verse ②
From the Place Pig-alle to Rue Genais and the Fauberg St Jerome, you can

1st X

2nd X

Verse ③

hear the people talking a-bout Thiers that naughty gnome.   I'm a brilliant poli-ti-cian, My

weapon is my brain, I know ev—ry trick there is to know a bout the power game.

© Helen Glavin

3. The Song of the National Guard

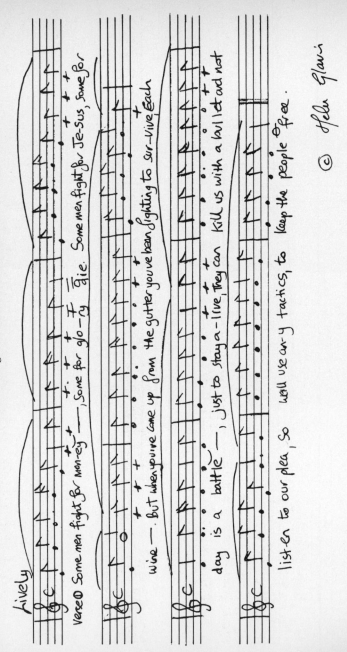

4. Masson's Song

5. Blow Winter Winds

a poem by Louise Michel, a Communard

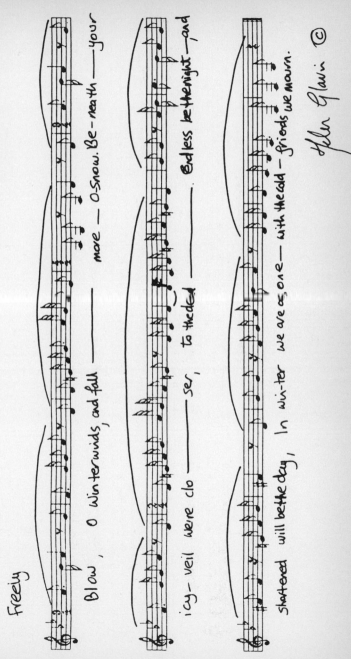

Freely

Blow, O winter winds, and fall — more — O snow. Be-neath — your

icy — veil were clo — ser, to the old — Endless be the night, and

shattered will be the day, In win-ter we are, one — with the old — friends we mourn.

Helen Glavin ©

6. Scum

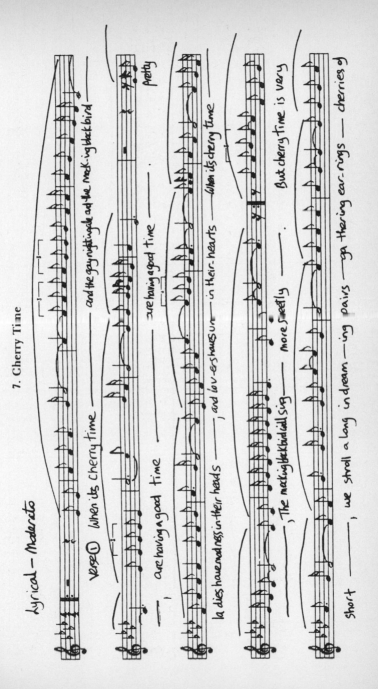

7. Cherry Time

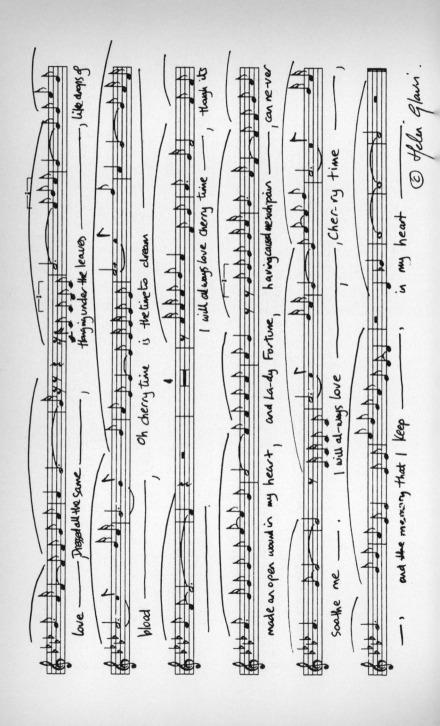

8. The Boulevards of Paris.

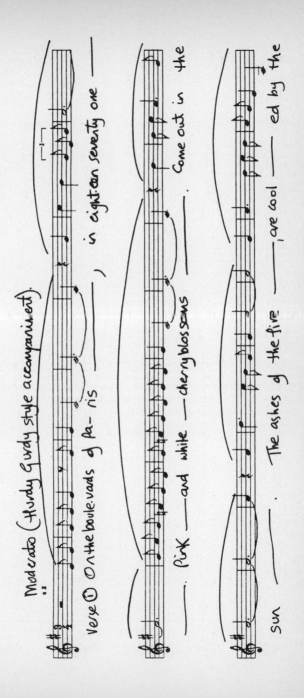

Moderato (Hurdy Gurdy style accompaniment).

Verse ① On the boulevards of Pa—ris —), in eighteen seventy one —

. Pink — and white — cherry blossoms — . Come out in the

Sun — . The ashes of the fire — , are cool — ed by the

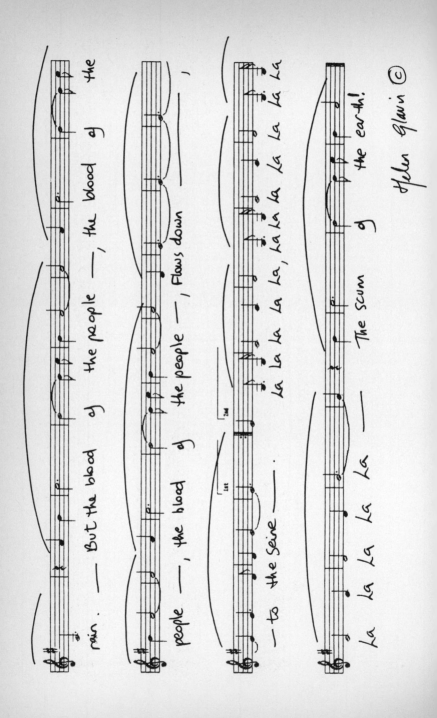

9. The Week of Blood.

Freely

Verse ① A - part from uniform-ers, and the pol-ice — all you saw on the streets now, are old men in tears. Widows and orphans crying in mis-sery — left all alone — they — weep in des-pair The Commune is in for a slaughter, have we no way — to stop the flood? — The all-rising war, and ev-ryone shaking — And the

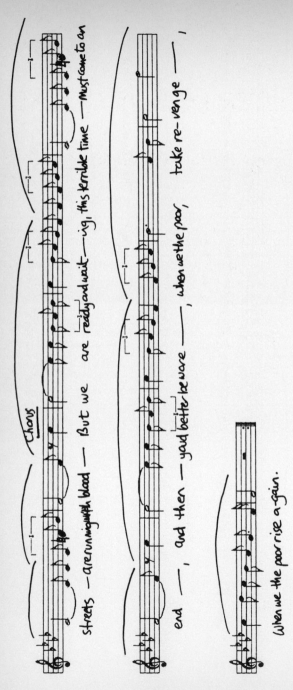

Helen Glavin ©

MY SISTER IN THIS HOUSE

by Wendy Kesselman

WENDY KESSELMAN's plays: *My Sister in This House, I Love You, I Love You Not, The Juniper Tree: A Tragic Household Tale, Maggie Magalita, Becca, The Griffin and the Minor Canon* (book) and *Merry-Go-Round* have been widely produced in this country and abroad. She received the Susan Smith Blackburn Prize and the First Annual Playbill Award, and is a four-time winner of the ASCAP Popular Award in Musical Theatre. she is the recipient of a Guggenheim, McKnight and two National Endowment for the Arts Fellowships, and is a member of the Dramatists Guild. She has recently completed a musical adaptation of Dickens' *A Tale of Two Cities*, which was commissioned by Stage One in Louisville, Kentucky and will be produced there in January, 1992. She has published nine children's books and a novel. *The Butcher's Daughter* was commissioned by the Ubu Repertory Theatre in New York, won the Jane Chambers Playwriting Award and was a finalist for the Susan Smith Blackburn Prize.

Characters

CHRISTINE
LEA (pronounced Léa), her sister
MADAME DANZARD
ISABELLE, her daughter

VOICE OF PHOTOGRAPHER
VOICE OF MEDICAL EXAMINER
VOICE OF JUDGE

The play takes place in Le Mans, France, during the early 1930's. It is based on an historical incident which occurred in Le Mans in 1933.

The play is performed without an intermission.

My Sister in This House was first produced in the USA by the Actors Theatre of Louisville on 18 February 1981, with the following cast:

CHRISTINE	Cristine Rose
LEA	Patricia Charbonneau
MADAME COTTIN	Eloise Terry
ISABELLE	Marianne Owen
MADAME DANZARD	Anne Pitoniak
PHOTOGRAPHER	Andy Backer

Directed by Jon Jory
Set Design Paul Owen
Costume Design Kurt Wilhelm
Lighting Design Paul Owen
Sound Design John North
Co-Property Masters Sam Garst
Sandra Strawn
Stage Manager Tom Aberger
Assistant Stage Manager Richard A. Cunningham

The play was later produced by The Second Stage Theatre Company, with the following cast:

CHRISTINE	Lisa Banes
LEA	Elizabeth McGovern
MADAME DANZARD	Beverly May
ISABELLE	Brenda Currin

Directed by Iverna Lockpez and Carole Rothman
Artistic Directors Robyn Goodman and Carole Rothman
Set Design by Jim Clayburgh
Lighting Design by Arden Fingerhut
Costume Design by Susan Hilferty
Sound Design by Gary Harris
Production Stage Manager Fredric H. Orner
Hair Design by Antonio Soddu
Stage Manager Judith Ann Chew

My Sister in This House was first performed by Monstrous Regiment, in association with the Leicester Haymarket Theatre on 1 April 1987. It then toured Birmingham (where it was performed at the Triangle), Glasgow (Mitchell Theatre at Mayfest) and the Hampstead Theatre, London, with the following cast:

LEA	Maggie O'Neill
CHRISTINE	Suzanna Hamilton
MADAME DANZARD	Maggie Steed
ISABELLE	Tilly Vosburgh

Written by Wendy Kesselman
Directed by Nancy Meckler
Designed by Stephanie Howard
Lighting designer Veronica Wood

Graphic designer Jo Angell/Paton Walker Associates
Costumes, set and props built by Leicester Haymarket Theatre
   Workshops

Production Manager and Sound Operator Gill McBride
Lighting Operator Debra Trethewey
Photographs (Rehearsal) Malcolm Andrew
Photographs (Production) Phil Cutts

Administration Sandy Bailey/Rose Sharp

ACT ONE

Scene One

CHRISTINE (*voice over. Sings*).
>Sleep my little sister, sleep
>Sleep through darkness
>Sleep so deep.

Lights come up slowly on the faces of CHRISTINE *and* LEA *as if framed in a photograph.*

>All the rivers find the sun
>My little sister
>Sleep for me.

>Dream my little sister, dream
>Dream I'm here now
>Dream your dreams
>All the things you want to be
>My little sister
>Dream for me.*

CHRISTINE *and* LEA *stand side by side at the edge of the stage.* CHRISTINE *wears a faded dress with a white apron,* LEA, *a simple childlike dress.* CHRISTINE's *hair is wound either in two buns, one on each side of her face, or in braids circling her head.* LEA's *hair hangs in a long braid.*

CHRISTINE *is just twenty,* LEA, *still an adolescent.* LEA *gazes vaguely into the distance.* CHRISTINE *looks straight ahead. They move apart.* CHRISTINE *begins polishing a brass candlestick.* LEA *looks out.*

LEA. Dear Christine. When Maman left me here on Friday, I thought I would die. They didn't want to take me at first, but Maman told Madame Crespelle I was fifteen. Christine, I wish

---

*Copyright © 1981 of 'Sleep My Little Sister, Sleep': lyrics and music by Wendy Kesselman. See p. 145–6 for music.

you could see what they eat. You can't imagine the desserts. The cook told me Madame's favourite dish is duck with cherries and Monsieur's, chicken with champagne. I'm hungry all the time. But it isn't as bad as I expected. I even have my own room. Do you think you could ask Madame Roussel to change your day off to Wednesday, like mine? (*She pauses.*) Today Madame Crespelle smiled at me. She was pleased with how the silver looked. I had been polishing it all morning. It was worth every minute for Madame's smile. When she smiles she looks just like Sister Veronica.

A bell rings. LEA *moves closer to* CHRISTINE.

Three days ago Maman came and took me away. She said I could earn more money somewhere else. I was just getting used to the Crespelles, but I'm getting four more francs a month and Maman's promised to let me keep one of them. The Cottins have one daughter, Mademoiselle Sophie. Her birthday is next week. She's only two months older than me. She's so pretty. Her skin is like milk. And Christine, you should hear her play the piano.

She pauses.

Madame Cottin counts everything. Even the chocolates in the glass bowl. But I remember everything you taught me. And I think Madame will be pleased with me.

She pauses.

Every morning Madame Cottin examines my fingernails before I make the beds. Her things are so delicate. So many ruffles. So many buttons. You wouldn't believe how many buttons. It takes me two hours to iron one dress. And even then Madame isn't satisfied.

She pauses.

In this house I'm always afraid I'll do something wrong. Not like you, Christine. You never make mistakes.

She pauses. Longingly.

Oh Christine, if only Maman would place us together.

A bell rings, almost interrupting LEA's *last sentence.* LEA *goes down on her hands and knees and begins polishing the floor.* CHRISTINE *looks out.*

CHRISTINE (*tender*). Don't worry, Lea. You don't have to worry. It's only a matter of time. Just time before you get used to it.

She pauses.

Don't worry what they say to you.

She pauses.

I mean . . . don't take it to heart. I know that's hard in the beginning. But you'll learn. It's just time.

She pauses.

You'll see. Remember what Maman says – 'When you've worked for them as long as I have – then you'll see.'

She pauses.

Some are better than others, Lea. Believe me. You just never know.

She pauses.

Don't worry about writing every day. I know how tired you must be. But don't hide anything from me. And if – if they make you cry – I want you to let me know right away.

A bell rings. Light comes up on the interior of the DANZARD *house in Le Mans, France. A combined dining room and sitting room is divided from the kitchen by a narrow staircase going up to a landing, and continuing to a maid's room. The house can also be created in a less realistic way. However, the staircase is an intrinsic element of the structure of the set.*

CHRISTINE *and* LEA *pick up shabby suitcases. They smile at each other. They go upstairs to the maid's room. The room is shabby, small. There is a single bed, a night table, a sink and a mirror. There is a small skylight.* LEA *opens the door and rushes into the room.* CHRISTINE *follows her.*

LEA (*excited*). I can't believe it. I just can't believe it. (*She puts her suitcase down on the floor.*) How did you do it? How did you get Maman to agree? Tell me.

CHRISTINE. Shhh. They'll hear you downstairs.

LEA. Tell me. You're always keeping something from me.

CHRISTINE *turns away.*

Tell me.

CHRISTINE (*turning back, smiling*). I told her there'd be more money for her this way.

LEA. You're so clever, so smart.

CHRISTINE. I said that till you learned, you had to have someone to protect you.

LEA. And that was you. That was you. Am I right, Christine? (*She reaches to hug* CHRISTINE.)

CHRISTINE (*shivering*). The room's cold. (*She lifts her suitcase onto the bed.*)

LEA. Remember what you used to call me? My feet still get cold at night. They get like ice.

CHRISTINE *opens her suitcase, starts putting her things away. She has few belongings.*

CHRISTINE (*smiling*). Come on. Put your suitcase up here with mine. I'll unpack it for you.

She picks up LEA's *suitcase and puts it on the bed. She begins to unpack it for* LEA.

LEA. Now they'll be warm.

CHRISTINE *takes a small crocheted blanket out of* LEA's *suitcase.*

CHRISTINE. What – you still have this old thing?

LEA. I had to take it. She was with me when I packed.

CHRISTINE (*turning away*). Well, I don't care. It has nothing to do with me.

LEA. Don't you like it?

CHRISTINE. It's old and falling apart. I never liked Maman's sewing. It's vulgar. (*Silently, she continues unpacking their things.*)

LEA (*watching her*). What's the matter? Aren't you glad that we're together?

CHRISTINE. Why didn't you take the other room? They offered it to you.

LEA. But I wanted to be with you.

CHRISTINE. The other room was nice. Nicer than this one.

LEA. Christine?

CHRISTINE *is silent.*

I don't understand. You worked the whole thing out and now you don't even want me with you.

CHRISTINE. Of course I want you with me.

LEA. What's wrong then?

CHRISTINE. Nothing's wrong.

There is a pause.

LEA. I'll throw the blanket away if you want. I don't care about it. I just want you to be happy.

CHRISTINE (*finally turning around*). But I am happy, little cold feet. (*She takes the blanket from* LEA.) We'll put the blanket right here. (*She lays the blanket at the foot of the bed.*) The main thing is that now we are together.

Slowly the light on CHRISTINE *and* LEA *dims. Light has begun to come up on* MADAME DANZARD *and* MADEMOISELLE ISABELLE DANZARD *downstairs in the sitting room.* MADAME DANZARD *is polishing* ISABELLE's *nails.* MADAME DANZARD *is in her early fifties,* ISABELLE *in her early twenties, the same age as* CHRISTINE.

MADAME DANZARD. This pink is lovely on you. So much better than the clear. Clear, clear, clear. It seems to be all everyone's wearing. This is such a bright colour.

ISABELLE. You don't think it's too bright, do you, Maman? Do you think it's too bright?

MADAME DANZARD. Too bright? Nonsense. Bright colours are coming back. Hold still. This is delicate work, my dear. Highly delicate. This has to be perfect.

She finishes the last nail of ISABELLE's *left hand.*

There! Now the other one.

ISABELLE *examines her hand.*

I'm waiting.

ISABELLE *holds out her other hand.*

So my dear, what do you think?

ISABELLE. About what, Maman?

MADAME DANZARD. What do you mean – about what, Maman? About them. About what else?

ISABELLE. Oh . . . they seem fine.

MADAME DANZARD. Fine? Is that all you can say? As a matter of fact, I think we may be in for a pleasant surprise.

ISABELLE. If you say so, Maman.

MADAME DANZARD (*after a pause*). Can't you at least express an opinion? You know how I value your opinion, Isabelle.

ISABELLE. Yes Maman. I know.

MADAME DANZARD. I wouldn't have taken the younger one. It's always a risk. But seeing that she's in the family. (*Putting the nail brush in the bottle and shaking it vigorously*). Sisters! What could be better? And two almost for the price of one. We'll save on everything. They didn't even want two rooms. (*Carefully touching up one nail.*) Just this little corner. Apparently the older one sews extraordinarily well. She's your age, you know. 'Such embroidery, such needlework,' they said. I've never seen recommendations like that from Saint Mary of the Fields.

ISABELLE. Sewing. That's all they ever teach them.

MADAME DANZARD. Well, it's all to the good. If there're any alterations on your new dress she'll make them. We won't even have to go to the dressmaker's.

ISABELLE. What luck.

MADAME DANZARD. I remember our neighbour Monsieur Blanqui hiding one of those convent girls. I saw her once from my window. She must have been just my age. She looked a little like the older sister. She'd run away from the convent.

ISABELLE. Run away. Really?

MADAME DANZARD. Every now and then one got away. I never understood how she escaped. That wall! There was not one place you could see inside. I used to hear her at night begging them not to send her back. 'Not there. Not to that place.' In the end even Madame Blanqui didn't want to give her up. Can you imagine – in this town? And believe me they came looking for her.

ISABELLE. They did, Maman?

MADAME DANZARD. They used to comb each house for those girls.

She lifts up ISABELLE's *hands.*

Look, my dear. Aren't they beautiful? How do you like my handiwork?

The light fades.

Scene Two

Early morning. CHRISTINE *and* LEA's *room is almost dark. They are asleep. The alarm clock rings.* CHRISTINE *turns it off. She reaches out to touch* LEA, *curled up beside her. Gently she touches her shoulder, strokes her hair.*

LEA *(turning toward* CHRISTINE*).* Is it time?

CHRISTINE. Sleep, turtle. Go back in your shell.

LEA. But –

CHRISTINE. Sleep. There's time. I'll wake you.

LEA *turns over again. She is holding the small blanket their mother has made.* CHRISTINE *covers* LEA's *shoulder with the blanket. Shivering she gets out of bed, stands on the cold floor. She puts on her shoes.*

Lea . . . it's almost six.

LEA. Mmmm. Another minute, Christine. Just one more.

CHRISTINE. Just one – all right. *(At the sink, she washes her face and hands. She shivers from the cold water, fixes her hair in the mirror. She removes her long white nightgown and puts on her maid's uniform. She goes over to the bed. Tickling* LEA's *feet.)* Come on now. Come on. *(She pulls the blanket off* LEA.*)*

LEA *(sitting up).* It's freezing here. Is it always like this?

CHRISTINE *(laying out* LEA's *uniform on the bed).* Always.

LEA. Everywhere you've been?

CHRISTINE. Everywhere.

LEA *(putting on her shoes).* I polished the banister yesterday. Did you notice how it shines?

CHRISTINE. I noticed. (*To herself.*) I thought it would be easier with two of us.

LEA. You're disappointed, aren't you? You're unhappy with me here. Tell me.

CHRISTINE. Don't be silly.

LEA. I can't seem to do anything right. I can't seem to please you.

CHRISTINE. You please me, turtle. You please me more than anything.

LEA. You're so quick. You get things done in a minute.

CHRISTINE. You're fine the way you are.

LEA (*struggling with her nightgown*). Maybe this was a mistake. I slow you down.

CHRISTINE. Stop it, Lea.

LEA (*still struggling*). Sister Veronica always said I was too slow. She said I'd never be as quick as you.

CHRISTINE. What did she know?

LEA. You used to think she knew everything.

CHRISTINE (*helping* LEA *take off her nightgown*). That was a long time ago. I've gotten over all that now.

LEA. You were famous at the convent. Your sewing! They still have that dress you made for the Virgin Mary. She's still wearing it.

CHRISTINE. And yet I remember, when I was at Saint Mary's, I could never go down the stairs like the others. One, two, one, two. I could never take a step with my left foot. It was always my right, my right, my right. I used to envy them running down the stairs when it took me forever.

LEA. Tell me a story, Christine. Just one – before we go down.

CHRISTINE. Which one?

LEA. When I was little.

CHRISTINE. You're still little.

LEA. No, I mean really little – you know – the story with the horse.

CHRISTINE. Again? Don't you ever get tired of it.

LEA. No – tell me.

CHRISTINE (*making the bed*). When you were just a tiny thing, Maman sent me out one day to get bread. You came with me, the way you always did. And as we were walking, you let go of my hand and ran into the street to pick something up.

LEA. Tell it slower. You're telling it too fast.

CHRISTINE. It was a *long* narrow street – you remember – on a hill. At the top of the street a horse and carriage loaded with bottles was coming down and galloping right toward you. I ran into the street and pulled you across and pushed you down into the gutter with me. (*Falling down on the bed with* LEA.) What a noise when the horse galloped by! Everyone was screaming. Maman said the horse had gone mad. And when we stood up, we were both bleeding. But it was the same wound. It started on my arm and went down across your wrist. Look – (*She lines up her arm with* LEA's.) We have it still.

LEA. And Maman. What did she say?

CHRISTINE. Oh Maman. Maman was terrified. You know how her face gets. She screamed at us.

LEA. And then – then what happened?

CHRISTINE. Then there was the gypsy – Mad Flower they used to call her.

LEA. And what did she say?

CHRISTINE. She said – oh you – you know it so well.

LEA. But tell me again, Christine. Tell me again.

CHRISTINE. They're bound for life, Mad Flower said. Bound in blood.

A bell rings.

Scene Three

In this scene the dining room and kitchen are seen simultaneously.
MADAME DANZARD *and* ISABELLE *are sitting at the dining room table, finishing the first course of lunch.* CHRISTINE *and* LEA *come into*

the kitchen. They are wearing their uniforms: CHRISTINE, *the long severe cook's apron,* LEA, *the delicate serving apron.*

MADAME DANZARD. Don't toy with your food, Isabelle. It's so disagreeable. Always making those little piles.

ISABELLE. I'm not, Maman.

MADAME DANZARD. You mean to tell me I don't see what you're doing.

ISABELLE. I'm not toying, Maman.

MADAME DANZARD (*coldly*). Very well, my dear, call it what you will. (*She rings a small round bell.*)

LEA *and* CHRISTINE *come into the dining room.* MADAME DANZARD *looks them over carefully.* LEA *is carrying a platter of veal on a tray. She presents the platter for* MADAME DANZARD's *inspection, as* CHRISTINE *stands to the side.* MADAME DANZARD *smiles to herself.* LEA *puts the platter down and she and* CHRISTINE *go back into the kitchen.* MADAME DANZARD *and* ISABELLE *serve themselves and eat in silence for a few moments.*

CHRISTINE (*following* LEA *into the kitchen*). She liked it. Did you see? Did you see her face?

LEA. She likes everything you do.

CHRISTINE. She sees everything.

She sits down at the kitchen table and begins to prepare string beans. Everything CHRISTINE *does in the kitchen is neat, quick, impeccable. The bowls and plates seem to move like magic beneath her fingers.* LEA *is clearly a beginner. She sits down beside* CHRISTINE *and begins, clumsily, to help her with the beans.*

MADAME DANZARD (*savouring the veal*). This veal is delicious.

ISABELLE. Of course, you love veal. (*She looks at her mother.*)

MADAME DANZARD. Don't you?

ISABELLE. You know I don't. It's too heavy in the middle of the day.

MADAME DANZARD. Not the way she's prepared it. Light as a feather.

ISABELLE. I've heard it ruins the complexion.

MADAME DANZARD. Where did you hear that?

ISABELLE. I read it.

MADAME DANZARD (*scornfully*). Really. Where?

ISABELLE. Somewhere. I don't remember.

MADAME DANZARD. Certain days of the month, my dear, you really are worse than others.

ISABELLE. That shouldn't surprise *you*.

MADAME DANZARD. Isabelle, if you continue in this vein you're going to ruin my meal. (*She eats with a certain relish.*) Wait till the Blanchards come to dinner. I'll have her make her rabbit paté. Won't that surprise them! The best cook we've had in years.

ISABELLE. Oh I don't know – Marie wasn't so bad.

MADAME DANZARD. Marie? Please. The way she cooked a pot au feu – ahhh – It still makes me shudder.

ISABELLE. You exaggerate, Maman.

MADAME DANZARD. Exaggerate? I'm being kind. Marie would have murdered a veal like this. (*Wiping her mouth with her napkin.*) Done to perfection. I hope we never lose her. And she always buys the best.

ISABELLE. I don't know how she does it with the money you give her.

MADAME DANZARD. It's what I've always given them. You have no idea how lucky we are, Isabelle. The servants I've seen in my day. (*She watches* ISABELLE *stuff potatoes into her mouth.*) They eat like birds. (*Looking at* ISABELLE.) Always looking so neat, so perfect. You wouldn't think they were maids at all. Though I must admit the younger one gives me trouble – she's so young.

ISABELLE. I like the younger one.

MADAME DANZARD. Well she's quiet. I'll say that for her.

ISABELLE (*mercilessly chewing on the veal*). Quiet? She never speaks. Neither of them do.

MADAME DANZARD. I suppose they must talk between themselves.

ISABELLE. I can't imagine about what.

MADAME DANZARD (*looking at* ISABELLE). Well, maybe they pray. (*She laughs.*) That's how it is when you're brought up by the nuns. (*They both laugh. Abruptly stopping the laughter.*) Will you stop it, Isabelle. Look at that plate. (*She rings the small round bell.*)

LEA *comes into the dining room with a platter of cheese.* MADAME DANZARD *and* ISABELLE *are instantly silent.* LEA *clears away the empty platter of veal and goes back into the kitchen.*

MADAME DANZARD. They're so discreet. Not the slightest prying. You can't imagine what it's like to have a prying maid. To have someone going through your things.

ISABELLE. The younger one washes my things so perfectly. Even my . . . And you know, she's almost pretty.

MADAME DANZARD (*cleaning her teeth with her tongue*). When your father and I were first married – she was something that one. But these two are different. Mark my words.

CHRISTINE (*rapidly snapping off the ends of the beans*). How lucky we are, Lea. The other houses I've been – they come into the kitchen and interfere. Madame knows her place.

MADAME DANZARD. I never even have to tell them anything.

CHRISTINE. I know what she wants before she says a word.

MADAME DANZARD. They take such pride in the house. Not a speck of dust under the carpet.

CHRISTINE. Madame checks everything. I like that.

LEA. You do? It scares me – the way she checks.

MADAME DANZARD. Not a speck.

CHRISTINE. Oh no, I like it. It's better that way. Believe me. In the end it's better.

MADAME DANZARD. Not under the lamps. Not a ring.

ISABELLE. Really?

MADAME DANZARD. Not one. They're extraordinarily clean.

CHRISTINE. Madame is so precise, so careful. Her lists! Everything down to the last second.

LEA. She doesn't let us get away with a thing.

ISABELLE. Well Maman, let's face it – you don't let them get away with a thing.

MADAME DANZARD. Why should I? I pay them enough.

CHRISTINE. Why should she? She wants the house a certain way.

MADAME DANZARD. This is my house.

ISABELLE. It certainly is.

MADAME DANZARD. Well, it will be yours one day, Isabelle.

CHRISTINE. But she always sees the little things we do.

MADAME DANZARD. The younger one may be pretty, but it's the older one who fascinates me. I've never had anyone like her.

CHRISTINE. I've never had anyone like Madame before.

MADAME DANZARD. Totally trustworthy. I never have to count the change when she comes back from marketing. Not one sou is missing.

CHRISTINE (*holding out her bowl to* LEA). Put them all in here, Lea.

ISABELLE. They don't seem to have any friends.

MADAME DANZARD. Thank heaven for that.

LEA *spills the beans on the floor. She gasps.*

CHRISTINE. You're so clumsy.

She begins picking up the beans. Upset, LEA *helps her.*

MADAME DANZARD. I've seen those people's friends, my dear. Believe me – it's bad enough with that mother of theirs.

ISABELLE. What a horror! It's a lucky thing they have each other.

CHRISTINE. I didn't mean it. You're so silly. What a baby you are.

MADAME DANZARD. And they do love us. They're so devoted to us. You'll see – the whole town will envy us. (*Laughing.*) We have pearls on our hands, Isabelle. Two pearls.

They clink their wine glasses. MADAME DANZARD *rings the small round bell.* ISABELLE *goes over to the sitting room area and takes an evening bag with tiny seed pearls out of a sewing basket.* LEA *and* CHRISTINE *come into the dining room and begin to clear away the dishes.* MADAME DANZARD *goes over to the sewing basket and takes out her needlepoint.*

MADAME DANZARD. Let me see, Isabelle.

ISABELLE *holds out the evening bag.*

I can't see it from here.

ISABELLE *leans closer and hands her the bag.*

CHRISTINE *and* LEA *work silently together in the kitchen.*

MADAME DANZARD. Nice. Very nice. It's coming along. Bit by bit.

She hands it back to ISABELLE, *sits down on the couch and begins doing needlepoint.*

You can't rush these things, my dear. Believe me. A bag like that could take you . . . (*She looks at* ISABELLE *labouring with the seed pearls.*) Two years.

ISABELLE *looks at her.*

Maybe more. But there's no hurry, is there? Nothing to hurry for. You have all the time in the world.

ISABELLE. Yes Maman.

MADAME DANZARD. All the time. When I was your age I made a bag just like that. Seed pearls too – but mine had a blue background. And when I held it up to the light, it . . .

ISABELLE. It what?

MADAME DANZARD. Shone . . . like little moons. Night after night I worked on that bag. But in the end it was worth it.

ISABELLE. Why, Maman?

MADAME DANZARD. I don't remember. An evening out. A dance.

ISABELLE. Oh what happened, Maman? Tell me.

MADAME DANZARD. I don't know. Maybe nothing. Maybe nothing *ever* happened. Listen to that rain. It's been raining like that for a week. A full week. Who knows when it will stop. Do you hear it, Isabelle?

ISABELLE. I hear it.

MADAME DANZARD. It could go on like this for a month. That's all we need. Are you listening to me, Isabelle?

ISABELLE. I'm listening, Maman.

MADAME DANZARD. Last year it went on for three months. Remember?

ISABELLE. That was the year before.

MADAME DANZARD. Was it? Was it really. Well, in Paris it's no better. After all, they're further north.

ISABELLE. Do you really think it rains more in Paris than here?

MADAME DANZARD. More, Isabelle. Much more. I'm sure of it.

After a pause.

Maybe we'll go up to Paris this year.

ISABELLE. Oh Maman, could we?

MADAME DANZARD. For a little shopping.

ISABELLE. Oh Maman. When?

MADAME DANZARD. Though I don't know. The things they wear in Paris. And you don't look well in those clothes, Isabelle. You know you don't. Even I don't look well in them. How could one? Hand me the scissors, would you.

ISABELLE *looks around.*

There. Right behind you. (*Impatient.*) On the table.

ISABELLE *stands up and drops everything.*

What's the matter with you? (*She rings the small round bell.*)

(*Pulling* ISABELLE *up, as she bends to pick up the seed pearls.*) Really, Isabelle.

LEA *comes in from the kitchen.* MADAME DANZARD *points to the floor.* LEA *kneels and starts collecting the tiny seed pearls that have fallen.* MADAME DANZARD *eyes the floor, making sure every last seed pearl has been picked up.*

Besides, I don't like to leave the house.

ISABELLE. But why, Maman? What could happen to it?

MADAME DANZARD. A lot can happen to a house when you're not there. And then – going to Paris – such a trip.

ISABELLE. A trip!

MADAME DANZARD. And such an expense. Think of the money. Mmm – Paris.

ISABELLE. Paris!

MADAME DANZARD. Yes, I think we'll just have to skip Paris this year.

A bell rings. MADAME DANZARD *and* ISABELLE *jump.* LEA *goes to the door.*

ISABELLE. Who's that?

MADAME DANZARD. Shhh. Let *me* listen. Who could it be? In this weather.

ISABELLE *puts her evening bag back into the sewing basket. She and* MADAME DANZARD *hurriedly sit down on the couch and wait, smiling, rubbing their cheeks to redden them.* LEA *comes back with the mail. She puts one letter in her pocket quickly, enters the sitting room with another letter on a tray. She presents the tray to* MADAME DANZARD *with a letter opener.*

MADAME DANZARD. Oh! Mail. (*She takes the letter.*)

LEA *goes up the stairs.*

ISABELLE. Anything for me, Maman?

MADAME DANZARD. Look at this. Would you look at this, Isabelle. No return address. And look at that handwriting. What do you think it could be? (*She waves the letter toward* ISABELLE.)

ISABELLE (*taking the letter*). Well, it's not a marriage.

MADAME DANZARD (*snatching it back. Excitedly*). Maybe a funeral. Whose I wonder?

ISABELLE. What is it, Maman?

LEA *comes into the upstairs room, sits down on the bed, opens the letter and eagerly begins reading it.*

MADAME DANZARD (*eagerly opening the letter*). Just a minute. Just a minute. (*Crushed.*) Another letter from the Little Shepherds of Le Mans. Will they never stop asking for money. Those children must be eating out of golden bowls. (*Reflecting suddenly*.) Hmm. I wonder how much the Blanchards are giving.

ISABELLE (*staring out at the rain.*) Do you really think it will rain straight through the winter?

MADAME DANZARD. You can never tell. But it looks it, doesn't it? (*Going to stand beside* ISABELLE.) It certainly looks it. Rain, rain, rain. Those clouds. I've never seen it so grey. Well, don't complain, Isabelle. At least we don't have to go out.

She walks out of the room. ISABELLE *follows her.* CHRISTINE *finishes putting everything away in the kitchen and goes upstairs into their room.* LEA, *hastily folding up the letter, looks at her guiltily.*

CHRISTINE (*softly*). What is it, Lea? Another letter from Maman?

LEA *looks away.*

(*Gently.*) Well, go on. Read it. There's no reason to stop just because I came into the room. (*She takes off her long apron and folds it neatly.*)

LEA. I'll read it later.

CHRISTINE. You won't have time later. You're exhausted by ten. Read it now.

LEA *looks at her.*

(*Smiling.*) Why don't you read it out loud?

LEA (*nervously*). Do you really want me to?

CHRISTINE. I wouldn't say it otherwise, would I?

LEA (*unfolding the letter, begins to read*). 'Lea, my pet, my little dove. I know I'll see you Sunday as usual, but I miss you. Little Lea. You'll always be little.'

CHRISTINE. Go on.

LEA (*continuing*). 'Don't forget to bring me the money. You forgot last week.'

CHRISTINE. Poor Maman.

LEA. Christine – Maman just –

CHRISTINE. Maman just what? (*Changing. Gentle.*) Go ahead. Keep reading.

LEA (*going on with the letter*). 'You can't wear your hair that way anymore, Lea. Like a child. All that long hair.' (*She stops.*)

CHRISTINE. Well? Don't leave anything out.

LEA (*going on*). 'Next Sunday, when you come, I'll fix it for you. It'll be better that way. Like Christine's. Won't fall in the soup.'

LEA *looks up, laughing.* CHRISTINE *doesn't smile.*

(*Going back to the letter. Quickly.*) 'Or get Christine to fix it for you. But –' (*She stops.*)

CHRISTINE. But what?

LEA. 'Tell her to be gentle.'

CHRISTINE (*snatching the letter from* LEA). I'm never going back.

LEA. Christine.

CHRISTINE (*folding the letter up very small*). You can go if you want to.

LEA. You know I wouldn't without you.

CHRISTINE. But you still care for her. She loves you.

LEA. But Christine, Christine. Maman loves you too. She's just . . .

CHRISTINE. What?

LEA. . . . scared of you.

CHRISTINE. Scared of me? (*Giving the tiny folded up letter back to* LEA.) You never stick up for me. But that's right. Defend her. Take her part. Like you always do. (*Moving away.*) Once she said that just to look at me made her sick. She couldn't even keep me after the first year. She hated when I cried.

LEA. Christine.

CHRISTINE. At Saint Mary of the Fields, I used to escape. Once a month. No one in this town would have brought me back – you know what they call it there. But your Maman – our Maman – she brought me back every time. In the end all I wanted was to be a nun. A nun! (*She smiles.*) That's all I wanted. But then of course she took me out. She hadn't expected that. That was against all her plans. I had to work. I had to make money. And she kept all of it. She placed me – and each time I got used to it, she took me out again. Sometimes I'd run away. I ran back to the Sisters. They wanted to keep me. It was

Maman, our beloved precious Maman, who would come and drag me out again.

LEA. Don't be angry with me.

CHRISTINE. I'm not angry with you.

LEA. Your face. It looks so –

CHRISTINE (*cutting in*). What? What's the matter with my face?

LEA. It just looked . . . Your face is beautiful. there's nothing wrong with your face.

CHRISTINE. No? (*She takes the hairbrush.*) I'll fix it for you. Just like she said. I'll fix it. (*Tenderly starting to brush LEA's hair. Longingly.*) If we didn't go back we could have all our Sundays together, just to ourselves. We could walk, we could go to the station and watch the trains come in. We could sit in the square, we could – But no – you wouldn't want that, would you? You want to go back. Don't you? (*Pleading.*) Don't you, Lea?

LEA *is silent.* CHRISTINE *changes, violently brushes LEA's hair.*

Of course you do. (*Roughly, she twists LEA's hair into two buns on either side of her face.*) There. Like this. That's what she meant. (*Pulling LEA over to the mirror above the sink. Raging.*) Look. How do you like it?

LEA (*tearing out her hair and sobbing*). I hate it! (*She grabs the brush from CHRISTINE and tries to fix her own hair, putting it back the way it was. She does this clumsily, jerkily – too upset to get it right. CHRISTINE watches her in silence, suddenly overwhelmed at what she has done.*)

CHRISTINE. I am a monster – aren't I? Just like she says.

LEA. You're not a monster. (*She stops fixing her hair.*)

CHRISTINE. Here. Let me. (*Cautiously, she reaches for the brush.*)

LEA *hesitates, turns away.*

I'll do it for you.

LEA *still hesitates.*

Let me do it – please.

LEA *is silent.*

Please.

Tentatively, LEA *holds out the brush.* CHRISTINE *takes it from her gently. Softly, slowly, she starts brushing* LEA's *hair.*

What did you mean when you said my face was beautiful?

LEA. What I said.

CHRISTINE. What's beautiful about it? Tell me one thing.

LEA (*looking up at her*). Your eyes.

Scene Four

The sound of a radio. In the sitting room MADAME DANZARD *is turning the dial of a radio. She stops at a station which is playing the overture of Offenbach's 'La Vie Parisienne'. She smiles. She stands beside the radio, listening, and starts humming along. She goes over to the dining room cabinet and takes out an old photograph album. She looks through the album, sighing to herself, gently tapping her foot. She puts the album down on the table in front of the couch and begins dancing to the music.* ISABELLE *comes down the stairs, slowly at first, then quicker, interrupting* MADAME DANZARD's *dance. Startled,* MADAME DANZARD *immediately switches to a station playing a Bach organ prelude.* She looks at* ISABELLE. ISABELLE *walks across the room and takes a chocolate out of a glass bowl, puts it into her mouth and looks at her mother.* MADAME DANZARD *snatches the bowl away and puts it in the dining room cabinet.* ISABELLE *sits down on the couch and starts looking through the photograph album.* MADAME DANZARD *takes a white glove from the cabinet and carefully puts it on. She rings the small round bell.* LEA *hurries in. She stands silently as* MADAME DANZARD, *wearing her white glove, slowly goes all around the room, testing the furniture and mouldings for dust.* LEA *smiles as* MADAME DANZARD *checks. On the radio, the Bach prelude continues.* MADAME DANZARD *walks up the staircase, smiling, checking the banister, kneeling down and touching the balustrades.* CHRISTINE *comes into the kitchen, carrying a heavy pewter pitcher with dried flowers.* MADAME DANZARD, *bending down in an awkward position on the staircase, finds a spot of dust on the white glove, stands up, shows it to* LEA. MADAME DANZARD *removes the glove, puts it on the table on the landing and goes downstairs to the dining room.* LEA *rushes up the stairs to clean the place where the dust has been found.*

**Nun Komm der Heiden Heiland (BWV659) a 2 Clav. e Pedale J.S. Bach

CHRISTINE *comes into the dining room, carrying the pitcher of dried flowers.* MADAME DANZARD *checks the flowers, rearranges one or two.* CHRISTINE *takes the pewter pitcher upstairs to the table on the landing. She picks up the white glove, looks at* LEA *dusting the staircase. Their hands touch for an instant.* CHRISTINE *goes down the stairs and out the hallway carrying the white glove, as* LEA *continues up the stairs dusting between the railings of the banister.* MADAME DANZARD *goes over to the radio and turns it off.*

ISABELLE. Who's this, Maman?

MADAME DANZARD (*looking over* ISABELLE's *shoulder*). Ah. Your great aunt Dominique, whom you never knew. Lucky for you. (*Sitting down beside* ISABELLE *on the couch.*) She owned half the houses on the Rue Dutois. When your father and I were first married, she wouldn't take one franc off the rent. That's the mentality of the people on your father's side. (*Pointing.*) That dress! Always pretending to be poor as church mice. (*Turning the page.*) Ah. The Rue Dutois. A quiet street. Almost as quiet as this one.

ISABELLE. No street is as quiet as this one.

MADAME DANZARD (*turning the page*). Oh. Look at you. Right here in the courtyard. Do you still have that little hat? Why don't you ever wear that little hat anymore, Isabelle?

ISABELLE. What hat? Oh. That hat. Of course not, Maman.

MADAME DANZARD. Too bad. You were delightful in that hat.

ISABELLE. Maman, do you know how old I was then?

MADAME DANZARD (*looking closely at the photograph*). Oh yes. Yes, I suppose so, Isabelle. I suppose you were.

ISABELLE. Exactly.

MADAME DANZARD *turns the page.*

MADAME DANZARD. Here you are again. Here we are. Oh look!

Together they laugh over the photographs. MADAME DANZARD, *still chuckling, continues to turn the pages of the photograph album. Suddenly* ISABELLE *smiles. She stifles a laugh.* MADAME DANZARD *looks up.* ISABELLE *begins laughing in earnest.* MADAME DANZARD *sees the photograph* ISABELLE *is looking at and stops laughing immediately. She slams the photograph album shut.* ISABELLE, *trying to stifle her laughter, leaves the room. After a few moments* MADAME DANZARD *goes up the stairs on tiptoe, silently opens the door to* CHRISTINE *and* LEA's *room, one foot stepping in, and stares at the immaculate perfect order, as the light dims.*

Scene Five

LEA *and* CHRISTINE *come into their room, wearing their faded dresses and coats of the first scene.*

CHRISTINE. I don't want to force you.

LEA. You're not forcing me. We can never go back.

CHRISTINE. She didn't mean you when she told us to get out. She only meant me. (*She takes off her coat.*)

LEA. She meant both of us.

CHRISTINE. Not you, Lea. Not ever you. She'll never stop loving you.

LEA. She'll never forgive me for the money. Never, Christine. You know she won't.

CHRISTINE. But why shouldn't you keep your own money – instead of giving it to her.

LEA *sits on the bed, upset.*

She'll forgive you. You'll see. She'll forgive you. She always has. (*Looking at* LEA.) And Lea, Lea, you know what we'll do with that money?

LEA *is silent.*

We'll save it. All of it, from now on. We'll put it together – yours and mine – and someday, Lea, someday we'll – we'll –

LEA *looks at her.*

LEA. Remember what you said – we could spend all our Sundays together.

CHRISTINE. I remember.

LEA. Promise?

CHRISTINE. Promise.

LEA *picks up the small blanket from their mother. She bites the wool with her teeth, loosening a strand. She pulls it, stops, pulls it again.*

LEA. Here. Hold this. (*She hands* CHRISTINE *the blanket.*)

CHRISTINE. What are you doing?

LEA *keeps pulling.*

You've had that since you were four.

As LEA *pulls, the loosely crocheted blanket begins to unravel.*

Lea!

LEA. Just hold it. (*She pulls harder.*) Now pull from your end.

CHRISTINE *hesitates.*

Go ahead. Pull it!

CHRISTINE. But –

LEA. Go on.

CHRISTINE *cautiously begins to pull*

That's it! That's right. Go ahead. Pull it. Pull it. Pull it harder.

CHRISTINE *looks at her.*

Harder.

CHRISTINE *really starts pulling in earnest.*

That's it. Harder. Oh harder. (*She pulls from her end.*) Harder.

As the blanket unravels faster and faster, they run around the room. They are constricted by the confines of the narrow room. They wind the wool around the bed, the sink. They wind it around each other. LEA, *laughing, falls on the bed.* CHRISTINE *falls beside her.*

CHRISTINE (*laughing*). No more, no more.

LEA *wraps* CHRISTINE *even closer to her with the wool.*

(*Breaking away suddenly.*) That's enough. I have to go downstairs.

LEA. It's not time yet. (*Playful.*) Don't you want to play anymore?

CHRISTINE (*putting on her apron. Abruptly*). No.

Scene Six

MADAME DANZARD *comes down the hall, dressed to go out. She is holding two hats. In the maid's room,* CHRISTINE *is sitting on the bed, embroidering a white chemise with delicate lace and wide intricate shoulder straps.* LEA *sits beside her, hemming a long white nightgown.*

MADAME DANZARD (*calling*). Isabelle! Isabelle.

ISABELLE *comes into the dining room.* MADAME DANZARD *holds out a particularly provincial hat.*

Charming, isn't it?

ISABELLE *is silent.*

Well, go ahead. There's no reason to be shy.

She lunges toward ISABELLE *with the hat.*

ISABELLE (*drawing back*). Oh. It's for me, Maman?

MADAME DANZARD. Of course it's for you. For whom else?

ISABELLE. And you want me to wear it now?

MADAME DANZARD (*very serious*). I don't want you to wear anything else. You haven't forgotten how pretentious the Loupins looked last Sunday in their monstrosities.

ISABELLE. I remember.

MADAME DANZARD. Well, I can't wait to see their faces today.

ISABELLE *puts on the hat.*

Perfect.

The bell rings.

ISABELLE (*anxious*). It's them!

MADAME DANZARD. Early, as usual. Hoping to catch a glimpse of something. Well, they won't see anything today. They'll just have to wait. (*She stands still for a few moments, delightedly looking at her watch. She puts on another hat, if anything even more provincial than* ISABELLE's. *Plunging in the stickpin of the hat.*) How do you like mine?

ISABELLE (*after a pause*). Adorable.

MADAME DANZARD. Well together – I must say – we make quite a pair.

The bell rings again. They go out.

LEA. I'll never sew like you. Look at this hem. (*She holds up the nightgown and laughs.*) Even my hems are crooked. All those years with the Sisters and I never learned.

CHRISTINE. The Sisters didn't know how to teach you. Give it to me. I'll do it.

LEA *gives her the nightgown.*

Remember when I used to visit you at the convent? You waited for me at the gate. You were so little and so hungry all the time. (*She laughs.*) You're still hungry all the time.

LEA. Christine.

CHRISTINE. Hmm?

LEA. Can I . . .

CHRISTINE (*knowing what* LEA *wants*). Can you what?

LEA. Can I look at them again?

CHRISTINE. Of course you can. They're yours.

LEA *jumps up and pulls an old trunk out from under the bed.* CHRISTINE *smiles.* LEA *pulls up the lid. The trunk is overflowing with beautiful white lingerie, undergarments trimmed with lace, nightgowns with fluttering ribbons, delicate ruffled chemises.*

LEA (*gathering it all in her arms*). All of it! All of it! No one sews like you.

CHRISTINE *stops sewing, watches* LEA.

Oh Christine. I can't believe how beautiful they are. (*She buries her face in the clothing.*)

CHRISTINE (*holding up the chemise she was sewing*). Look, it's almost finished.

LEA (*raising her head*). Already?

CHRISTINE. Yes. Come try it on.

LEA. Now?

CHRISTINE. Don't you want to?

LEA. I want to.

CHRISTINE. Well then.

LEA *comes forward.*

Go ahead. I'll close my eyes.

She looks at LEA.

I want to be surprised.

She closes her eyes. LEA *takes off her dress and slowly, carefully, puts on the chemise.*

LEA. Christine . . . you can look now.

CHRISTINE. Can I?

LEA. Yes.

CHRISTINE *opens her eyes.*

It's beautiful.

CHRISTINE. It's you who are beautiful.

LEA *(tentatively reaching out her hand).* I'm cold.

CHRISTINE *(going toward her).* I know.

Scene Seven

Light comes up on the empty sitting room. Off-stage ISABELLE *is playing 'Sur Le Pont D'Avignon' badly on the piano. She hums off key to the music, continuing to make mistakes as she goes along. Abruptly, the music stops.* ISABELLE *peeks her head out into the sitting room. She comes in and goes over to the dining room cabinet. She opens the cabinet and takes out the glass bowl of chocolates. She takes one, unwraps it and gobbles it up. She takes another, unwraps it, pops it into her mouth.* LEA *comes in, carrying a dusting cloth. She sees* ISABELLE *with the chocolate in her mouth.* ISABELLE *looks away, awkwardly chewing the chocolate.* LEA *begins dusting the couch.* ISABELLE *takes a chocolate from the bowl and, hesitatingly, holds it out to* LEA. LEA *doesn't move.* ISABELLE *continues to hold out the chocolate.* LEA *hesitates, cautiously looks around. She looks back at the chocolate, still hesitating. Suddenly she snatches the chocolate and puts the glass bowl back in the cabinet and leaves.* LEA *goes up the staircase to the landing. She takes the chocolate out of her pocket, smiles to herself.* CHRISTINE *comes into the kitchen, holding a mortar and pestle. She starts pounding. Off-stage,* ISABELLE *begins playing 'Sur Le Pont D'Avignon' with one finger on the piano. She plays quickly, badly.* LEA *begins dusting the banister. Accidentally she hits the pewter pitcher. It rolls off the table and clatters down the stairs. The dried flowers scatter.*

LEA *(closing her eyes and screaming).* CHRISTINE!

In the kitchen CHRISTINE *stops pounding instantly. She runs to the stairs.*

CHRISTINE. What's wrong? What happened?

LEA *(frantic).* The pitcher. The pewter pitcher. Madame will be so angry. Madame will –

CHRISTINE. Shhh. *(She goes down on her knees and apprehensively, picks up the pitcher.)* Look, Lea. Come here. It's not even broken.

LEA, *unbelievingly, opens her eyes, goes down the stairs to* CHRISTINE.

My angel, my dove.

She pulls LEA *down beside her.*

Don't be frightened. Look at me. Look.

The bell rings. The piano stops. LEA *looks into* CHRISTINE'*s eyes.* CHRISTINE *gathers the dried flowers and puts them back in the pewter pitcher.*

Don't worry. Nothing is broken. Believe me.

ISABELLE *appears and sees* LEA *and* CHRISTINE. LEA *rushes down the hall.* CHRISTINE *puts the pewter pitcher back on the table on the landing. She comes down the stairs, goes to open the front door.* ISABELLE *goes after her.* MADAME DANZARD *comes into the house.* ISABELLE *runs ahead.* CHRISTINE *goes out of the hall.*

ISABELLE. Anything for me, Maman?

MADAME DANZARD *takes off her hat. She smiles delightedly, raises her finger in anticipation. She puts her hat, gloves, coat, bag and package on the dining room table. Smiling with excitement she opens the package.* ISABELLE *leans forward expectantly. Happily,* MADAME DANZARD *holds up a photograph in a frame. It is a picture of herself and* ISABELLE *in their two hats.* ISABELLE *looks at the photograph and grimaces.* MADAME DANZARD *sets the photograph down on the radio table. She turns on the radio, as* ISABELLE *takes the clothing and* *wrapping paper off the dining room table. 'C'est La Saison D'Amour'* blares out over the radio.* MADAME DANZARD *smiles, bursts into song. Blackout.*

Scene Eight

LEA *and* CHRISTINE *stand side by side. They are dressed identically in dark wool dresses. Each dress has a wide yolk of intricate white lace. Their hair is arranged in exactly the same way. Their eyes are wide. They look frightened, shy. They have come to have their photograph taken.*

LEA (*whispering*). Do you really think we should have come?

CHRISTINE. Why not? I wanted a photograph of you – of us together.

LEA. Suppose someone should find out?

CHRISTINE. Suppose they should? We're allowed to have a photograph taken, aren't we?

LEA. It's so expensive.

CHRISTINE. We can afford it.

LEA. I'm nervous.

CHRISTINE (*holding her hand for a moment*). It's all right.

LEA. My hair – is it –

CHRISTINE. It's perfect.

LEA. But did you get it right on top?

CHRISTINE. You look like an angel. I'm going to fix it like that every Sunday.

LEA. I hate that iron.

CHRISTINE. Shhh. He's coming back.

*'C'est La Saison D'Amour' Copyright ©1936 by Musikverlag und Bühnenvertreib Zürich, A. G. Zurich. Reproduit avec l'autorisation de 'ROYALTY' Editions Musicales, 25, Rue d'Hauteville, Paris, Musique de Oscar Strauss d'après Johann Strauss père. Paroles de Albert Willemetz et Léopold Marchand.

LEA. Oh Christine, I'm frightened.

CHRISTINE. Of what? It's only a photograph. (*For a moment she clasps her hands tightly together. She straightens her dress.*) We should have done it long ago.

PHOTOGRAPHER (*voice over*). I'm sorry that took so long. Now look this way. That's right. You're sisters, aren't you?

CHRISTINE. Yes.

PHOTOGRAPHER (*voice over*). I knew right away. This should make a lovely photograph. Just step a little closer to each other.

CHRISTINE *and* LEA *move very close.*

Not quite so close.

They move slightly apart.

That's it. Perfect. Don't move.

There is a burst of light as he takes the photograph.

Did your mother always dress you like that?

They are silent.

Hmmm?

CHRISTINE. Like what?

PHOTOGRAPHER (*voice over*). In the same clothes.

CHRISTINE. She never did.

PHOTOGRAPHER (*voice over*). You look like twins.

LEA *smiles.*

No, not twins. But sisters. Sisters, certainly. Such a resemblance.

CHRISTINE. We're not twins. I'm six years older than my sister.

PHOTOGRAPHER (*voice over*). Six years? Look up please.

Again there is a burst of light.

You look practically the same. But I guess a lot of people have told you that.

CHRISTINE. Some.

PHOTOGRAPHER (*voice over*). Not very talkative, are you? What about your sister? Cat got her tongue?

CHRISTINE (*warningly*). She's shy.

PHOTOGRAPHER (*voice over*). Well, I always wanted a sister – shy or not.

LEA *looks in the direction of the* PHOTOGRAPHER.

A sister sticks by you. Even when you're in trouble. Isn't that true?

LEA *smiles.*

Can she talk? Such a shy thing. I bet you're your mother's favourite.

LEA (*nervously*). No . . . I . . .

PHOTOGRAPHER (*voice over*). Still a child, isn't she? I can see that. What a sweet smile. Please now, both of you smile. And look at me.

LEA *smiles.* CHRISTINE *looks directly at the* PHOTOGRAPHER.

That's good.

There is a burst of light, as he takes the final photograph.

That will be fine. No one would ever know the two of you were servants. At the Danzards, aren't you?

CHRISTINE (*nervously*). Yes.

PHOTOGRAPHER (*voice over*). Excellent people, the Danzards. I've known them for years. Photographed the whole family. Photographed the daughter when she was just a child.

He pauses.

I hear she's going to be married soon.

CHRISTINE *and* LEA *are silent.*

Of course I've been hearing that for years.

He waits. They don't speak.

Well – seeing is believing I always say. Who knows if it's true.

They remain silent. He chuckles quietly.

You two certainly are discreet. They're lucky to have two such discreet young ladies. Especially in this town.

CHRISTINE. Hurry, Lea. I still have the shopping to do. (*She puts on her coat.*)

PHOTOGRAPHER (*voice over*). You've been there a long time, haven't you?

They are silent.

How many years is it now?

CHRISTINE. A few.

PHOTOGRAPHER (*voice over*). I'm sure they treat you well.

They remain silent.

Very fine people. Excellent people. But of course you know that.

CHRISTINE. Certainly, we know it. Come Lea, don't be so slow.

LEA *turns her back to the* PHOTOGRAPHER *and puts on her coat. It is exactly the same as* CHRISTINE's.

PHOTOGRAPHER (*voice over*). No need to be shy with me.

He laughs.

Madame Danzard makes you work hard enough, I imagine. For the money she pays you.

CHRISTINE, *eager to leave, starts taking out her money.*

CHRISTINE. You said fifty francs, didn't you?

PHOTOGRAPHER (*voice over*). For you girls, I'll make it twenty-five. You can pay me when you come for the photograph.

CHRISTINE. Fifty is what you said, fifty is what we pay.

PHOTOGRAPHER (*voice over*). I see. Very well. Come back in two weeks.

LEA (*smiling*). Thank you.

They go out.

Scene Nine

Before the scene opens, the slap of cards hitting a table is heard. Light comes up on MADAME DANZARD *and* ISABELLE *sitting at the dining room table. They are each armed with a pack of fifty-two cards. They sit facing each other. They are engaged in playing an elaborate game of réussite, a card game similar to double solitaire, the difference being that with réussite, each player secretly asks a question about the future before the game starts. Whether the question is answered affirmatively or not depends on the outcome of the game. When the scene opens,* MADAME DANZARD *and* ISABELLE *are laying out the last row of cards. As all but three cards are used from the very beginning, the cards almost completely cover the table.*

MADAME DANZARD (*as she finishes laying out her cards, deftly, neatly, straightening them as she goes along*). What did you wish for this time? If you don't tell, you won't get it.

ISABELLE (*sloppier as she finishes laying out her cards*). That's not true. You don't have to tell what you wish for.

MADAME DANZARD. Well, I think I can guess. I'm not telling my wish either. Not even if I win.

ISABELLE. Ready Maman?

MADAME DANZARD. I'm ready. But you're not. Look at those cards.

ISABELLE. Which cards?

MADAME DANZARD. Those over there. They're going to fall off the table.

ISABELLE *straightens the last cards.*

Good. Now we're ready.

She and ISABELLE *tap their remaining cards on the table three times.*

ISABELLE. One, two, three . . . begin. Maman – that is not fair.

MADAME DANZARD. What's not fair?

ISABELLE. You started at two.

MADAME DANZARD. I did not. I absolutely did not. However, if you insist, we'll start again.

ISABELLE. One . . . two . . . three . . . start.

MADAME DANZARD (*inspecting her cards*). I don't have anything to start with.

ISABELLE. You always do that. Start first.

MADAME DANZARD. Never. That's your imagination.

ISABELLE (*shrieking*). I saw you!

MADAME DANZARD. Quiet, Isabelle. (*Looking at her cards.*) This is absurd. I can't move a thing.

She looks over at ISABELLE's *cards.* ISABELLE *sits pondering.*

Look at you. You have a million things. Don't you see? (*Disgusted.*) Aah.

ISABELLE. Where Maman?

MADAME DANZARD. There. Right there. Right before your eyes. Oh Isabelle, sometimes you're so slow.

ISABELLE. You think so, Maman?

MADAME DANZARD. Well I'm stuck. Wait a minute. Why didn't I see that seven. Just a minute now. (*She transfers a large block of cards.*) That certainly should make things a little easier. (*Looking at* ISABELLE's *cards.*) What's happening over there? That six is still sitting there.

ISABELLE. I see it, Maman. (*She moves the six.*)

MADAME DANZARD (*directing as* ISABELLE *moves her cards.*) And now the nine. Go ahead.

ISABELLE. What nine?

MADAME DANZARD. The nine of diamonds onto the ten of clubs. What's the matter with you?

ISABELLE. Maman please. I can't concentrate.

MADAME DANZARD. What are you talking about? Of course you can concentrate. This is a game of concentration. You have to concentrate. You have to concentrate on every little detail. Otherwise all will be lost. (*Looking over her own cards like a hawk. Excited.*) Red eight on black nine on red ten on – Perfect! That frees my queen and now I can take all these with the jack – (*She lifts a huge block of cards.*) – put them on the queen and . . . let's see what's under here. What's been hiding from me. (*She turns up a card. Disappointed.*) Three of spades. Now what am I going to do with that? (*Suddenly.*) You got an ace, Isabelle. How did that happen? Clubs. My two is buried under that nine. I'll never get it out.

ISABELLE. I've got it, Maman. Look. And the three.

MADAME DANZARD. How did you get them so fast?

ISABELLE *laughs gleefully.*

You're not cheating, are you?

ISABELLE. Maman.

MADAME DANZARD (*checking the cards*). Where is the ace of diamonds? Where is that ace?

ISABELLE. Not the ace of diamonds, Maman. But I've got the ace of spades. And the two, and the –

MADAME DANZARD. Three!

ISABELLE (*overlapping and getting there first*). Three!

MADAME DANZARD. Isabelle! How could you. Blocked again. Incredible.

ISABELLE. What are we having for dinner tonight, Maman?

MADAME DANZARD. Blanquette of veal.

ISABELLE. Veal again?

MADAME DANZARD (*looking at her watch*). They'll be down soon. Ah – there's the four. (*Slapping down the four of spades.*) They never speak anymore. Have you noticed? Not a word. The older one walks by me as if I'm not there.

LEA *comes into the upstairs room, lays a delicate, handmade white coverlet on their bed, places the photograph of herself and* CHRISTINE *taken at the* PHOTOGRAPHER's *on the night table, and goes out again.*

ISABELLE. I have the five. And the six! The older one was always that way.

MADAME DANZARD (*slapping down her cards*). Seven, eight!

ISABELLE (*tapping her mother on the hand*). One hand, Maman!

MADAME DANZARD. Every Sunday – up in that room alone – it's amazing.

ISABELLE. They've always stuck to themselves.

MADAME DANZARD. They haven't seen their mother in years.

ISABELLE (*looking at her mother. Quietly*). That's just as well.

MADAME DANZARD. You know – I found the older one in the hallway trying to rub a stain off the door.

ISABELLE. I know that stain. It's been there for years. It'll never come off.

MADAME DANZARD. And she knows it. (*Smacking down three more cards as* ISABELLE *shrieks.*) And the nine, ten, jack! (*She takes a small titbit from a dish on the table and pops it into her mouth. Making a face.*) What's wrong with her? She's put too much salt in these again.

ISABELLE (*laying down a card*). The queen!

MADAME DANZARD. Have you turned up your three cards yet?

ISABELLE. Not yet. (*She sneaks a card into her lap.*)

MADAME DANZARD. Well, I absolutely refuse to turn – Isabelle! You cheated. I can't believe my eyes.

ISABELLE. I did not.

MADAME DANZARD. You did. You moved that jack of hearts onto the queen of diamonds.

ISABELLE. And – ?

MADAME DANZARD. What do you mean – And? You know you can't move red onto red. Move it back.

ISABELLE. It was there before, Maman. I started the whole game that way.

MADAME DANZARD. Isabelle, please stop this lying at once. And just what was happening at the Blanchards the other night?

ISABELLE. Nothing was happening, Maman.

MADAME DANZARD. Nothing? Of course they're so blind –

ISABELLE *sneaks her ace of hearts onto the edge of the table.*

But with a marriage coming, you can't just smile at anyone.

ISABELLE. I wasn't smiling, Maman.

MADAME DANZARD. No? Wait! You put out the ace of hearts without even telling me. Where's my two? Here it is. My two, my three. (*She slaps them down.*) Where's that four?

ISABELLE. Here Maman. I have it. (*She puts it down.*)

MADAME DANZARD. You don't? You do. Well, I'm turning over my three cards. It's finally come to that. (*She turns up one of the three cards.*) Jack of hearts. What use is he? Looks just like Jacques Blanchard, doesn't he? Not a place for him here. (*Looking at her watch again.*) Where are they? Have they forgotten the Flintons are coming? What's wrong with them? Do you know that yesterday, coming back from the Loupins, I saw them sitting in the square. At eleven o'clock in the morning! Can you believe that?

ISABELLE. Unbelievable.

MADAME DANZARD. Eleven o'clock in the morning. I didn't say anything when they came back. But they knew. (*She turns over the second card.*) Four of diamonds. Too soon for that. Should I look at the third one? Yes or no?

ISABELLE. Go ahead Maman. Take a chance.

MADAME *turns over her last card. It is the ace of hearts. She smacks it down in the centre.*

MADAME DANZARD (*ecstatic*). Hearts! Just what I was waiting for.

ISABELLE (*slapping down an ace of diamonds*). Diamonds!

MADAME DANZARD. What?

ISABELLE. My ace, my two, my –

MADAME DANZARD. I can't do a thing till you move that queen.

ISABELLE. Queen? What queen?

MADAME DANZARD. Your queen, your queen. Use your eyes, Isabelle. (*She stands up and moves* ISABELLE*'s queen into the centre.*)

ISABELLE (*watching her mother*). There. My queen.

MADAME DANZARD. And *my* king! That frees everything. Now we can really go ahead!

The game builds to a frenzied finish with ISABELLE *feverishly manoeuvring her cards, and* MADAME DANZARD *laughing wildly and madly slapping down card after card with amazing speed. Reaching the end of the game, she triumphantly hugs the despairing* ISABELLE. LEA *comes down the stairs wearing a pale pink sweater. She places a lace cloth on the table in front of the couch.*

ISABELLE (*whispering to her mother*). Maman, do you see?

LEA *looks up, aware they are whispering about her.*

MADAME DANZARD. Of course I see. What do you think I am
– blind? What in heaven's name allows her to think she can
wear a sweater like that in this house.

LEA *clumsily finishes laying down the lace cloth and goes to the kitchen.
In the kitchen,* CHRISTINE *is preparing dough for a tart. She stops
when she sees* LEA.

LEA. You told me I could wear it.

CHRISTINE. When I gave it to you, I never told you to wear it in
this house, did I? I never told you to wear it downstairs.

LEA *is silent.* CHRISTINE *goes back to kneading the dough.*

MADAME DANZARD. Just where did she think she was going?
And how did she have the nerve, the extreme nerve to buy
such a thing?

ISABELLE. Maman –

CHRISTINE (*wetting the dough too much, her hands getting messy*). Why
did you? Why would you want to wear that sweater anywhere
but in our room? What were you thinking?

MADAME DANZARD. What is the world coming to? I couldn't
believe my eyes.

ISABELLE. But Maman –

LEA. I wasn't thinking of anything but us. (*Carefully, she takes off the
sweater.*)

CHRISTINE (*pulling her violently into a corner of the kitchen*). You're
lying.

MADAME DANZARD. There are no buts involved here.

CHRISTINE. Don't think I haven't noticed. I have eyes. I can
see. When I come into the dining room, you're polishing the
table looking off into nowhere. When you sew, you prick your
fingers, when you wax the floor, you get the wax on your shoes.
You drop plates, you spill water, you chip cups, you burn
yourself with the iron –

LEA. I dropped that plate six weeks ago.

CHRISTINE. What about the cup?

LEA. The cup was chipped when we came here. I do things. I get
things done.

CHRISTINE (*wiping her dough covered hands on her apron*). But you look good. That I can see. Your apron neat as a pin. Immaculate. (*She circles* LEA.) The collar just right in front. The cuffs folded just so. You keep yourself perfect, don't you? And why?

LEA. I've always dressed this way. Look at me. We've always dressed this way.

CHRISTINE. You're different. Believe me. I know.

CHRISTINE *goes out the hall.* LEA *follows her.*

ISABELLE. Maybe she didn't know, Maman.

MADAME DANZARD (*gathering up the cards*). Of course she knew. She deliberately put it on and wore it. That sweater must have cost –

ISABELLE (*interrupting*). Maybe –

MADAME DANZARD. I wonder if I pay them too much.

ISABELLE. Maybe she didn't buy it, Maman.

MADAME DANZARD. What?

ISABELLE (*rising and walking to the staircase*). Maybe it wasn't her.

MADAME DANZARD. What are you talking about? Make yourself clear, Isabelle.

ISABELLE. Maybe it was her sister who gave her that sweater. Didn't you see? It was handmade.

MADAME DANZARD (*softly*). Oh. Yes. Yes. Now I see. (*Softer yet.*) I believe you're right, Isabelle.

ISABELLE. I think so, Maman.

MADAME DANZARD. Handmade! Of course. And such expensive wool. I saw wool just like that in the Dupin's shop window. You don't think she bought it there, do you?

ISABELLE. Maybe, Maman. I wouldn't be surprised.

MADAME DANZARD. What an extravagance! Can you imagine if someone had seen . . .

ISABELLE. Oh Maman, you go too far. (*She starts up the staircase.*)

MADAME DANZARD (*following her*). Do I? Do I, my dear? You don't know this town like I do. Imagine if the Flintons had been here. Or Madame Blanchard. Or . . . I can't even think of it . . . Madame Castelneuve. You think I go too far. No my dear, you haven't lived here nearly long enough.

Scene Ten

It is night. Silence. LEA *moans in the darkness.*

CHRISTINE. Lea.

LEA. I can't breathe.

CHRISTINE. Lea.

LEA. I can't breathe. I can't.

Light comes up in their room.

Someone behind me, pulling my coat. Even before I turn around I know. She grabs my hand and starts running. Her hand like iron around mine. I make myself heavy, but she holds me tight and I can feel all her little bones. She snatches me into the house and I run from corner to corner but she gets everywhere first. She grows and grows till she's as big as the room. And then I hear the door open but I can't move, Christine. I can't breathe.

CHRISTINE (*rocking* LEA). Hush. Hush now. It's over. Try and sleep. Go to sleep.

LEA. I can't.

CHRISTINE (*sings*).
　　Sleep my little sister, sleep
　　Sleep through darkness
　　Sleep so deep

LEA. You won't ever leave me, will you, Christine?

CHRISTINE (*sings*).
　　All the rivers find the sea
　　My little sister
　　Sleep for me.

LEA (*touching* CHRISTINE'*s face*). You won't, will you?

CHRISTINE (*holding* LEA *close*). Never.

LEA. I don't think I could bear it – being alone in this house. In any house.

MADAME DANZARD *appears at the top of the stairs. She is wearing a bathrobe and slippers and is carrying a kerosene lamp. She comes down the stairs on tiptoe and goes into the dining room.*

CHRISTINE (*sings*).
    Dream my little sister, dream
    Dream I'm here now
    Dream your dreams

LEA. Do you hear me, Christine?

CHRISTINE (*sings*).
    All the things you want to be
    My little sister
    Dream for me.

Softly, MADAME DANZARD *moves across the floor to the cabinet, opens it quietly, takes out a long black box, on top of which lies the white glove, opens it, and silently begins counting the silverware.*

LEA. I was so scared when Madame was waiting when we came back from the square. Weren't you scared, Christine?

CHRISTINE. Madame doesn't speak to us anymore. She hasn't said a word in months.

LEA. She never did, Christine. Oh Christine, she never did.

CHRISTINE. Shhh. Sleep now. Sleep my angel. (*Continues the song.*)
    Somewhere there are meadows
    Somewhere there are hills
    Somewhere horses run
    And sheep are still

MADAME DANZARD *closes the box, lays the white glove carefully on top, returns the box to the cabinet, picks up the kerosene lamp, and quietly goes up the staircase. Sings.*

    Sleep my little sister, sleep
    Cows will moo
    And lambs will bleat
    I will never leave your side
    My little sister
    Close your eyes.

*As the light dims, LEA's eyes remain wide open, staring into the
darkness.*

Scene Eleven

The sound of a 1930's song, 'Chez Moi' is heard on the radio. Light comes
up on an empty house. A door fans open and shut to the music. ISABELLE
dances out into the sitting room, carrying a hairbrush and an ivory mirror.
In a 1930s pose, she brushes her hair and gazes at herself in the mirror. She
puts the hairbrush and mirror down on the table, flings herself onto the couch
and plucks an imaginary cigarette out of the air. She dances over to the
staircase, tests the banister for imaginary dust. She goes quickly to the
cabinet and takes out a chocolate. She throws the wrapper on the table and
pops the chocolate into her mouth. CHRISTINE comes down the hallway
on her hands and knees, dusting the moulding of the staircase. ISABELLE
puts on MADAME DANZARD's hat, plunges in the hatpin, and dances
over to the bottom of the stairs. CHRISTINE sees ISABELLE and stands
up. ISABELLE stops dancing immediately. They stare at each other.
ISABELLE turns off the radio. A soft drip of water begins. CHRISTINE
starts polishing the banister. ISABELLE stands in the sitting room. LEA
appears carrying a silver centrepiece. She puts it on the dining room table,
not noticing CHRISTINE on the staircase. ISABELLE looks at
CHRISTINE. She picks up the hairbrush and the mirror. She holds out the
brush to LEA. LEA hesitates. Finally she takes the brush from ISABELLE
and starts brushing her hair. ISABELLE smiles, luxuriating in LEA's
brushing her hair. CHRISTINE watches them. MADAME DANZARD
appears at the top of the stairs. She sees CHRISTINE polishing the
banister, the same spot over and over again. CHRISTINE sees
MADAME DANZARD, stops, and goes into the kitchen. She begins to
struggle with the cover of a canister. She cannot get it off. MADAME
DANZARD comes all the way down the stairs and stands watching LEA
brush ISABELLE's hair. ISABELLE sees MADAME DANZARD and
takes the hairbrush from LEA. She goes out. LEA, finally seeing
MADAME DANZARD, follows her. ISABELLE closes the door in
LEA's face. LEA comes back, stands still, nervously watching MADAME
DANZARD. MADAME DANZARD takes the chocolate wrapper from
the table and flicks it onto the floor. She looks at LEA. Confused, LEA
doesn't move. Pinching LEA's arm, MADAME DANZARD drags her*

---

*'Chez Moi' (Venez Donc Chez Moi) Copyright © 1935. Fox-trot avec
refrain chanté (P. Misraki – J. Feline)

over to where the chocolate wrapper has fallen. She pushes LEA *down on her knees.* LEA *picks up the wrapper. There is a loud banging sound. In the kitchen,* CHRISTINE *is struggling desperately with the canister. She bangs it several times on the table.* MADAME DANZARD, *hearing the noise, goes into the kitchen. Seeing her,* CHRISTINE *places the canister carefully on the table. The sound of the drip grows louder.* MADAME DANZARD *checks a pot, opens the door of a cabinet and closes it. Holding the chocolate wrapper,* LEA *goes out of the hall.* MADAME DANZARD *turns off the dripping tap.* CHRISTINE *watches her.* MADAME DANZARD *looks at* CHRISTINE, *leaves the kitchen and goes down the hall. The light dims.*

Scene Twelve

ISABELLE *stands on a stool in the middle of the sitting room. She is trying on a drab mauve dress, much too large on her.* CHRISTINE *is on her knees, pinning up the hem of the dress. Around her neck hangs a large pair of tailor scissors.* LEA *holds the pins and hands them to* CHRISTINE. MADAME DANZARD *stands looking up at* ISABELLE. *Throughout the scene,* CHRISTINE *makes adjustments on the dress – hem, sleeves, waist, bodice. Never, during any point in the scene, is a word addressed to* CHRISTINE *or* LEA.

MADAME DANZARD. What did I tell you? It's perfect.

ISABELLE. Yes Maman. (*After a pause.*) Do you really think so?

MADAME DANZARD. Of course I think so. You're always so difficult when it comes to clothes.

ISABELLE. I'm not difficult. (*Looking down at the dress.*) I just didn't like it.

MADAME DANZARD. Well you see – you were wrong. You really should trust me, Isabelle. Have I ever chosen anything you didn't like?

ISABELLE *is silent.*

Eventually?

ISABELLE. It looks better at home.

CHRISTINE *starts taking in the right sleeve of* ISABELLE's *dress.*

MADAME DANZARD. Of course it does. Everything always looks

better at home. I want you to wear it Friday when we go to the Flintons'.

ISABELLE. But it won't be ready in –

MADAME DANZARD *(interrupting)*. It will be ready. She hardly has anything to do.

ISABELLE. Must we go, Maman? The Flintons are so –

MADAME DANZARD. We're going. And put your arm down, Isabelle. Remember how long she took the last time. *(She touches the bodice of the dress.)* You know my dear, I think it's too tight around the chest.

CHRISTINE *moves to* ISABELLE's *right side and undoes the pins around her chest.*

Yes, I really think so. You don't want to wear these things too tight. Though they are wearing them tight these days. I saw Mademoiselle Loupin on the Rue Mafort just yesterday. I couldn't believe my eyes.

ISABELLE. Oh you can't count her. Everything looks tight around her chest.

CHRISTINE *moves behind* ISABELLE.

MADAME DANZARD *(barely restraining a laugh)*. Isabelle! How unlike you. I never even thought you'd noticed Mademoiselle Loupin.

ISABELLE. Of course I've noticed her. Who hasn't?

CHRISTINE *moves to* ISABELLE's *left side.*

MADAME DANZARD. She's getting married in September Monsieur Bouttier told me at the pharmacy. The date is definitely set.

ISABELLE *(smiling)*. So they say.

MADAME DANZARD. Why – do you have any reason to doubt it?

ISABELLE. None.

MADAME DANZARD. You sounded so . . . Anyway I know one marriage that's going to take place. *(She smiles to herself.)*

CHRISTINE *trembles suddenly, holds the pins out to* LEA *who is not paying attention to her. The pins fall to the floor in front of the footstool.*

CHRISTINE and LEA *bend down to pick up the pins.* CHRISTINE's *hands are shaking.* MADAME DANZARD *watches.*

Those first few months of being married, my dear. (*Looking at* CHRISTINE *and* LEA.) Some people will never know.

ISABELLE (*smiling*). Maman.

LEA *looks up at* ISABELLE. CHRISTINE *stands up, and looks down at* LEA. LEA *moves to* CHRISTINE. ISABELLE *watches her.* MADAME DANZARD *and* CHRISTINE *look at each other.*

MADAME DANZARD (*moving closer*). Now how am I going to take you to the Flintons with a crooked hem? Hmm? Just tell me that.

ISABELLE *tries to look down at the hem.*

(*Glaring at* CHRISTINE.) Don't move, Isabelle. Don't budge.

Hastily, CHRISTINE *starts redoing the hem.*

(*Watching her.*) Incredible how long it takes to do a simple hem.

CHRISTINE *continues to fix the hem.* MADAME DANZARD *suddenly moves in and rips the bottom of the dress out of* CHRISTINE's *hands. She points to the neck of the dress.*

The neck should be lower. Definitely lower.

CHRISTINE *takes the tailor scissors and slowly begins cutting away the fabric around the neck.*

(*Stepping forward.*) Impossible.

She takes the scissors from CHRISTINE, *with them gestures her away, and begins cutting the fabric around the neck herself.* CHRISTINE *starts up the stairs.*

(*Loudly, as she cuts.*) Really. And with crepe going for seven francs a yard. Next time we'll go to the dressmaker's.

On the stairs, CHRISTINE *stops. She continues up.* LEA *follows her.*

(*Taking a few steps back from* ISABELLE.) Your grandmother's pearls will look just right. You shall have them as a present.

ISABELLE. Maman!

In their room, CHRISTINE *sits down on the bed, facing out.* LEA *stands behind her.*

MADAME DANZARD. I can already see you. And those pearls. A perfect match.

The light dims slowly on MADAME DANZARD *and* ISABELLE.

CHRISTINE. There was nothing wrong with that hem. Nothing. You saw it. That hem was perfectly straight.

LEA *is silent.*

Wasn't it?

LEA. Of course it was.

CHRISTINE. She sees things. Things that aren't even there. Her and her daughter.

She pauses.

You won't go, will you?

LEA. Go where? Where would I go?

CHRISTINE. Even if she goes, you won't go

LEA *is silent.*

Lea! You're thinking about it all the time, aren't you? That's why you're always dreaming. Why you're always off in that other world.

LEA. There is no other world, Christine. (*Coming closer.*) Christine – darling. Don't be upset.

CHRISTINE. You heard Madame. You heard what she said.

LEA. What did she say?

CHRISTINE. You heard her. Don't pretend you didn't.

LEA. I didn't hear anything.

CHRISTINE. Nothing about her daughter.

LEA. Mademoiselle Isabelle, you mean?

CHRISTINE (*turning on her*). Who else?

LEA. (*drawing back*). Don't be like that, Christine. You sound just like Maman.

CHRISTINE. You smiled at her. I saw you.

LEA. I didn't smile –

CHRISTINE (*interrupting*). She makes you do everything for her. You're always with her.

LEA. I –

CHRISTINE (*cutting in*). Promise me you won't go. When she goes.

LEA. If she goes. She may never go. We've been over this a hundred times, Christine. She may never get marrie –

CHRISTINE (*overlapping*). Answer me!

LEA. Christine.

CHRISTINE (*breaking in*). Answer me! Don't just keep saying Christine. (*Anguished.*) Sometimes . . . every morning . . . I think of – I imagine – things . . . that you . . .

LEA. Christine.

CHRISTINE. You're all I have, little Lea. All I'll ever have. (*Holding* LEA). Sometimes I think we'll never have enough time. Do you think we'll have enough time, Lea? The days seem to be getting longer. And the nights, ah Lea – the nights – (*Jumping up suddenly.*) There'll never be enough time for us. (*She starts pacing the room.*)

LEA. Come and sit with me.

CHRISTINE. In a minute.

LEA. When you walk like that it reminds me of Sister Veronica. I used to hear her when I went to sleep. And when –

CHRISTINE. What?

LEA. She was angry when Maman took me away.

CHRISTINE. Angry?

LEA. I tried to talk to her. I followed her after morning mass. Remember the garden, Christine? Remember the path?

CHRISTINE *is silent, watching her.*

My shoes . . . my shoes kept clicking on the stone. I followed her all the way to her room. She was walking so fast her habit moved like a wind was blowing it. I got so close I almost tripped on it. But she wouldn't stop. She wouldn't turn around. She never turned around.

CHRISTINE. You never told me.

LEA (*after a moment*). Christine.

CHRISTINE. Yes?

LEA. I . . . um . . .

CHRISTINE. What is it?

LEA. (*swallowing*). I want you to . . . Would you . . .

CHRISTINE. What? (*Softly.*) Tell me. (*Watching her.*) Tell me.

LEA. Let's . . . Oh Christine, let's . . . let's pretend you're her.

CHRISTINE. Her?

LEA. Just be her.

CHRISTINE. Sister Veronica.

LEA. Yes.

CHRISTINE. I – (*Turning away. Smiling*) Idiot!

LEA. Christine. Please.

CHRISTINE. Now?

LEA. Yes, now.

CHRISTINE. All right. (*Hesitating.*) Close your eyes. (LEA *closes her eyes.*)

LEA. Can I look yet?

CHRISTINE. Wait a second. (*She unties her long apron from around her waist.*)

LEA. What are you doing?

CHRISTINE. Just a minute. You'll see. Don't be so impatient. (*She ties the apron around her head, so that it falls in front of her face, then slips it back so that it resembles a nun's habit.*) Now look.

LEA. You're ready?

CHRISTINE (*turning toward* LEA). I'm ready.

LEA *opens her eyes, looks at* CHRISTINE. *The light dims.*

Scene Thirteen

Sunday morning. Church bells are ringing. ISABELLE *is downstairs, ready to go out.*

ISABELLE (*picking up a calling card*). Maman. Look! Madame Castelneuve was here.

MADAME DANZARD (*coming down the stairs*). No!

ISABELLE (*picking up another calling card*). And Madame Richepin.

MADAME DANZARD. How did they get in? When? The new curtains aren't even here yet. What's the matter with those two? They didn't even tell me. (*Irritated, tapping* ISABELLE *on the back.*) Don't slump, Isabelle. You know how I hate that. She asked me for another blanket yesterday.

ISABELLE. Incredible. Why should they complain about the cold? They're hardly ever in their room.

MADAME DANZARD (*taking two heavy prayer books, one for her, one for* ISABELLE). No one in this town has a radiator in the maid's room. It's unheard of. Have you ever heard of such a thing?

ISABELLE. Never.

MADAME DANZARD (*putting on her gloves*). They're in the kitchen from six in the morning till ten at night. They have the stove to keep them warm.

ISABELLE. You worry too much, Maman.

MADAME DANZARD. As if I don't make life easy for them in every way.

ISABELLE. You do everything for them. You're too good to them.

CHRISTINE *and* LEA *come running into the house, laughing. They are dressed in their identical coats and hats, and wear white gloves. They stop when they see* MADAME DANZARD *and* ISABELLE. *Quietly they go up the stairs into their room.*

ISABELLE. Did you see them? Coming back from church.

MADAME DANZARD. Spotless – with their white gloves. They don't even look like maids anymore.

Softly LEA *closes the door. She laughs and whirls* CHRISTINE *around.* CHRISTINE *puts her hand over* LEA's *mouth.* LEA *begins pulling off* CHRISTINE's *gloves.*

MADAME DANZARD. But they're losing their looks, my dear. Have you noticed? Have you seen how thin they've become? Especially the younger one.

LEA *takes off* CHRISTINE's *hat.* CHRISTINE *sits still, watching her.* LEA *smiles, takes a few steps back.*

MADAME DANZARD. And those circles under their eyes.

ISABELLE. They look like they never sleep.

LEA *takes off her gloves. She turns and looks at* CHRISTINE.

ISABELLE *(suddenly touching the banister).* Look at this, Maman.

MADAME DANZARD. At what?

ISABELLE. Don't you see? *(Pointing.)* There. Right there.

MADAME DANZARD *(turning back).* What is it?

ISABELLE *points again.*

MADAME DANZARD *(looking carefully).* Oh yes. I see. Yes. They're getting careless.

LEA *takes off her hat. The* DANZARDS *go out. The heavy front door slams.* LEA *undoes her hair. It falls around her. Slowly, she unbuttons her coat, pulls it open. She is wearing the elaborate white chemise with the wide shoulder straps* CHRISTINE *sewed for her.* LEA *begins to move around the room. Her movements have a strange grace of their own. She moves all over the small room, her hair flying.* CHRISTINE *watches her. Suddenly, she pulls* LEA *down to her. The light dims.*

Scene Fourteen

The sound of water dripping. Slowly CHRISTINE *comes down the stairs. She goes into the kitchen and turns off the tap. From the cabinet she takes a tray and places it on the kitchen table. From the sink she takes four drying wine glasses. She polishes them, places them on the tray. The fourth glass breaks in her hand. She draws her cut hand to her mouth, licking away the blood. She wraps her hand in a napkin. With the other hand, she puts the broken pieces of glass in the sink. She takes the tray with the polished wine glasses to the cabinet. Upstairs, in their room, the lights go out.*

LEA (*voice over. Screaming*). Christine!

CHRISTINE (*almost dropping the tray*). What is it?

LEA (*screaming*). Oh no, no! Christine!

CHRISTINE (*running to the bottom of the stairs*). What is it? What happened?

LEA *comes down the stairs to the landing.*

LEA. The iron. It blew the fuse.

CHRISTINE. Oh no.

LEA. What will Madame do to us? What will she do?

CHRISTINE *goes to the kitchen cabinet and takes out a candle and matches.* LEA *comes down the stairs.*

LEA. I was right in the middle of her satin blouse.

CHRISTINE (*whirling around, the candle in her hand*). Did you burn it?

LEA. It's the second time something's gone wrong with that iron.

CHRISTINE. Answer me, Lea. Did you?

LEA. First Mademoiselle's dress and now –

CHRISTINE. Did you burn it?

LEA. Madame will be so angry. Madame will be furious.

CHRISTINE. How can Madame be angry? It's not your fault. She can't be angry. (*She starts up the stairs with the candle.*) Let me see the blouse.

LEA *grabs at her arm.*

Let me see it. (*She goes up the stairs.*)

LEA (*frozen on the staircase*). Is it all right?

CHRISTINE (*voice over*). Just a minute.

LEA (*nervous*). Is it? (*Panicked, running up the stairs.*) Is it?

CHRISTINE *comes into their room, spent.* LEA *comes in after her.*

CHRISTINE. Don't worry.

LEA. Are you sure?

CHRISTINE. It's all right, Lea.

LEA (*sitting down on the bed*). I'm so tired. That was the last thing left. And what will happen now, Christine? What will happen now?

CHRISTINE. Nothing will happen. There's nothing we can do. Don't worry, Lea. They've gone to the Blanchards for dinner. They'll play cards all night. We just have to wait.

LEA. Christine – how much money do we have saved?

CHRISTINE. Not enough.

LEA. I know it's not enough. But it will be one day.

CHRISTINE *is silent.*

It will be, won't it?

CHRISTINE. Hush, hush. Rest. Rest now.

LEA. And then   then we'll go away from here and –

CHRISTINE *is still.*

And –

CHRISTINE (*quietly*). Yes. Yes my Lea.

She begins to undo LEA's *long braid.*

Someday.

There is a pause.

LEA (*devastated, beginning to cry*). I burned it, didn't I? Didn't I? Tell me.

CHRISTINE. My angel. My love. It's all right.

CHRISTINE *puts her arms around* LEA. *On the bed they undo each other's hair. There is the sound of hairpins falling on the floor. A pause. The sound of a key turning in a lock.* MADAME DANZARD *and* ISABELLE *enter downstairs. They are carrying several small packages tied with string. In one hand,* MADAME DANZARD *holds a set of heavy keys.*

MADAME DANZARD (*impatient*). Where is she?

ISABELLE. How do I know?

MADAME DANZARD. Don't answer me like that. Go and find her.

ISABELLE *doesn't move. There is something ominous about the house.*

MADAME DANZARD (*putting down her package and gloves*). Did you hear what I said? This is absurd. She should be here to take these packages. She should have been here to open the door. At five thirty in the afternoon – what time is it anyway?

ISABELLE (*looking at her watch*). Five forty-five.

MADAME DANZARD (*looking at her watch*). Five forty-five. I mean really. Five forty-five and not a sign of them. I never heard of anything like it. Go into the kitchen, Isabelle. They must be there.

ISABELLE *goes into the kitchen. On the bed upstairs,* LEA *and* CHRISTINE *are in shadow.* ISABELLE *finds the broken glass and a dish in the sink.*

CHRISTINE (*sitting up*). Lea! Listen.

LEA *sits up.* ISABELLE *comes back from the kitchen.*

MADAME DANZARD. Well? What took you so long?

CHRISTINE. It's them.

LEA (*her eyes wide with terror*). Oh no.

ISABELLE. They're not there, Maman. And –

LEA *and* CHRISTINE *sit huddled together.*

MADAME DANZARD. Impossible. *I'll* look. They must be there . . . And what?

ISABELLE. There's a dish in there . . . And a glass. Broken.

MADAME DANZARD (*going to the kitchen and picking up the broken glass in the sink*). Broken. Nerve. What can they be doing?

LEA. Maybe they'll go away.

MADAME DANZARD (*listening*). Shhh. Listen.

CHRISTINE. Shhh.

MADAME DANZARD (*looking out into the audience*). Maybe they're upstairs.

LEA. What will we do, Christine?

CHRISTINE. Lea.

LEA. What will we do?

CHRISTINE. Little Lea. Wait, let me think.

MADAME DANZARD. I'm going up there this minute.

CHRISTINE *stands up.*

CHRISTINE. I have to go down.

ISABELLE. Maman – wait.

LEA. Wait.

MADAME DANZARD. Wait? What for?

CHRISTINE. Do you want them to come up here?

ISABELLE. I don't think you should.

MADAME DANZARD. This is my house. Of course I'm going
upstairs. Right now. (*She starts up the stairs.*)

CHRISTINE. If I don't go down, they'll come up.

MADAME DANZARD. You don't have to come if you don't want
to.

ISABELLE *follows her slowly.*

LEA. I'm frightened, Christine. I'm frightened.

MADAME DANZARD *stops.*

MADAME DANZARD (*looking up*). What's this? The lights are off
up here.

CHRISTINE *leaves.*

LEA (*terrorized*). Don't leave me!

MADAME DANZARD (*quietly but furiously*). This is really
something.

She and ISABELLE *start down the staircase.* CHRISTINE *appears at
the top of the stairs, her hair loose for the first time.*

CHRISTINE. Madame.

ISABELLE *lets out a little shriek.*

CHRISTINE. Madame has come back.

MADAME DANZARD. What is this? How dare you expect me to come back to a dark house?

CHRISTINE (*coming down the stairs, putting her right foot first on each step*). It was the iron, Madame.

MADAME DANZARD. *Again?* Unbelievable. That's the second time. That iron was just repaired. What about my satin blouse?

ISABELLE. She came back to change into it.

MADAME DANZARD. Your sister didn't burn it, did she? She didn't burn my blouse?

CHRISTINE. Madame's blouse isn't finished yet.

MADAME DANZARD (*interrupting*). Not finished? I'm wearing it to the Blanchards. What's the matter with your sister?

CHRISTINE *is silent.*

And why weren't you downstairs? Where's your apron?

CHRISTINE (*covering her uniform with her hands*). I finished early, Madame.

ISABELLE. There's a dish in there. A glass. Broken.

MADAME DANZARD. Don't lie to me. I won't have a liar in this house.

CHRISTINE. Madame knows I don't lie.

ISABELLE. She is lying. I can tell.

MADAME DANZARD. You disappoint me. Send your sister down with my satin blouse at once.

CHRISTINE *doesn't move.*

Did you hear me? Go.

CHRISTINE. Madame can't see my sister now.

MADAME DANZARD. What?

ISABELLE. Are you going to let her speak to you like that?

MADAME DANZARD. I will see your sister this instant. And she will explain how she ruined my iron for the second time.

CHRISTINE. I already explained to Madame about the iron.

MADAME DANZARD. You call that an explanation?

CHRISTINE. It wasn't our fault, Madame.

MADAME DANZARD. Not your fault? No? Whose fault was it then? (*She turns to* ISABELLE.) Did you hear that?

ISABELLE. I heard. Who knows what else they've done.

CHRISTINE. We haven't done anything.

MADAME DANZARD. How dare you? How dare you speak to my daughter like that?

CHRISTINE. If Madame can't trust us, if she suspects anything –

MADAME DANZARD (*interrupting*). Suspect what?

CHRISTINE (*quickly*). We'll leave this house.

MADAME DANZARD. You'll leave? And just where do you think you'll go?

CHRISTINE. We'll find another house.

MADAME DANZARD, *clenching her fists, is silent for a moment.*

MADAME DANZARD. Will you? Not with the recommendation you get from me. Don't think you'll get out so easily. Not after what I've seen tonight.

CHRISTINE (*breaking in*). Madame has seen nothing.

MADAME DANZARD. Nothing? (*Snorting.*) That face, that hair. You smell of it, my dear.

CHRISTINE. Madame, stop. Madame. Please.

MADAME DANZARD (*pushing* CHRISTINE *down and going up to the landing*). Not another word out of your mouth. Breaking my iron. The house in darkness.

CHRISTINE (*looking up at her*). I told Madame. It wasn't our fault.

MADAME DANZARD (*looking down at* CHRISTINE, *starting to yell*). Going to church every Sunday. Thinking you were a child of God. (*Raging, crossing herself.*) Forgive me God for what I have harboured here.

CHRISTINE. Madame. You have no right.

LEA *leaves their room.*

MADAME DANZARD (*shrieking*). No right? You must be mad.

ISABELLE. She is mad. Just look at her.

MADAME DANZARD. *You* have no rights, Christine.

LEA appears at the top of the stairs. ISABELLE *gasps.*

ISABELLE (*grabbing her mother's arm*). Maman!

CHRISTINE *runs up the stairs to* LEA.

MADAME DANZARD. Look at that sister of yours. Dirt. (*She spits at them.*) Scum. Scum sisters.

Her face twitching, CHRISTINE *holds onto* LEA.

CHRISTINE (*continuously*). Not my sister, not my sister.

She steps forward. LEA *comes down the stairs.*

MADAME DANZARD. You'll never work with your sister again.

ISABELLE (*trying to push past her mother*). No one will take you.

LEA *tries to push past* CHRISTINE *toward* ISABELLE.

CHRISTINE (*overlapping*). Not my sister, not my sister.

LEA (*lifting the pewter pitcher high above* ISABELLE'*s head*). CHRISTINE!

At the same moment, in a violent gesture, CHRISTINE *leaps toward* MADAME DANZARD'*s face. Blackout.*

CHRISTINE. NOT MY SISTER!

ISABELLE (*overlapping*). MAMAN!

MADAME DANZARD *screams wildly. Certain gestures may be made clear, others not. In the darkness are sounds of footsteps, screams, the thump of pewter on flesh. The screams gradually turn into moans in the quiet black house.*

Scene Fifteen

Light comes up on CHRISTINE *and* LEA, *standing separately.*

MEDICAL EXAMINER (*voice over. A flat anonymous voice*). On the last step of the staircase, a single eye was found, intact, complete with the optic nerve. The eye had been torn out without the aid of an instrument.

He pauses.

The bodies of Madame and Mademoiselle Danzard were found on the landing. On the ground were fragments of bone and teeth, a yellow diamond earring, two eyes, hair pins, a pocketbook, a set of keys, a coat button. The walls and doors were covered with splashes of blood reaching a height of seven feet.

JUDGE (*voice over*). Is this the pewter pitcher with which you struck them down?

LEA *looks up.*

MEDICAL EXAMINER (*voice over*). Madame Danzard's body lay face up, Mademoiselle Danzard's body face down, the coat pulled up, the skirt pulled up, the underpants pulled down, revealing deep wounds on the buttocks and multiple slashes on the calves. Madame Danzard's eyes had been torn out of their sockets.

JUDGE (*voice over*). The carving knife with which you slashed them?

CHRISTINE *looks up. They are silent.*

JUDGE. What did you have against Madame and Mademoiselle Danzard?

He pauses.

Was Madame good to you?

He pauses.

Did anything abnormal happen between you and your sister?

He pauses.

You understand me, don't you? Was it simply sisterly love?

He pauses.

How did you tear out their eyes? With your fingers?

CHRISTINE *clasps herself and rocks back and forth.*

Speak! You are here to defend yourselves. You will be judged.

CHRISTINE. Lea. I want Lea. Please. I beg you. Forgive me. I'll be good. I promise. I won't cry anymore. Give me Lea. Give me my sister. (*With a terrible, long drawn out cry.*) LEA!

LEA *moves to the centre. Her face is pale, her eyes vacant.*

JUDGE (*voice over*). Lea Lutton. You will perform ten years of hard labour. You are refused the right to enter the town of Le Mans for twenty years.

He pauses. CHRISTINE *stands beside* LEA.

Christine Lutton. You will be taken barefoot, wearing a chemise, your head covered by a black veil, to a public place in the town of Le Mans. And there, before your fellow citizens, your head will be severed from your body.

LEA (*gazing straight out, sings brokenly*).
     Sleep my little sister, sleep
     Sleep through darkness
     Sleep so deep
     All the rivers find the sea
     My little sister
     Sleep for me.

CHRISTINE *looks directly out.* LEA *gazes vaguely into the distance. They stand as if framed in a photograph.*

'Sleep My Little Sister, Sleep'

*Copyright © 1981 of 'Sleep My Little Sister, Sleep'
Lyrics and Music by Wendy Kesselman

'Sleep My Little Sister, Sleep'   page two

ISLAND LIFE
by Jenny McLeod

JENNY McLEOD, born in Nottingham in 1963, won the competition *Writing '87* set up by Nottingham and Derby Playhouses with her first play *Cricket at Camp David*, which was later given a full production by the Bolton Octagon Theatre in 1988. She was commissioned to write *The Mango Tree* for Strange Fruit Theatre Company and *Island Life* for Monstrous Regiment. *Island Life* opened at Nottingham Playhouse as a co-production in 1988. Her children's play, *Just Like a Genie*, toured schools and was performed at the Lilian Baylis Theatre and her television play, *The Wake*, produced by Phillipa Giles and Vicky Licorish was screened in 1990. She is currently working on a television play with the producers of *The Wake*, writing a studio play, a situation comedy, a radio and a stage play.

Characters

SOFIA, EMMY and VERA, residents in an OAP home.

KATE, a young woman.

The action takes place in an OAP home, over a Bank Holiday weekend.

Island Life was first performed by Monstrous Regiment in co-production with the Nottingham Playhouse at the Nottingham Studio Space from 19–29 October 1988. It toured from 13 March–22 April. The cast was as follows:

SOFIA	Joanna Field
EMMY	Corinne Skinner Carter
KATE	Marcia Tucker
VERA	Stella Tanner

Written by Jenny McLeod
Directed by Jane Collins
Designed by Iona McLeish
Lighting and technical advice by Veronica Wood
Graphic Design by Jo Angel at Paton Walker Associated
Lighting Technician: Janet Cantrill
Stage Manager: Lesley Chenery
Administration: Ferelith Lean
              Rose Sharp
Photographer: Mary Tisserand

Cast changes for the tour

EMMY	Joan Hooley
KATE	Irma Inniss

ACT ONE

Scene One

A lounge in semi-darkness. A light shines from outside in through a window. Slowly the window is opened from the outside and hands appear on the ledge, climbing up.

SOFIA. Go on . . . go up!

VERA. Is it enough to say I'm stuck?

SOFIA. Stuck! You can't be stuck.

VERA. Well stuck I am . . . Oh hang on. There . . . there . . .

EMMY. You alright Vera?

SOFIA. Wouldn't believe you were only two feet off the ground.

VERA. I told you I don't like heights.

SOFIA. Vera, in no way could two feet be construed as a height. Now get your leg over! Surely you've had enough practice in that department.

VERA. Oh! I've somehow managed to sit on the ledge.

SOFIA. Despite being stuck.

   VERA *sits straddling the window ledge.*

VERA. Wasn't that clever. Oh but I've pulled a stocking. Look!

SOFIA. Vera, get off the ledge and let us in.

VERA. Five pence from Oxfam and look at them, ruined!

SOFIA. Now!

VERA. Alright, don't shout.

   VERA *jumps down, switches on the light and then exits. Shortly she returns with* SOFIA *in a wheelchair and* EMMY *on foot.*

SOFIA. Switch that light off. No lights until the curtains are drawn.

VERA *switches the light off and* SOFIA *puts the torch on.*

VERA. Who's gonna see with that wall out there?

SOFIA. The lights stay off. Got it? Check upstairs.

VERA. Why me?

SOFIA. 'Cause I say so.

VERA. But it's dark.

SOFIA. Get moving.

VERA. Only if I can borrow the torch.

SOFIA. And leave me in the dark?

EMMY. It really dark.

VERA. But you'll have Emmy.

SOFIA. Emmy is a fool!

EMMY. We have night like this back home. When it so black you can hold the darkness with two hand.

SOFIA. Sooner you go, sooner we can get the lights on.

VERA. Will you listen out for me then?

VERA *moves to the door.*

VERA. I said . . .

SOFIA. Vera!

VERA. Alright, I'm going.

SOFIA. Well go!

VERA. You promise to listen out for me?

SOFIA. Vera unless you've got one of your geriatric boyfriends up there, you should be perfectly safe.

EMMY. Me will promise you.

VERA. Thanks Em . . . I won't be long . . . Sofia you listening?

SOFIA. If you don't move your . . .

VERA. I'm going, see I'm gone!

Exit VERA.

SOFIA. How the hell am I gonna get through a whole weekend with her?

EMMY. Is just her way.

You don't say things for the sake of saying, Miss Sofia?

SOFIA. 'Course not.

EMMY. Sometime me just like talk. That alright though . . . The house look funny tonight.

SOFIA. You can't see anything.

EMMY. Then it no feel funny to you Miss Sofia?

SOFIA. What you on about? On second thoughts I don't really care.

EMMY *moves away from* SOFIA.

Now where are you? I can't see you

EMMY. Me is here, Miss Sofia.

SOFIA (*fiddling with the torch*). I think the batteries are going. You think the batteries are going?

EMMY. Me don't know. You think the battery them going?

SOFIA. That's what I asked you.

EMMY. Maybe is the battery them?

SOFIA. Oh shut up . . . What's keeping Vera?

EMMY. Make me go look for her.

SOFIA. No! Get back over here where I can see you.

EMMY *moves back and* VERA *comes rushing in.*

VERA. Oh . . . ! It's, all, clear.

And I turned the bedclothes down in our room Em.

EMMY. Oh good! Me like the bed to catch breeze before me lay down.

SOFIA (*imitating* VERA's *voice*). 'I turned the bedclothes down Em'. Lights!

VERA *puts the lights on.*

Doubt if anyone'll see the lights with that wall out there anyway.

VERA (*aside*). I said that all along.

SOFIA. What?

VERA. What?

SOFIA. What did you say? I can guess and I'm not gonna put up with it.

EMMY. Maybe you should.

SOFIA. What?

EMMY. Put up with it. We should put up with each other.

SOFIA (*to* EMMY). What are you going on about?

VERA. Put up or shut up!

SOFIA. What?

VERA. Lord Hawthorne-Wood! 'Vera, either put up or shut up.' I did neither and that really got his pecker up – only time too I remember.
I had a quick peep in Phipps' room when I was upstairs. Reminded me of a room I once shared with him. Both let in little warmth and little light even at the height of summer . . . The infants hated it. Why I left him really, because of the infants. He never treated them right and a mother should always put her infants before any man . . .
And Phipps, she has this beautiful vase of fresh flowers just waiting for me to bring down. Beautiful they are . . .
Maybe I'll bring them down for the table.

SOFIA. No flowers!

EMMY. You ever sit an' wonder why anyone would want build a big everlasting wall like that?

SOFIA. Unlike you, most of us don't have to sit down to think.

EMMY. Me think the person who build that wall must full up a pure darkness. How else you explain it?

SOFIA. It's to keep us in and them out.

VERA. Them, what them do you mean Sofia? Let me say I've never found any 'them' to fit the silly confines of that 'them

and us' phrase, since I've always found that people were the
same wherever you went and I've been and seen plenty.

SOFIA. Nonsense!

EMMY. Me never see no wall big so till me come a England.

SOFIA. Curtains!

VERA. You saying they don't have walls on your Jamaican island
Emmy, because if you are I can't believe it; people as I said are
the same anywhere in the world and they build walls. Take for
instance . . .

SOFIA. Curtains! Draw the damn curtains and stop staring at that
wall!

EMMY. When me was pickney back home, me never see none. Is
only now me turn old an' come a England me see so many.

EMMY *pulls the curtains.*

SOFIA. Look how long it's been there and you are just decide to
hold an inquest.

EMMY. Sometime these things just come to you. You see them,
but you no see them, then one day you just see them.

VERA. I thought to myself the other day, how long has that wall
been there and what has it seen? It must have seen a lot of life
and it's still standing.

SOFIA. Oh God!

EMMY. Is long time it stand up there.

VERA. What, sweet?

EMMY. The wall.

SOFIA (*to* VERA). Isn't it a good thing one of us can cut through
your incessant ramblings and remember the question.

VERA. What question? I was talking about people and how alike
they are. Take me for instance, I can't believe there's only one
of me, there must be two or three or even more all with
beautiful arses!

SOFIA. God forbid!

EMMY. Well looking at it from here it look about . . .

SOFIA. About Vera's age.

VERA. You and your silly jokes, Sofia. They can't hurt me; you only have to look at the ripeness of my beautiful arse to see that I'm only fifty-four and a bit, so if that was a joke . . .

SOFIA. Judge for yourself.

EMMY. An' it strong, you know. Me know storm back home that lift up whole house, wash 'way beast and flatten banana crop, but I bet it wouldn't touch that wall.

VERA. Sounds a touch like my second husband: he could stand up to anything and everyone, except me, and he always used to say . . .

SOFIA. Shut up!
When're you two gonna stop this dismal trip down memory lane?

VERA. Trip! Oh, I wonder how Phipps is getting on with the others. Bet it's dire; bet she's wishing I'd gone now, only I can get them going and stop them from going too, for that matter. Do you know she couldn't even let Mrs Sherman have her tea before they set off and that's sad really because Mrs Sherman can't do without . . .

SOFIA. Vera?

VERA. Yes, sweet?

VERA has a personal hi-fi set which she now plugs in and puts over her ears.

SOFIA. We have come back for a reason, or have you forgotten?

EMMY. Me no forget, Miss Sofia.

SOFIA. Pass my bag; let me get the table ready. Vera, take those bloody things off and get the chairs.

EMMY passes the bag over.

VERA. Oh this is the one . . .

She rushes over to EMMY and puts her arms around her ready to dance.

This is the one . . . The one I used to dance to with Finnbar Willis . . . Come on Em. Hold me tight. Tighter, Em.

VERA. Finnbar had a masterful hold right here in the small of my back. Dadadadaaa . . .

They begin to dance.

EMMY. But you know me can't hear the music. Me can't dance so.

VERA. 'Course you can, sweet. Come on now follow me, sweet. Dadadadaaa . . . Finnbar Willis! What a man! He used to bring me kippers. He was a fishmonger and he always used to save the best kippers for me, said it made my hair shine. Long and black it was and it did have a shine . . . Said it enhanced my beauty.

SOFIA. And foolishly you believed him.

VERA. And my hair's remained the same all these years. I'm convinced it's because of the kippers Finnbar always brought me.

SOFIA. Really!

VERA *and* EMMY *begin tripping over each other's feet.*

VERA. You're not concentrating, sweet.

EMMY. But me can't hear the music.

VERA. 'Course you can, sweet. Dadadadaaa . . .

Ow! Emmyryha!

They part.

SOFIA. I ask again. Have you both forgotten why we're here?

EMMY. Me remember, Miss Sofia.

VERA (*taking her head-sets off*). You remember what, sweet?

EMMY. Why we come back.

VERA. And so do I, who's been saying I don't, because I remember as much as anyone.

SOFIA. What do you remember?

VERA. I . . . I . . . I remember it all.

She puts her head-sets back on and begins dancing around by herself.

SOFIA. Tell her to get those things off and pay attention.

EMMY. Yes, Miss Sofia.

EMMY *moves to* VERA *and stops her.*

EMMY. Miss Sofia soon ready to start the talking.

VERA. What, sweet?

EMMY. Miss Sofia soon ready to start the talking.

VERA. Oh yes the seance! It might turn out fun if we approach it right. I did something like this once. We all wore long black gowns, stood at altars and drank this red stuff. I thought it was red wine but how wrong, it was blood!

SOFIA *spreads a cloth over the table.*

SOFIA. Well, nothing like that will go on here.

VERA. Oh, and I was looking forward to inviting some of the boys from next door; I know if I did everyone would enjoy themselves, even you Sofia.

SOFIA. Take one step near that place and you'll have me to answer to. Got it?

VERA. If you expect me to stay cooped up in here with you all weekend you're wrong.

SOFIA. We'll see about that.

EMMY. But me a consider now whether we should . . .

VERA. Whether we should what, sweet?

EMMY. Do what we come to. Me no sure 'bout it. Me kinna afraid.

SOFIA. You got more to be afraid of sharing a room with her – and I use the word sharing in its loosest form.

EMMY. Me to be afraid of Vera? How you mean, Miss Sofia?

VERA. I know what she means and there's nothing wrong with me . . . any more!

SOFIA. Oh no?

VERA. And I can get medical evidence to prove it . . . if you want.

SOFIA. I don't want nothing from you, 'sweet'! And just you remember, I want you cooking all my food this weekend, Emmy.

VERA. I don't have to take this.

SOFIA. You take worse. Why you can't take this is beyond me.

VERA. Everything's beyond you.

SOFIA. Except the fact that you're a walking, talking, breathing, disgrace!

EMMY. Oh, Miss Sofia!

VERA. Jealous!

SOFIA. Me?

VERA. Because they need me.

SOFIA. I can do without that kind of need.

VERA. And you frequently do, since no one needs or wants you.

EMMY. Oh Vera!

VERA. Just as well she's never had a man with her wetting the bed the way she does. Imagine the embarrassment of waking up the next morning to find you've pissed over him.

SOFIA. Bitch! Bitch!

SOFIA stares at VERA and then wheels herself away to one side of the room for a sulk.

VERA. Did you hear what she called me?

EMMY. You shouldn't say that, Vera.

VERA. But did you hear, Emmyryha?

EMMY. You shouldn't say it.

VERA. She goads me!

EMMY. And you still shouldn't. It not nice.

VERA. She's one of the least nicest people I know and I know plenty.

EMMY. She not so bad.

VERA. Why're you always sticking up for her when she treats you as bad as me? You shouldn't take it.

EMMY. Maybe me should.

VERA. What?

EMMY. Call her and beg her pardon.

VERA. No.

EMMY. Do it, no?

VERA. I will not!

SOFIA *wheels herself forward again.*

SOFIA. I don't wet the bed. Got it?
But speaking of food, as we were, where is it?

EMMY. Where the food?

SOFIA. Who's job was it to take the food out the freezer?

EMMY. Well . . . well me did have to leave the latch on the
window open and you Miss Sofia, did have to get the things
ready for later and . . .

VERA. She knows it was me because I remember her looking
straight at me and saying . . .

SOFIA (*to* EMMY). Ask her where it is.

EMMY. . . . Me? Me to ask Vera, Miss Sofia? (*Giggling.*) But . . .

SOFIA. Do it!

EMMY. Vera . . ?

VERA. The food's in the kitchen where I left it. Now I'm off to
get that vase of flowers I saw in Phipps's room: should brighten
up the place no end.

SOFIA. No flowers!

Exit VERA.

EMMY. Miss Sofia. Vera say . . .

SOFIA. Start cooking.

EMMY. Yes, Miss Sofia.

Exit EMMY. SOFIA *goes back to the table and continues arranging.
Shortly* EMMY *returns; standing uncomfortably at the door she stares at*
SOFIA.

SOFIA. What?

EMMY. You hear exactly where Vera say she put the food?

SOFIA. What you on about?

EMMY. The food! Me don't see it.

SOFIA. It's not there?

EMMY. No.

SOFIA. So! The silly old cow did forget.

Re-enter VERA *with the vase of flowers.* SOFIA *turns her back to her and continues arranging the table.*

EMMY (*whispering*). Where you put the food?

VERA. What?

EMMY. Where you put the . . . ?

SOFIA. I'll deal with this.

SOFIA *turns to them now.*

The food's missing.

EMMY. Me look high and me look low.

SOFIA. She look high and she look low.

VERA. What're you talking about?

SOFIA. There's no food in the kitchen.

VERA. Of course there is, I put it there myself on the work top and . . . and . . . I remember, I moved it out by the back door because Phipps was snooping around and if I'd left it on the work top she would've found it. A leg of lamb, three pork chops, a chicken for Sunday dinner and some vegetables.

SOFIA (*to* EMMY). Look!

EMMY. Yes, Miss Sofia.

Exit EMMY. VERA *moves further in with the vase of flowers and places them on the table.*

VERA. Leg of lamb, three pork chops, chicken for Sunday dinner, and some vegetables, all in two white carrier bags . . . I remember how easily they fitted . . . Don't the flowers look lovely?

VERA *stands back admiring them.* EMMY *returns.*

By the back door, weren't they sweet, just like I said by the . . . Where are they . . . ?

EMMY. Me don't see them.

VERA. By the back door, sweet?

SOFIA. You did forget.

VERA. You sure you looked properly, sweet, maybe I should look because I know exactly where I put them, I put them by the back door against the . . .

Exit VERA.

EMMY. Maybe me never look good?

SOFIA. I'm sure you did.

Shortly VERA *returns.*

EMMY. Maybe is dog thief them?

SOFIA. Vegetables as well?

EMMY. Back home dog eat anything. Even turn cornmeal!

SOFIA. Well you are not bloody back home now. What are we going to do? All the cupboards locked and no food – except the things for Daphne's tea, and we can't eat them can we?

EMMY. No we can't eat them.

SOFIA. That was the sole idea of getting the food out before, because the cupboards would be locked when we came back.

VERA *sits down.*

EMMY. It no that bad Miss Sofia. We can go down the village go buy more.

VERA *looks agonised at* SOFIA. SOFIA *smiles.*

We cannot be seen in the village. We are not supposed to be here. Remember?

SOFIA. And even if we could, which one of us could make the journey there and back?

EMMY. Oh . . .

EMMY *comforts* VERA, *who is sobbing.*

Don't worry! We will get through.

VERA. But I put them there. Where could they have gone?

SOFIA. Vanished maybe?

EMMY. But things just don't vanish, Miss Sofia.

SOFIA. Well maybe . . . Maybe, someone stole them. Some pedlar who deals in frozen lambs and so forth.

VERA. Really?

SOFIA. He hides in wait for old women putting food out and then when they've gone, he emerges like a sick coward . . .

VERA. Sick, you say?

SOFIA. . . . Sick coward – he emerges from his hiding place and pounces on the neat white plastic bags.

VERA. That would make sense.

EMMY. But . . .

SOFIA. They say it's the smell of white plastic that urges him on. The urge is so strong sometimes, that he has been known not to wait for these elderly women to leave and he jumps out in full view of them and . . .

VERA. And what?

SOFIA. And is gone! In a puff of white plastic . . . (SOFIA *laughs*.) Gone! Just like you, you silly old cow!

VERA *begins crying loudly*.

EMMY. Done, done. We will get through.

VERA. But I'm not, I'm not a silly old cow.

EMMY. No, you not.

VERA. I'm not, am I?

EMMY. No.

SOFIA. Alright, for the sake of peace and quiet you're not.

VERA *still sobs*.

Oh shut up!

EMMY. Take time with her, no, Miss Sofia?

SOFIA. Time? Thanks to her we don't have any food.

EMMY. But is not Vera fault.

SOFIA. If only you knew.

EMMY. Know what, Miss . . . ?

VERA. . . . That Miss Sofia's right! I am a silly old cow.

EMMY. Maybe me can open one of the cupboard? Break the lock with hammer or something. Make me go look . . .

Exit EMMY. SOFIA *wheels herself in front of* VERA *and* VERA *looks up at her.*

SOFIA. Go and help her with that lock.

VERA. Yes Miss Sofia . . .

VERA *moves to leave.*

SOFIA. And take those bloody flowers with you.

VERA. Yes, Miss Sofia.

VERA *moves back to the table and picks up the vase of flowers and begins to leave.*

SOFIA. I did say, no flowers!

Exit VERA.

Scene Two

EMMY *enters with a tray of food. She is followed by* VERA *who has her head-sets on, carrying the tea.*

EMMY. Oh Miss Sofia all we could manage to get out is little flour, so me make . . .

SOFIA. What the hell are those?

EMMY. Fry dumplings.

SOFIA. They're foreign!

EMMY. Is not really foreign, is Jamaican.

SOFIA. How much more foreign can you get?

VERA (*begins eating, taking her head-sets off*). Tastes nice.

EMMY. Is only flour and water. Smell just like back home.

SOFIA. This is your home. Like the rest of us.

You live here because no one wants you.

EMMY. That not true. You shouldn't say that Miss Sofia . . . You should never say a thing like that. My Daphne coming for me.

VERA. 'Course she is, sweet. She wrote and said she was, didn't she?

EMMY. She coming to take me out!

EMMY *opens her handbag and takes out a letter and reads it.*

'Dear Mum, Coming to take you shopping tomorrow. Love Daphne.'

SOFIA. Postmarked July nineteen seventy-one!

EMMY *begins sobbing.*

VERA. That is an absolutely vicious observation!

SOFIA. Truth usually is. Sooner you both wake up to your pathetic little selves, the better. No one wants us, difference between me and you two is that I've accepted it and not let it bother me.

VERA. Don't worry Em, I'm here and so will Daphne be. Sofia's only jealous. Our infants mean the world to us, I understand.

SOFIA. And you have a very short memory. (*To* EMMY.) Throw that muck out. The smell of it gets everywhere, and I don't want it everywhere. Got it?

EMMY. Yes Miss Sofia.

EMMY *begins clearing the plates.*

SOFIA (*to* VERA). Get the chairs to the table.

Exit EMMY *with the plates.* VERA *stands moving the chairs.*

VERA. She'll be alright soon. You know how she gets when she's expecting Daphne . . . But maybe if you had infants, you'd understand. What I like best is having them all around. I always have liked that. And I always wanted a picture, with me sat in a big armchair, a really comfortable one and they'd be sat and stood around me, all fully grown men and women and we'd all be smiling and there I'd be in the exact middle of all my infants . . .

SOFIA. So why didn't you?

VERA. Oh we will. We will! It's not easy arranging a time for me to smile in the middle . . . when we all lead such busy lives . . . If you had infants you'd understand that. But you don't, do you?

You know you should've tried one of Emmy's fried dumplings.

SOFIA. Never! I've always kept myself to myself. It wouldn't suit me.

VERA. Well I liked it; it tasted like bread.

SOFIA. Some of us are more choosy.

VERA. Like me, I'm very choosy. You like the blouse?

VERA *begins combing her hair.*

Nice isn't it. Chose it myself at the Oxfam shop; fifty pence, should go well with that skirt I bought last month.

Re-enter EMMY.

EMMY. Me dash it away Miss Sofia.

SOFIA. Good! We'll start.

Emmy you sit there, between me and her.

EMMY. Here so, Miss Sofia?

SOFIA. Yes.

They all sit down.

And you stop combing that bloody hair and pay attention.

VERA *stops.*

Relax . . . I'll ask the questions. Are you ready?

VERA . . . steady, go!

SOFIA. If you can't act in an adult manner, then leave the table. Now . . . is there anyone there? . . . Is there anyone there?

EMMY. We must answer Miss Sofia?

SOFIA. For the last time. Shut your stupid mouths.

VERA. Just because no one's answering there's no need to take it out on us. Perhaps they don't want to talk to you; wouldn't be the first time.

SOFIA. One more word, just one more . . . Now . . . Is, there, anyone, there? Give two knocks if there is anyone there.

Nothing is heard for a while.

Is, there, anyone, there? Give two knocks if there is anyone there . . . !

Shortly, two loud knocks are heard.

Which one of you did that?

EMMY. Not me!

SOFIA. Vera?

VERA. Sofia, I know it was you, you don't expect me to believe you've actually . . .

SOFIA. It was not!

VERA. Then who was . . . ? Holy Mary, Mother of God, pray for me for I have sinned, Sofia hold my hand.

EMMY. She already have mine.

There comes another two knocks.

EMMY. Speak to it, Miss Sofia.

VERA. Before it strikes us dead or something.

SOFIA. Alright . . . Is there anyone there?

Unnoticed by the three a shadow enters and stands by the door.

KATE. Yes.

SOFIA. Oh Christ!

VERA. Should we bow or something?

SOFIA. Don't be stupid. Keep quiet, I'm getting quite good at this. (*Looking at her book.*) Now, what's the next question? Oh yes! Who do you wish to speak to?

KATE. I don't know, anyone . . .

VERA. Anyone? Well how about me?

SOFIA. Me! It must be me.

EMMY *becomes aware of* KATE *and stands, letting go of* SOFIA's *hand.*

SOFIA. Don't let go of my hand. Emmy hold my hand!

VERA (*to* EMMY). What you looking at?

EMMY. The duppy!

VERA. What?

VERA *also stands looking at* KATE.

SOFIA. Keep quiet!

EMMY. Miss Sofia, look. Open you eye and look!

SOFIA. And make me lose my train of thought?

VERA. I think you should lose it.

EMMY. Miss Sofia?

SOFIA (*turning*). Oh what? What is it?

EMMY. The duppy!

SOFIA. What . . . ? Ararar . . . !

EMMY. You is who?

KATE. I saw your light and . . .

EMMY. You want Miss Phipps, the supervisor? Well she away on a trip with all the other ladies and won't be back until the day after . . .

SOFIA. Leave, this, to, me!

KATE *takes a step forward.*

Stay, where, you, are! What, do, you, want?

EMMY. She must be the new nurse, Miss Sofia.

SOFIA. What're you on about?

VERA. You mean she's not a, I thought you were a . . .

KATE. What?

SOFIA. Noth . . . nothing . . . You the . . . police?

EMMY. Or the new nurse?

KATE. Could you shine that somewhere else?

VERA. I'll put the lights on since you're not the police.

VERA *puts the lights on.*

SOFIA. We haven't established that, have we?

VERA *turns the lights off and* SOFIA *again shines the torch at* KATE.

Well, are you?

KATE. No.

SOFIA. Lights on.

The lights come on again and SOFIA *switches the torch off.*

EMMY. Maybe is the new nurse?

SOFIA. Doesn't look like any nurse.

KATE. Can I sit down?

EMMY. Of course. Sit in my chair.

KATE *moves to the chair offered and sits down.*

KATE. Could I have a drink? Feels like I've been walking miles. How long is that wall?

SOFIA. One, we don't fetch, and two, this place is as dry as Vera's ovaries.

VERA. Take no notice. She's jealous because I'm only fifty-four and a bit.

EMMY (*moving forward and offering a hand*). You must be the nurse? And concerning the wall, I don't think anybody really know how long it is, or how old it is.

SOFIA. She doesn't look like a nurse, new or otherwise.

EMMY. She must be the new nurse. Who else could she be?

SOFIA. She looks familiar.

VERA. Not to me.

SOFIA. Who are you and what do you want?

EMMY. If you're the new nurse . . .

SOFIA. She's not.

EMMY. But if she is. (*To* KATE.) If you is, you should know 'bout Miss Phipps. She's the supervisor.

SOFIA. Emmy, shut up. She's not the new nurse.

EMMY. But if she is . . .

KATE. I'm not the new nurse.

EMMY. Oh! Well my name is Emmyryha. Emmyryha C. Waspkiss! Them call me Emmy and sometime Vera she call me Em.

You visiting? Maybe me know you kin? Although is holiday weekend and everybody gone beside we. And not even we is really here. Maybe you should a rung first? You did ring first?

KATE. I'm not visiting anyone.

EMMY. You not the police, and you not the new nurse, and you not visiting no kin. Oh! So you come to stay?

VERA. Well kiss my beautiful arse! Another young beauty just like myself.

SOFIA. You should tell Vera your secret, 'sweet!' With you looking so young and pretty, I'm sure she's gonna want to know how. Aren't you Vera, 'sweet'?

VERA *rushes to sit beside* KATE.

VERA. Fruit or just good old fashioned vanishing cream? Bet it's vanishing cream isn't it, I tried that a couple of months ago . . .

KATE. Tried what?

SOFIA. One of Vera's favourite words, couple.

VERA . . . but I don't need much help with my complexion. (*Holding her face up.*) What d'you think sweet? A good female friend of mine . . .

SOFIA. She always distinguishes between her friends by calling them male or female, it's the way her world's constructed.

VERA. . . . well she died a virgin 'bout our age (*She gestures to herself and* KATE.) and young-looking just like us and do you know she swore by it – saying no I mean, swore it kept her young she did. Personally, I find it's the complete opposite with me 'cause that little word 'no' just doesn't do for me.

SOFIA. We all know about your inability with that word Vera.

EMMY. What Miss Sofia mean is that Vera's still active.

KATE. What?

EMMY. She still do things . . .

SOFIA. She's a prostitute.

EMMY. . . . with men!

KATE. What?

SOFIA. Prostitute. Serving Crompton Park for retired and almost defunct gentlemen.

VERA. The pay's not great because of the pension you see, but I manage.

KATE. You manage?

VERA. And very well too, since I'm only fifty-four and a bit!

EMMY. You know something? If I never knew you before, I would've took you for the new nurse.

KATE. You don't know me.

SOFIA. I'm sure I do. What you say your name was?

EMMY. You alright?

KATE. Emmy is it?

EMMY. Emmyryha C. Waspkiss. But them call me Emmy and sometime Vera she call me Em. What them call you?

KATE. Kate . . .

EMMY. Kate? Is you did married to sweet Winston Pickett?

KATE. What?

EMMY. Sweet Winston Pickett! Him did married to a woman name Kate.

SOFIA. Hell, that must be over fifty years or more.

EMMY (*peering into* KATE's *face*). She wear well eeh! Sweet Winston . . . Him was going married to me you know! But Kate she go get herself pregnant, an' sweet Winston did have to married to she instead . . . And that's why me get left with Husband.

VERA. These days us girls have abortions.

EMMY (*to* KATE). You ever have one?

SOFIA. Where're you from anyway?

KATE. What?

SOFIA. Where're you from?

EMMY. You want to lay down? You look tired. Which room she to have, Miss Sofia?

SOFIA. Apart from mine, any.

VERA. And apart from ours, too. We share don't we Em?

EMMY. Yes, we share.

SOFIA. Why're you staying in a place like this? Although it's a nice place. Nice isolated place.

VERA. Nice place my beautiful arse, if you know what's good for you you'll start walking, I've been trying for years.

SOFIA. Gets as far as the men's dormitory and turns back . . . exhausted.

VERA. Ignore Sofia, everyone usually does.

SOFIA (*to* KATE). And your biggest mistake would be to listen to that old bat.

VERA. Fifty-four and a bit, that's me.

SOFIA. Really? I'm gonna get some proper food. Food I can eat.

Exit SOFIA.

VERA. I'll show her. She's always criticising; as if I ever mention the fact that she never gets invited out.

EMMY. Oh Vera!

VERA. I will, I'll show her.

VERA *puts on her head-sets and exits.*

KATE. Something wrong?

EMMY. Is just them way. Miss Sofia have a way 'bout her, but she not so bad when you get to know her. And Vera and she always a cuss and quarrel. You feeling alright? You don't look good.

KATE. I am. I'm alright.

EMMY *looks out through the curtains.*

EMMY. The wall look dark tonight.

KATE. I had to walk round it.

EMMY. Maybe you should climb over?

KATE. Climbing walls is for the young.

EMMY. You alright?

VERA *returns dressed to go out, wearing an extravagant hat.*

You going out?

VERA. Yes!

EMMY. But Miss Sofia not going 'llow you.

VERA. Miss Sofia can kiss my beautiful arse! It's because of her I'm going. I can't stand being stuck here under orders with her, and anyway just remembered I've got a date with Tucker and if I know old Tucker he'll be up pacing the floor on his ricketty old legs. Sometimes he gets so impatient . . . gives a girl heart it does . . . Maybe I'll bring us back some drink?

EMMY. Food would be better.

VERA. Oh dear I forgot . . . I mean I . . .

EMMY. Don't worry yourself. We will get through.

VERA. I'll bring some back if I re . . . Well I'll see you all later!

VERA *begins to leave, putting her head-sets on as she goes.*

EMMY. If Miss Sofia ever find out say Vera gone out, we never hear the end of it. She don't like Vera to go next door. But it good for Vera. Vera start to forget things. Nothing much. Except she forget the food and now we don't have much to eat. She think me don't know she getting that way, and me make she think it. 'Cause it suit her. It important that me don't know. We all alike in that respect, even Miss Sofia . . . But me glad she gone out. She can't do without her friends from next door . . .

VERA *returns.*

VERA. Oh Em, I forgot. If any of my infants call, take a message and say I'll call back. Okay!

EMMY. Alright Vera.

Exit VERA.

She call them her infants . . . And she call him ricketty . . . Just like one grandaddy me did have. Ricketty as hell, but was he the brute a that word MAN! Joshua them call him. Joshua! What a damn confounded name. Damn confounded name, for a damn confounded man, with a damn confounded piece a manhood.

Re-enter SOFIA.

EMMY. Me remember the time him have one wound. One foot long or more. From thigh to groin, groin to thigh. An' him lay down inna the yard, naked as the day, for me grandmother to dress it. Him hand them stretch out so . . . And the high Jamaican sun just a bawl down 'pon him, and him a bawl down profanities 'pon me grandmother. And she! She a scurry come, black, shine and stink with sweat, and the white crepe bandage inna her hand. Days later the foot turn yellow and them chop it clean off!

SOFIA. If you stay long enough, you'll get used to Emmy rambling on and then declining.

KATE *stands and picks up her case.* SOFIA *watches her.*

It can't be that bad . . . whatever it is . . . Well what is it?

KATE. What's what?

SOFIA. The reason you're here.

KATE. What reason?

SOFIA. There must be one.

KATE. Well there isn't.

SOFIA. People don't just turn up.

KATE. Whatever the reason, it's my business.

SOFIA (*smiling*). So there is one?

KATE (*to* SOFIA). You did say any room?

EMMY. You want sleep with me, Kate? My bed big you know

SOFIA. 'Course she bloody doesn't. Who ever heard of two grown women sharing a bed? Unless they're a bit queer.

EMMY. Sometime me and Vera sleep.

SOFIA. Just show her to the room next to Phipps's.

EMMY. Yes, Miss Sofia.

KATE (*to* EMMY). Thanks, all the same.

SOFIA. By the way, where is she?

EMMY. Miss Phipps gone on the trip, Miss Sofia.

SOFIA. Vera you idiot!

EMMY. She . . .

SOFIA. She what?

KATE. She's gone to bed.

SOFIA. Oh, what a pity. 'Cause I've just broken the lock on the freezer and guess what I've found? Two white carrier bags of food . . . frozen food!

EMMY. But where you find them, Miss Sofia?

SOFIA. The freezer, dummy. One leg of lamb, three pork chops, some vegetables and a chicken for Sunday dinner . . . all frozen solid. Silly old cow locked them back in. All neat in two, white, plastic bags, just waiting to be lifted and she locks them back in. Well at least we won't have to endure any more of your foreign muck, Emmy.

EMMY. No.

SOFIA. And now I've found them, I'll cook my own dinner.

EMMY. But you can' reach the stove Miss Sofia?

SOFIA. 'Course I bloody can.

Exit SOFIA.

EMMY. I hope she will reach this time. Last time her sleeve catch fire and if it wasn't for nine, nine, nine and Vera, she would dead. Vera say she go in the kitchen the morning and Miss Sofia was cooking breakfast. Miss Sofia have on her gown and because she low down in her chair she have to lean it catch fire. Well Vera never see the fire at first and when she turn round, she see Miss Sofia eye them full up her head. Vera say all Miss Sofia a do is bat, bat the fire. 'Bat, bat, bat!' Vera say. Miss Sofia down in her chair and the flame a ride her, and she couldn't even call out for help. So Vera grab the towel, dash it over Miss Sofia and wrap it tight round her and kill the fire dead. And that's when Vera run out go call nine, nine, nine and Miss Sofia save.

KATE. You like it here?

EMMY. It alright. Is where them put we. But my Daphne coming for me, you know. She coming to take me out this weekend. (EMMY *takes a letter out of her handbag and reads.*) 'Dear Mum, Coming to take you shopping tomorrow. Love Daphne.'

And Miss Sofia, she get this notion . . . She always get them. Me remember one notion she get. She used to write these letters – chain letter she call them. She used to like write them, but she stop. Cost too much she say . . . That was years ago. Then she start write these other letters. She hide write, but me see. And though Miss Sofia always first for the letters and newspapers, me never one day see any reply come from foreign for her . . . Me know is foreign she write, because the envelope them blue and red . . . Now this new notion she have is talking to the dead. She get book from library and everything. Me not too sure though, cause me kinna fraid . . . But is what Miss Sofia want.

KATE. That's what you were doing when I came in?

EMMY. Yes. Why you laughing?

KATE. Nothing. Show me the room.

EMMY. Come then.

   KATE *picks up her case and they leave.*

Scene Three

SOFIA *is waiting for* VERA.

A loud noise outside and VERA *enters staggering and clutching her bag –
she looks a mess.*

VERA. Oh!

SOFIA. . . . Oh! Here she comes, blacker and bluer, repentful as hell, two pounds more in the kitty and full of nevers! Thought I told you not to leave this house?

VERA. Never, never again that trumped up little Hitler bastard! He's gonna have to beg for my services the next time he's feeling randy, 'cause till then he can kiss my beautiful arse!

SOFIA. Sure you remember which he it was this time?

VERA. Of course I do!

SOFIA. You're sure now? Because your memory's not . . .

VERA. Tucker! I remember!

SOFIA. Perhaps it's the beatings before you remember?

VERA. I said I remember!

SOFIA. You said you took the food out, but do you know where I found it?

   Ask me where I found the food, Vera.

VERA. I don't want to talk about food.

SOFIA. Well I do. I spent the good part of ten minutes breaking into the freezer to rescue food you had locked back in. I think your memory's getting worse.

VERA. I'm fine!

KATE *enters.*

KATE. What's the matter?

VERA. Sofia?

SOFIA. Well ask me where I found the food.

VERA. But my head hurts.

SOFIA. Ask me!

VERA. Where then, where?

SOFIA. . . . Did I find the food, Sofia?

VERA. Where did you find the food, Sofia?

Enter EMMY.

SOFIA (*to* EMMY). Bed ah? I'll deal with you later, liar.

KATE. I said that, not Emmy.

SOFIA. And she condoned it.

VERA. Where then?

SOFIA (*to* EMMY). Later!

VERA. Where?

SOFIA. In the freezer.

KATE. Is there something going on?

VERA. No.

SOFIA. Oh, I think they should know, don't you Vera? Especially sweet darling Em!

VERA (*looks at* SOFIA). Don't.

KATE. Don't what?

SOFIA. It's just . . .

VERA. Did my infants call?

KATE. What?

VERA. My infants, did they call?

KATE. What's happened?

SOFIA. Just, just Vera back from one of her illicit sojourns. Illicit being the operative word.

KATE. She's been attacked.

SOFIA. I reckon it does something for her. Aren't I right Vera . . . sweet?

EMMY. Me will go for the aid box.

Exit EMMY.

KATE. Shall I call the police?

SOFIA. Do no such thing.

VERA. I'm alright.

Re-enter EMMY *with the First Aid box. She begins attending to* VERA.

I am really . . .
But my infants? Did they call while I was out? I was expecting
. . .

EMMY. Husband used to beat me. Used to beat me bad. If Husband never beat me, me never used to feel it was a real week. The week just never feel right . . . One time me even go blind. Me just close me eye them so. Doctor tell me is nothing. All in me head. And favour it was true, cause it just get better. Soon as Husband died it get better. Husband was a big everlasting black man who did so black, him kinna blue with it . . . Black blue, with a dullness over him whole self. Him eye them red and weak and all day long them run water . . . Every morning him wake them stuck shut with yellow matter and him can't see. Blind! That's when me used to bathe them. The closest we ever get was me bathing him eye . . . So anyway, Husband used to bawl, 'Emmyryha!' Him would bawl, 'Emmyryha! Get the switch!' An' me go for it; me go for it, just like me a one a him pickeny. Then Husband would whip me. And when him done, him ask me if me know why him whip me. And me say, 'yes Sir! Yes Sir, cause you a Husband.' Then he died on me. I know the exact second Husband died. It was when I turned oak on him . . . The switch broke on my back – wood on wood . . . Afterwards he lingered for a few days, like a pestilence: moaning and fawning for food, but dead! Eyes stuck shut and me refusing to bathe them. No ordering,

no beatings . . . dead! He just never knew the sap of a weed
could up and turn oak on him. And when he did, it killed him.
Killed him, biff!
(*To* KATE.) You should find out 'bout oak. Best way to kill a
man like Husband . . . But if it wasn't for all them pickeny
Husband gimme, me think me would a turn oak on him long
before. Twelve a them! And no girls.

SOFIA. Kids! Nature's way of slapping women in the face. Every
year or so, 'slap', right in the face. 'Slap!' Right in our beautiful
liberated arses, ah Vera!

EMMY. You got babies, Kate?

KATE. No . . . I have a husband though. It's our anniversary
tomorrow.

SOFIA. So that's why you're here.

KATE. What?

SOFIA. The reason you've run away.

KATE. My husband doesn't have much to do with it.

SOFIA. So you have run away?

EMMY. How long you married, Kate?

KATE. Eight years.

SOFIA. But more like eighty, ah?

KATE. There's nothing wrong with my marriage.

SOFIA. Really?

KATE. Really!

SOFIA. Married! You don't look old enough. But you look young
enough, fool enough.

VERA. My longest lasted three years. He died. He was good to
me and I was good to him. Whenever we walked out he would
put his arm around me and in those days you looped arms and
that was it, but he would always put his arm around me. He
liked to touch me. It was like he needed to touch me. Like his
whole life depended on . . . touching me . . . Made me feel
needed. Had my first orgasm with him. Thirty-eight and losing
control. But you can do that with someone who cares.

SOFIA. Sex! Sex! Sex! Anything and you turn it round to sex!

EMMY. How you meet you husband, Kate?

KATE. He was my father's best friend.

> But it was stupid because as soon as I married him my father stopped being his best friend. And then I realised that was why I'd married him.

SOFIA. You're not happy with him are you? Go on admit it; you're not ecstatic with him.

KATE (*to* EMMY). Let me finish that for you.

> KATE *takes over attending to* VERA.

EMMY. I have a girl. Only one . . . Daphne!
She coming tomorrow. (EMMY *takes the letter out of her handbag and reads*) 'Dear Mum, Coming to take you shopping tomorrow. Love Daphne.'
She look just like her father. Beautiful!

> SOFIA *wheels herself away.*

EMMY. She wearing a thin summer dress and her lovely shiny black hair tie up with ribbon, and she six months pregnant with her first child . . .

KATE (*to* VERA). How's that?

VERA. Oh better, sweet.

EMMY. . . . she says her ankles are swollen. But they look just the same, slim and strong.
And then she smiles; as I take the picture she smiles . . .

> EMMY *takes a picture out of her handbag staring at it.*

VERA. There's no bruising is there sweet? (*She takes a mirror out of her handbag and looks at her face.*)

KATE. Not much.

VERA. No, not much . . .

EMMY. . . . And as me click done . . . she start laugh.
She got a beautiful smile, but she got a laugh you can feel with you two hand them . . .

> (EMMY *now has her hands up*). Feel with two hand.

SOFIA. Emmy . . . go to bed . . .

EMMY. Yes, Miss Sofia.

Exit EMMY.

VERA. My head still hurts. But I got a call from one of my infants today, one of my sons, says his wife has just given birth to a lovely girl and could I come over as soon as possible . . . They're going to call her Vera, what an honour ah . . . ! But how can I go over like this? I'm all bruised and . . . What do you think Sofia, you think make-up will help?

SOFIA. Make-up? Stop talking bloody nonsense. Look at you. Just look at you. You're a disgrace.

VERA (*looking in her mirror*). Oh . . .

SOFIA. I'm gonna see about some food, don't be here when I get back.

Exit SOFIA.

Scene Four

The next morning. Present is SOFIA *looking out the window. Enter* EMMY *dressed in a fancy dress and made up.*

EMMY. How me look, Miss Sofia?

SOFIA (*still looking out the window*). Fine.

EMMY. I hope Daphne going like it. You think she going like it, Miss Sofia?

SOFIA. You haven't seen that wretched paper boy have you?

EMMY. Me see him last week.

SOFIA. This morning!

EMMY. No. But when me see him last week, him tell me him don't name Richard, him name Edwin!

SOFIA. That wretched boy I said dummy.

EMMY. Edwin! Him no name Richard. Him name Edwin.

SOFIA. Oh shut up.

EMMY. You like these?

EMMY (*she holds up a string of pearls around her neck*). Vera lend me. Them nice eeh! Vera say them got style. That mean me going have style too?

SOFIA. Impossible!

EMMY. And Vera was going lend me the ears ring to match, but me tell her me ears don't bore. She even make up me face . . . she say Daphne going like it.

SOFIA. Where is he?

SOFIA *turns now.*

What the hell're you doing?

EMMY. Doing?

SOFIA. We're supposed to be making contact with the other side, not scaring them half to death.

EMMY. But them dead already, Miss Sofia.

SOFIA. Keep quiet! Look at the state of you!

EMMY *looks down at herself.*

EMMY. Then it no look good, Miss Sofia?

SOFIA. No it bloody doesn't. Get upstairs and scrub that muck off before it sets fast. You let Vera do that to you?

EMMY. But she say it look good.

SOFIA. Vera is a whore. She would, she doesn't know any better. But you!

EMMY. Yes, Miss Sofia.

Enter KATE *with the newspapers.*

SOFIA. There they are. Hand them over.

KATE *drops them on the table and* SOFIA *picks them up and starts reading.*

EMMY. Kate, Miss Sofia say me no look good.

KATE. You look as good as you feel is what my mother always said. Never said an original thing, my mother.

SOFIA. You have one of those weird and wonderful creatures.

And the relationship doesn't sound too good from that last
remark. You should abstain, like me.

EMMY. Miss Sofia no have no mother. Is inna toilet them find
her and call her Sofia. No true Miss Sofia? Miss Sofia live inna
children's home all . . .

SOFIA. It was not a home of any kind. I lived in an orphanage.

EMMY. Three months old, that's all she was.

SOFIA. And I don't see why I should have to apologise for it.

EMMY. No Miss Sofia. You no have to sorry for nothing.

SOFIA. There are some who would've benefited from my
upbringing. That Vera for one. She flits from one disgusting
liaison to another . . . as if her life depended on it. If she had
had my upbringing that would've set her right.

KATE. I think Vera would've been Vera, even if she had had your
upbringing.

SOFIA. And what the hell do you know about Vera or any of us
to be saying that?

KATE. Well . . .

SOFIA. You don't know anything. Nothing!
And all I can say is I'm glad I have none of the needs or
desires that seem to have afflicted her.

EMMY. Is just her way, Miss Sofia.

SOFIA. Just her way indeed!

Exit SOFIA.

EMMY. She no mean it, but because she no have no one, it kinna
rest on her mind and . . .

KATE. I don't care.

EMMY. Me and Vera have we memories . . . And even though
Vera infant no come look for her, she know them out there . . .
But sometimes the thought of them not enough, and only the
touch of them will suffice . . . I think the newspaper help Miss
Sofia. She read 'bout other people and them life and she can
pretend . . . And me call her Miss Sofia. That make her feel
good. And she and Vera cuss and quarrel, but that good for her
too. I wonder sometime if Vera know the tonic she is to Miss

Sofia. Me scared to ask in case she don't and she stop out of spite. Vera little bit quick tempered . . . But maybe talking to the dead will help Miss Sofia . . .

KATE. My father's just died.

EMMY. Maybe you want talk to him?

KATE. No.

EMMY. You don't want talk to him?

KATE. We never had much to say to each other when he was alive.

EMMY. Maybe is time? You never like you father?

KATE. It's not that simple. You wouldn't understand.

EMMY. When you old, people think you can't grasp anything. You going help me with the tea and sandwich for when Daphne come? You will like my Daphne. She nice. Just like you.

KATE. You think I'm nice?

EMMY. Of course you nice.

KATE. You only think so because you don't know me.

EMMY. Me no have to know you to know you nice. You going help me with the food?

KATE. Okay then.

EMMY. Good. Vera tell me last night that she have a new granddaughter and them going call her Vera. You want see her when she tell me. She kick up her heel and we hold each other and we dance. Me glad for her I can hardly tell you . . . Anyway come we make the tea before Daphne come.

Exit KATE *and* EMMY.

Scene Five

Enter VERA. *She hobbles over to a chair and sits. She takes a hand mirror out of her handbag and peers into it, applies some make-up and combs her hair. After a while* KATE *and* EMMY *enter talking together and carrying plates of sandwiches, they stop when they see* VERA.

VERA. What you two staring at?

EMMY. You.

KATE. How're you feeling?

VERA. I'm used to it. Did any of my infants call?

EMMY. No. We make tea for Daphne. You want some now?

VERA. No I'll wait. Anyway I'm on a diet. You think I'm gaining
weight, sweet?

EMMY. No.

VERA. Oh I think so, I'm sure this extra cheek wasn't on my
beautiful arse, or maybe I don't remember . . . ?

EMMY. You look alright.

VERA. You're only saying that because you don't want me to
worry. She knows I worry, she's a good friend . . . but I worry
. . . Even now, don't know why. You worry yourself too, don't
you sweet? Worse than me. She worries about anything . . .
Dear God, why am I babbling?

EMMY. Why worry? You have me.

VERA. Because my head feels like shit and I look like shit and I
sound like Sofia.

KATE. Maybe you got up too soon?

VERA. No I'm fine and anyway I've got my new granddaughter
to cheer me up . . . Oh I didn't tell you did I Em? One of my
infants called, my daughter. She's had a girl! Called and wanted
me to go over, said her husband would come and fetch me,
wanted me to come over right away. Today! But I said, this is
what I said Em, I said 'No sweet, I can't, not without my best
friend Emmy.' And then do you know what she said when I
said that?

EMMY. What?

VERA. She said, 'Bring your friend.' That's what she said.

EMMY. Really?

VERA. Really! But then I said, 'No we couldn't, Emmy's having a
treat herself today, her daughter Daphne's visiting.' So we
agreed on another day. Some time next week. Hope you'll
come.

EMMY. Oh yes. Me will come . . .

VERA. What an honour, ah! Vera!

EMMY. Is really a honour.

VERA. But right now we've got a tea to organise for when your Daphne comes haven't we, sweet?

EMMY. Oh yes. Make me go for the tea.

> EMMY *puts her sandwiches down and exits.* KATE *also puts her sandwiches down and begins laying the table.*

KATE. She's looking forward to seeing her daughter.

VERA. Mmm?

KATE. Emmy, she's looking . . .

VERA (*laughing*). She's not really coming, sweet.

KATE. Who?

VERA. Daphne! Em's daughter, she's not really coming.

KATE. I don't understand.

VERA. God, Emmy hasn't seen or heard from her Daphne in years. There's nobody coming to tea except us, sweet. (*Touching her head.*) It's all up here.

KATE. What do you mean?

VERA. Well there's me, you, Sofia and Emmy. One, two, three, four for tea.

KATE. But . . .

> EMMY *returns with the tea.*

VERA. Oh Em, sweet, there're only four places set. There'll be five for tea remember? You mustn't forget Kate. Me, you, Sofia, Daphne and Kate, makes five.

EMMY. Oh yes, you right. And me remember Daphne like her tea well mash, so me put the water on it.

VERA. Yes put the pot in the middle of the table next to the flowers, by the way where are they? I remember flowers somewhere.

> EMMY *puts the tea down.*

EMMY. Make me go for the extra setting. Little most me forget you Kate.

Exit EMMY *who then returns with extra tea things and lays them on the table.*

Daphne soon come now.

EMMY *looks out the window.* KATE *watches her.*

VERA. You wouldn't think so to look at me but I'm a Lady. The last man I married was a Lord so that makes me a Lady. Lady Vera Hawthorne-Wood! Horrendous! So was he. Meanest man I ever lived with, he didn't have a stately house or anything, but he had a big enough one. We lived in three rooms, one bedroom each and a dining room. Separate bedrooms were his idea . . . I don't think he liked me. Couldn't tolerate me and I needed the company, all I ever needed from them really, so I left . . . Left them all one way or the other, all six of them!

KATE. What does a woman do with six husbands?

VERA. If she's clever she'll kill four, divorce one and leave the other one. Beautiful infants though. They really look after me . . . Because they love me . . . because I was a good mother, because I am a good mother . . .

No sign yet, Em?

EMMY. Not yet.

VERA *goes to* EMMY.

VERA. You know my eyes're younger, let me.

EMMY. Maybe we should wait outside?

VERA. Yeah, that way we'll see her as soon as she gets round the wall.

Exit VERA *and* EMMY. KATE *moves to the window and looks out.* SOFIA *enters. She moves to the table and begins eating the sandwiches.*

SOFIA. So! You're still here.

KATE. Emmy's looking for Daphne.

SOFIA. Great sandwiches. Want one?
We might get somewhere tonight. We'd better anyway. Last night before they all come shuffling back. And you won't know the place once they all get back. All that dribbling and pissing

and a terrible waiting silence . . .

KATE. They're waiting . . . for Daphne.
Vera told me. About Emmy and her daughter. Her Daphne.

SOFIA. Bet that's all she told you.

KATE. She waits every holiday then?

SOFIA. Try one, they're really nice. Oh Emmy'll be upset for a
few days but she'll carry on . . . Until the next holiday . . .
when it'll all start up again . . . If she's lucky . . .

KATE. Lucky? It can't be good for her . . . Everytime . . . Every
holiday . . . Why, why don't you tell her she's dead or
something? That Daphne's dead.

SOFIA. You don't know what you're talking about.

KATE. I suppose you enjoy it?

SOFIA *throws the sandwich on the table.*

SOFIA. I was.

KATE. I'm going to talk to her. You can't let her go on like this.

SOFIA. Just stay out of it. You don't know anything about it. She
needs it.

Enter VERA *comforting* EMMY *who is sobbing.*

VERA. Don't worry, sweet. She'll come, she's probably just been
delayed.

EMMY. You think so?

SOFIA. Vera, stop talking nonsense and get the chairs, we've
wasted enough time as it is.

KATE. Is that all you're bothered about? Your seance?

SOFIA. What else is there? Oh she's fine. I've seen it all before.
Vera get the chairs.

VERA. I'm busy.

SOFIA. Busy mothering her, because you don't have your own to
mother.

VERA. You never know when to stop do you?

SOFIA. Says the woman with her face hanging off.

Quickly VERA *lets go of* EMMY, *opens her handbag and takes out her mirror peering into it.*

VERA. My face isn't hanging off. Em's my face hanging off?

VERA *begins applying some make-up.*

EMMY. I feel so tired.

KATE *rushes over to* EMMY *and sits her down in a chair.*

KATE. Why? Why do it? You shouldn't put yourself through this.

EMMY. Maybe she late or maybe is tomorrow she coming? She never reach nowhere on time you know! Me remember the night she born . . .

KATE. Emmy . . .

EMMY. Three week over me carry her and still she take the whole night. But in the end she come . . .

KATE. Em . . .

EMMY. In the end . . . (*She begins sobbing again.*)

KATE. Em look. I've got some bad news. Hold my hand.

SOFIA. Keep out of it.

KATE. Hold my hand. Tighter Em!

SOFIA. I said . . .

KATE. There was a phone call. While you were outside. About your daughter.

VERA. My daughter? My daughter?

SOFIA (*to* KATE). Keep out!

KATE. About Daphne.

EMMY. Daphne?

KATE. I'm sorry, Em. She's dead. She died on her way to see you. Car crash. She didn't suffer . . . She did love you and she needed you and she . . .

EMMY. Oh Daphne . . .

EMMY *begins breathing heavily and then slumps back in the chair.*

Ohohoh . . . !

SOFIA. You bitch!

VERA. Emmy!

VERA *rushes to* EMMY.

SOFIA (*to* KATE). Look at her.

EMMY. Uhuh . . . !

KATE. But . . . Emmy . . . ?

SOFIA. Get out! Get out!

VERA. Emmy what's wrong?

SOFIA *wheels herself towards them.*

SOFIA. How stupid are you? Sit her up. You do realise this is
our last night?

VERA. She's not up to it.

SOFIA. Just a little shock. Wasn't it Em? Go and put the kettle
on.

VERA. But . . .

SOFIA. Do it!

Exit VERA.

(*To* KATE.) Satisfied?

KATE. I didn't think she'd . . .

SOFIA. No you didn't. Just get out and leave her to me.

KATE. Emmy, I'm sorry. I'm . . .

SOFIA. Get out!

(*To* EMMY.) Just a little shock. And your friend Vera's gone to
make the tea.

EMMY. Ohohoh . . .

Exit KATE.

EMMY. Daphne dead . . . !

SOFIA. But I'm sure we can get in touch for you. Talk to your
Daphne.

EMMY. Talk to Daphne . . . ?

SOFIA. If we do the seance . . .

VERA *returns.*

VERA. I've put the kettle on. How is she?

SOFIA. Better. She wants to do the seance.

VERA. You don't have to, Em.

SOFIA. She wants to. Get the chairs. Sit her on one.

VERA. But . . .

SOFIA. Do it!

VERA *puts the chairs up to the table and helps* EMMY *on to one and then sits down herself.*

Now! Same procedure as last night. Place hands on the table and we'll begin.

Hands are placed on the table.

VERA. How you feeling, sweet?

SOFIA. Keep quiet. I'm not having you talk through the whole thing again.

VERA. I did not talk through the whole . . .

SOFIA. Quiet! I think I'm getting there.
Is there anyone there? Is there anyone there?

Nothing is heard for a while.

Knock twice if there is anyone there.

SOFIA. Is there anyone there?

After a while EMMY *begins to breathe heavily and then she gasps and falls off her chair.*

EMMY. Uhuhuhu . . . ! Uhuhu . . . !

VERA. Oh no!

SOFIA. What now?

VERA *stoops over her.*

EMMY. Uhuh . . . ! Uhuh . . . !

VERA. Emmy?

ACT TWO

Scene One

EMMY *is still on the floor and* VERA *is still over her.*

VERA. Oh Christ!

   EMMY *appears to be choking, gasping for breath.*

EMMY. Uhuh . . .

SOFIA. What's the matter now?

VERA. I think she's choking.

SOFIA. Oh God, no!

VERA. What should I do?

SOFIA. Get her up and lay her out.

VERA. Don't you mean down?

SOFIA. What?

VERA. Lay her down!

SOFIA. Down! Out! What's the difference at her age?

   VERA *helps* EMMY *up and lays her on the sofa.*

SOFIA. Maybe she's thirsty?

VERA. Do you want some tea Em?

EMMY. Uhuhu . . .

SOFIA. Told you she was.

VERA. I'll get the tea then.

   Exit VERA. SOFIA *wheels herself to* EMMY, *peering at her.*

SOFIA. I bet you're having us on. Aren't you? Trying to ruin it for me.

Are you listening to me Emmyryha C. Waspkiss? Are you?

SOFIA *slaps* EMMY's *face.*

Can you hear me? Bet you can, can't you?

The slaps become harder and faster. EMMY *sobs and* SOFIA *peers at her.*

SOFIA. Maybe you can't.

Offstage VERA *is heard.*

VERA. Here it is, sweet.

Enter VERA *with* EMMY's *tea.* SOFIA *moves back as* VERA *rushes over to* EMMY.

There there don't cry. You drink this up and you'll be fine, I know you will. Lots of sugar and no milk, ah sweet!

VERA *kisses* EMMY *and* SOFIA *moves even further away.*

EMMY. Feel sick.

VERA. It was just a turn and I haven't even sent for the doctor because I know it was just a turn, wasn't it Sofia?

EMMY. Hold my hand.

VERA (*grabbing* EMMY's *hand*). I am sweet, I am I'm holding on for the two of us . . .

EMMY. Feel nice.

VERA. I know, something I first discovered with my mother, she always held my hand. It's good holding hands.

EMMY. Me dead?

VERA. No. What would I do without you to snuggle up to?

SOFIA. Find someone else.

VERA. 'Course you're not dead.

EMMY. I think so.

VERA. No!

EMMY. Me go look for Daphne and me see Husband instead! See him walking . . .

VERA. Your imagination.

SOFIA (*to* EMMY). What did you say?

EMMY. Him put him hand round me throat and me drop down and me can hardly breathe for life . . . Me never drop down?

VERA. Yes, but . . .

SOFIA. You're telling me you saw your husband? You made contact with your rotten husband?

VERA. She needs to rest.

SOFIA. Rest? You bitches! You planned it didn't you?

VERA. Planned what?

SOFIA. Soon as I told you what I wanted, what I needed, you both started planning how to ruin it. How to make it work for yourselves!

SOFIA *wheels herself forward.*

VERA. What're you talking about?

SOFIA. You hijacked my seance!

VERA. We did what?

SOFIA. Don't pretend. My seance!

EMMY. . . . And him hand cold, and them squeeze and squeeze and all me can do is drop down. And me feel a warmth . . . Like a quick fire. It run through me. And someone dragging me back and squeezing me hand and is you . . .

VERA. Don't say any more. Sofia's finally lost her mind.

SOFIA. And why don't you want her to say any more? Afraid she'll let it slip? And you with the brain of a fruit cake. How did you manage it?

VERA. Let what slip? Quite frankly I'm appalled at your attitude, hounding me and Emmy like this, and Emmy not well . . . !

SOFIA. You bitches! You stole my seance!

VERA. Stole? We did nothing of the kind; we only joined in for your sake and now you accuse us, accuse me . . .

SOFIA. Shut up.

VERA . . . accuse me of stealing your seance. I never stole a thing in my life and what would I want with a seance of all things, not exactly one of the most appealing things to steal is . . .

SOFIA. Quiet!

VERA. . . . shouting! And Emmy not well, Emmy flat out on her back because she's lost her daughter and you shouting at the top of your . . .

Suddenly SOFIA *slaps* EMMY *around the face and* VERA *screams out and is then quiet.*

SOFIA. Keep quiet I said . . . please . . . keep . . . quiet . . .

EMMY. Uhuhuh . . .

VERA. You hit her.

SOFIA. You have her. She has you. You have each other.

I only wanted to talk to my mother . . . I only wanted . . . to ask her . . . And you wouldn't even let me. You couldn't even let me do that . . .

EMMY. Me don't see Daphne.

VERA. It's alright Em. Don't worry, sweet.

Quickly VERA *helps* EMMY *up.*

SOFIA. Where're you taking her? Vera where're you taking her?

SOFIA *moves to them.*

You going now? I'm sorry Vera, Vera, I'm . . .

VERA *exits with* EMMY, *ignoring* SOFIA. SOFIA *goes to the window and sits alone looking out and then she looks down at her hands and clasps them together, shaking them as she raises them.* KATE *enters and stands watching her.*

You caught me.

KATE. Doing what?

SOFIA. Holding hands. Apparently there's something to be had from it.

KATE. It helps if you have someone with you.

SOFIA. I thought I told you to get out?

KATE. I came back.

SOFIA. What for?

KATE. To see Emmy. I thought . . . I mean I . . .

SOFIA. It doesn't seem to be working.

KATE. What doesn't?

SOFIA. Do you like my hands? A little bit even? They pretty? They hands you could hold on to? In case you're wondering they've ruined everything and gone to bed . . . together! Was my last chance too.

KATE. What was?

SOFIA. The seance! They did it for themselves. They didn't do it for me . . . And now they've gone off together. Which is quite normal. As this, me alone here, is quite normal. And though it doesn't get any easier, everything is quite normal.

KATE. Sofia . . . ?

Enter VERA.

SOFIA. What's wrong with you? Is she dead?

KATE. Who?

VERA. Why?

SOFIA. She's dead, isn't she?

VERA. Why are you you?

SOFIA. What?

VERA *begins to move slowly forward all the while she is speaking.*

VERA. I said why're you you? I thought it was me. But it's Emmy too. You hate Emmy too.

SOFIA. Well is she or isn't she?

VERA. You hate Emmy.

SOFIA. Nonsense!

VERA. I thought it was me rubbing you up the wrong way. But you hate Emmy.

SOFIA. She's dead, isn't she? And you don't know how to say it. Well let me: 'she's dead!' There, it's been said. Now let me say it's a blow, but you'll need someone, not to take her place, but someone to ease your pain. Take it from me, the worst way is trying to get through alone and you'll grieve and you'll pine, but let me say, let me tell you straight, I will not shirk my duty;

I am willing, more than willing to take Emmyryah's place and become . . . your friend!

VERA. She's not dead.

SOFIA. What?

VERA. She's not dead.

SOFIA. 'Course she is.

VERA. You hate her.

SOFIA. I know she is. She is! And you don't know how to say it.

VERA. Why do you hate her?

SOFIA. What . . . ?

VERA. You've hated her for years. Haven't you? I know you have.

SOFIA. I don't know what you're . . .

VERA. I know!

SOFIA. What?

VERA. That you hate my friend.

SOFIA. Shut up!

VERA. I know!

SOFIA. Emmy's not dead?

VERA. Say you hate her.

SOFIA. She should be dead. If she were . . .

VERA. Say it!

SOFIA. Yes! Yes!

VERA. Why?

SOFIA. Because . . .

VERA. Why?

SOFIA. Because . . . it's not natural the way you two carry on. Kissing. Holding bloody hands. Dancing . . . together! Whispering. Telling each other things. Keeping sordid . . .

VERA. Sordid . . . ?

SOFIA. Sordid, little secrets. Like spiteful children . . .

VERA. I went to your room . . .

SOFIA. But I bet there're some secrets you haven't told your dear, sweet, darling Em!

VERA. Emmy was cold. I went to a room. Got a spare quilt. She was still cold. Went to another room. Got another. But she was still cold . . . Then I went to your room. To get an extra quilt . . . that's all I went for . . .

SOFIA. Scared she won't want you if she knows that at the drop of one of your ridiculous hats you become a blithering idiot?

VERA. I said I went to your room! I found these.

VERA *opens her hands and reveals a bundle of letters and photographs –* SOFIA *doesn't really look.*

SOFIA. But I thought best friends told each other everything.

VERA. I went to your room!

SOFIA. I thought! But it's no good asking me. What would I know . . .

VERA. What are they?

SOFIA. . . . never having had a best friend. And you two keeping spiteful, sordid secrets and . . .

VERA. What are they?

SOFIA. What're what?

SOFIA *turns now looking at them.*

VERA. These. I read them, but I don't know.

SOFIA. Neither do I . . . know.

VERA. Ask me where I found them, Sofia.

SOFIA. No.

VERA. I want you to.

SOFIA. No.

VERA. Ask me!

SOFIA. Where then? Where?

VERA. Did I find them, Vera?

SOFIA. Go away . . .

VERA. Say it! Ask it! Ask me!

SOFIA. Where, did you find them, Vera?

VERA. In your room.

SOFIA. They are mine . . . that's all.

VERA. What're yours?

SOFIA. Those. In your hand!

> SOFIA *wheels herself forward to take them but* VERA *sidesteps her.*

They are . . . are mine.

VERA. And I found them. Under your mattress. Pushed under. Emmy was cold. I went to your room. To get an extra quilt. I pulled and I pulled and I pulled. I couldn't get it off . . . I lifted the mattress. Found these. Pushed under.

SOFIA. You had no right.

VERA. I found them under your mattress.

SOFIA. It's none of your business! (*She begins sobbing.*) They are mine . . .

VERA. Don't cry. Please don't cry Sofia. You bitch!

> VERA *rushes at her but* KATE *stops her.*

KATE. What?

> As VERA *is pulled away the photographs and the letters fall to the floor.*

VERA. She even has the nerve to sit there and cry.

> VERA *tries to rush at* SOFIA *again, but* KATE *holds on to her.*

KATE. Stop it.

VERA (*pointing to the letters*). Those! Under her bed! All of them! Stuffed under her bed.

KATE. So?

VERA. Stuffed under her sodding bed. And you do piss the bed you incontinent bitch.

KATE. Vera . . .

VERA. God! They're Emmy's!

SOFIA. She's lying. They're mine.

VERA. Letters from Daphne! And now she's dead . . .

KATE. What? I don't under . . .

VERA. All these years. Stealing Emmy's letters. And we all thought Daphne didn't care.

KATE looks now at SOFIA *and then picks up one of the pictures, looking at it.*

SOFIA. They are mine you know. (*She holds out her hand for* KATE *to pass it to her.*) They really are.

KATE hands it to SOFIA *and on seeing this* VERA *rushes between them and the picture falls to the floor again.*

VERA. She's not supposed to have it. She's not supposed to!

KATE holds on to VERA.

KATE. Vera . . .

VERA. And now Daphne's dead . . .

KATE. No she's not . . .

VERA. What?

KATE. Daphne's not dead.

VERA. Oh no! Is it all in here again? (*She touches her head.*)

KATE. No. It's not your fault.

KATE begins to lead her away.

VERA. Em loves her, Daphne. I love my infants . . . They really love me . . . They do. And they look after me. All of them, they do . . .

Exit VERA *and* KATE. SOFIA *looks down at the pictures and letters on the floor.*

SOFIA. They are mine. They are.

She reaches out for them and topples helplessly out of her wheelchair. She lays flat out and then begins sobbing. Unobserved KATE *returns and watches her.*

I don't need any of you anyway. I can do it on my own. I always have and I always will. I can.

KATE watches as SOFIA *reaches for her walking stick. It is too far and she has to shuffle along her stomach to reach it.* KATE *moves forward to help her.*

SOFIA. Don't come any closer.

KATE *stoops to help her.*

KATE. Let me . . .

SOFIA. Take, your, hands, off, me!

KATE. Sofia.

SOFIA. Get off me! I never asked for help.

KATE *stands up from her and watches her.*

And I don't piss the bed. I don't!

At some point she reaches her stick and manages to use it to slowly haul herself up into a sitting position on the floor. KATE *watches as she begins collecting the letters and pictures into some kind of order.*

SOFIA. One two, three. Picture letter (*She turns one of the pictures over reading the back.*) Dear Mum, this is me and the brood around the barbecue on Angela's sixteenth. Angela's the one in the silly hat. Write soon. Love Daphne.

KATE *moves to leave, but stops when* SOFIA *speaks.*

You can't bear it can you? Can't bear to look at what you'll one day become. Me! You remind me of me.

KATE. I'm not like you.

SOFIA. Of course you are. They hate me. Both of them, they do. They never kiss me. Emmy never kisses me the way she kisses Vera; Vera never dances with me the way she dances with Em.

KATE. But you won't dance Sofia, you can't dance.

SOFIA. I could've learned, maybe. A little bit, perhaps. Have you seen them dance?

KATE. No.

SOFIA. They're not very good. They're always tripping over each other's feet. But one thing; one thing they do; they hold each other a certain way and . . . I don't know how to describe it. I spied on them one night. Emmy was sitting in that chair over there. Vera came in. Beaten by Tommy Tucker. She was shaking and couldn't stand. Em sat her down and took her hands. Then one finger at a time she kissed them. Emmy kissed them all. All ten of them really slow and gentle. When she finished, Vera was sobbing on her shoulder, but she seemed so calmer.

That bloody Vera! Who does she think she is? Just because she's a sodding Lady. Imagine being a whore and a Lady! And wearing a wig! I'd suspected a long time and then one day when we were alone. 'Pick that up for me Vera.' And the silly old cow did. I yanked it clean off with my walking stick. Clean being the operative word. As a baby's backside. And she a Lady too! She screamed, thrashed about and cursed just like she was drowning or something . . . And I flung it away and she chased after it like it was her lifeline . . . Like it was her lifeline . . . But no matter how she preens and prods it, it'll never be her hair. Because it's not hers . . . Not really. And that's one of her secrets. You see she has them too and she comes shouting at me. Who does she think she is?

(*Looking at a picture*). I could've been your mother.

Enter EMMY, *a quilt around her.* SOFIA *looks at her.*

EMMY. Miss Sofia, what you doing down there? You alright?

KATE. Emmy . . .?

SOFIA. Keep quiet. You'll only confuse her.

EMMY. It cold up there. You cold too?

EMMY *sits beside* SOFIA *on the floor and wraps the quilt around the both of them.*

EMMY. Vera say she gone get cover for me. But me don't see her come back yet.

SOFIA. She hates me.

EMMY. You not to mind her so much, Miss Sofia. Is just her way.

SOFIA. Look. (*She hands* EMMY *one of the pictures.*)

EMMY. Is who? Is Daphne. Is she this?

SOFIA. I stole her . . .

KATE. Sofia . . . ?

SOFIA. Stay out of it this time.

EMMY. Is where you get Daphne?

SOFIA. I stole her.

EMMY. You bring back Daphne.

SOFIA. I thought she could be mine for a week or so. Then it got to months, then years.

EMMY *stands rushing to* VERA *showing her the picture.*

VERA *has returned and stands watching them unobserved.*

SOFIA. She does you know, Vera hates me.

VERA. Yes I do.

EMMY. Vera, look. Miss Sofia bring back Daphne!

EMMY *stands rushing to* VERA *showing her the picture.*

VERA. I know.

EMMY *rushes back to* SOFIA, *and sits beside her kissing and holding her hands.*

EMMY. Daphne! Me know her straight away.

EMMY *kisses* SOFIA *and embraces her*

VERA (*to* EMMY). What're you doing? Has she told you? Has she explained?

EMMY. How you mean?

VERA. What she did.

EMMY. Bring back Daphne?

VERA. She stole your daughter!

EMMY. But Miss Sofia bring back Daphne.

VERA. You don't understand Em.

(*To* SOFIA.) You haven't explained to her have you? Haven't told her what you did.

(*To* EMMY.) All these years she hid the letters because she didn't want you to be happy.

SOFIA. That's a lie.

EMMY. No Vera, Miss Sofia bring back Daphne.

VERA. Emmy listen. Listen to me. She stole . . .

EMMY. Miss Sofia bring back Daphne.

VERA. You forgive her?

EMMY. What else me to do . . .

>EMMY *embraces* SOFIA *again*.

>. . . when she bring back Daphne?

VERA. You can't! I won't! I won't forgive you!

SOFIA. But you have nothing to forgive me for.

VERA. I know what you want. Emmy, I know what she's after.
She's been wearing me down for years. Wearing us down . . .

>(*To* SOFIA). Emmy's my friend. She is my friend!

EMMY. Miss Sofia look Daphne put on weight. (*She shows* SOFIA
the picture.) Vera look, look how Daphne put on weight.

>VERA *turns and leaves quietly.*

>Vera look! Look!

>*Exit* EMMY *after* VERA.

Scene Two

KATE *enters and goes to the window looking out and then* SOFIA *walks
in aided by two walking sticks. She looks very unsure and* KATE *watches
her closely.*

KATE. Where's your chair, Sofia?

>*Ignoring her* SOFIA *stands staring at an armchair unable to reach it.*

SOFIA. So! The papers haven't arrived yet?

KATE. No.

SOFIA. How did you sleep?

KATE. Not so well.

SOFIA. I slept well . . . In fact it was the best night's sleep I've
had for years.

KATE. Have you seen Emmy this morning? How is she?

SOFIA. No and I don't know.

>KATE *watches* SOFIA, *who is shaking.*

KATE. Why don't you sit down?

SOFIA. When I'm good and ready.
I thought maybe I'd take a walk outside. Perhaps to the wall
and back. It's been years. Arthritis. It makes me weak.
Somehow I've just let it come on me. Just let it override me. It
was easier than fighting it. Now it has me . . .

KATE. It wasn't something you could help.

SOFIA. Oh I think so. I think so.

Enter VERA, *taking her head-sets off.*

KATE. Morning.

VERA. So it is.

KATE. Didn't you sleep either?

VERA. Went next door and had some sex.

VERA *takes some money out of her pocket and throws it on the table.*

Fifty pence! All he had the old bastard! But the old fools can't
do without me. They'd go quite blind, if you know what I
mean . . . I suppose I can get some new stockings with that.
And I've made a decision. I'm getting married.

KATE. Who to?

VERA. Tucker. He asked. I said why not. He's asked before and
I've always said no. But then I said yes. So here I am, getting
married. Soon as I can. Maybe next weekend.

SOFIA. Looks like a lovely morning. Very dry, bright, and warm.
I can feel myself. Hot, sticky and sweaty . . . Feel like I'm awash
with it. But somewhere there's a lovely, fresh line of washing
drying in the sun.

VERA. I'll be leaving in a week or so. And I've got so much to do
before I go and all in a week. Write to the infants, and of
course they'll all want to come to their mother's wedding and
. . . Tucker has a good pension so we should get a nice
bungalow. Look what he gave me. Pure silk. (*She holds up a
headscarf.*) I've got just the dress and gloves to go with it.

Enter EMMY *reading the letters.*

EMMY. Vera look, look at Daphne grandson.

VERA *ignores* EMMY, *puts her head-sets on and walks out.*

KATE. She's getting married. To Tommy Tucker. Next weekend.

Exit KATE.

EMMY. Me never know say Vera love Mr Tucker. She never tell me.

SOFIA *now makes her way slowly to a chair.*

SOFIA. She's not talking to you.

EMMY. Why? What me do her?

SOFIA. How stupid are you?

EMMY. How you mean?

EMMY *sits beside* SOFIA *and* SOFIA *reaches for one of the pictures in* EMMY's *hand.*

SOFIA. That's Jerry, Daphne's only grandson. Isn't he beautiful?

EMMY. Him look just like sweet Winston Pickett. How much him weigh when him born?

SOFIA. Nine pounds five ounces. He was a big boy. He stays at Daphne's every weekend.

EMMY. She always been happy?

SOFIA. In general.

EMMY. It hard for me to think of her in America. Now, which one of Daphne daughter this?

SOFIA. That's Angela, she's the one studying law . . .

Scene Three

Enter KATE *with her case, followed by* VERA *who is dressed in her red dress, gloves and new scarf.*

VERA. This is the dress. Will it do? What do you think? Tucker likes me in red. Says it suits me. I've gone and lost my batteries though.

KATE. Looks okay.

VERA. Only okay? Not very free with your compliments, sweet. I put them down somewhere.

KATE. Okay, it looks like Vera. Like you.

VERA. And I always look great so the dress and me together must look doubly great. What do you think about me having my hair up for the day? Perhaps with my new scarf round it? I like a man who gives presents don't you?

VERA *begins looking around under the table down the sides of chairs etc.*

KATE. Suppose it could be pleasant.

VERA. Pleasant! Where is your enthusiasm, sweet? Take it from me, men who give presents are a phenomenon.

KATE. I've only ever had one. What you looking for?

VERA. Only ever had one present, sweet? What a disgrace . . .

KATE. Only ever had one man.

VERA *suddenly stops searching.*

VERA. One man?

KATE. My husband.

VERA. One?

KATE. Yes.

VERA. Well, kiss my beautiful arse . . . one man!

KATE. What's wrong with that?

VERA. Wrong? Did I say anything was wrong, sweet? In fact it sounds quite . . . sweet.

Enter EMMY. VERA *starts searching again.*

EMMY. Vera, you look lovely. That frock did always suit you. What you looking for? You lost something?

VERA (*to* KATE). Did you hear someone speak?

EMMY. Kate tell me you getting married.

VERA. There it is again.

KATE. There what is?

VERA. That voice.

EMMY. Vera, is me.
Me think me will wear the purple frock with the frill round it. And you can make me up and fix me up and . . .

VERA walks around, performing a mock search.

VERA. Sounds like someone talking, but not to me, it couldn't be to me and the strangest thing is I don't see anyone do you?

EMMY. See me here, see me here Vera! And me was wondering what you and Mr Tucker want for the wedding present? Me have a set of bath towel that me never use upstairs in me trunk. Or if you want we can go choose something together. But me have some news too. After you married and gone, me think me might go look for Daphne in America.

VERA. You're going?

EMMY. Daphne say, 'Come and stay six months or for good if you want.'

VERA. For good?

EMMY. After the wedding, though. Daphne say she will pay for me and one of me friend to come out.

VERA. You're leaving me?

EMMY. Sofia say maybe she would like go with me for a month and come back. When she talk it seem like is she alone should go and not me. Fancy we going travel at our age.

VERA. Fancy!

EMMY. So you think the purple one will do?

KATE. Purple what?

EMMY. Me purple frock. I think is chiffon make that frock. That sound alright to you Kate?

KATE. Sounds great.

VERA. Oh so you are free with your compliments as long as they're for the right person.

EMMY. You remember the frock me talking Vera? You think it will do?

VERA. Go! Go to bloody America. See if I care. I can get by without you. I don't need you. I can cope on my own.

Exit VERA.

EMMY. Something wrong with Vera?

KATE. Why do you think she suddenly said yes to him?

EMMY. How you mean?

KATE. Nothing. Have you never thought of getting married again?

EMMY. Me? No love. Husband married me when me young. Then him dead and me get Daphne. And then me come to England with the big belly before me.

KATE. You never been back?

EMMY. Thirty-five years and never. Sometimes all me remember 'bout back home is how it nice, then another time me remember Husband and how him a beat me. But me have my Daphne now. Me have my Daphne . . .

KATE. I have a child.

EMMY. You have baby?

KATE. He's nine months. He's not a baby; he never was to me. I keep him in his play pen. Upstairs. In his room. All day. Where he can't spill out into me. My husband comes home, picks him up, brings him down, throws him up, and he's sick on the sofa. The first thing I do is rush for a wet cloth.

EMMY. Oh child. Make me hold you. Make me hold you.

EMMY *embraces* KATE *and then* VERA *returns with her personal hi-fi and begins searching again.*

VERA. I still haven't found them.

KATE. Found what?

VERA. My batteries. I left them here. On the table. And now they've gone. Someone's moved them. Deliberately.

KATE. Who?

VERA. I can think of two names.

KATE. You've mislaid them.

VERA. Just here is where I left them. And now they've gone.

VERA *bends looking under the table.*

I know they sometimes roll off but not this time.

EMMY. Vera . . .

VERA. And you know, Kate, that's the reason I moved my things to another room.

KATE. What reason, Vera?

VERA. People interfering. Trying to take my things, trying to make it affect me. I've always wanted that room, but I've always been afraid alone . . . But I have to be now they've forced me . . . But if I can get settled before Phipps comes back she won't have the heart to put me back will she, 'cause it'll only be a few days before I leave and get married. I can't wait to go before they take everything. They've taken my batteries and now they want everything else.

EMMY. But me think you would stay with me till you married, Vera. You not going stay with me any more? Eeh Vera?

VERA. No I'm not.

EMMY. But why?

VERA. My batteries, Kate! I need my batteries! (*Pointing at* EMMY.) And I'm not talking to you until you give them back. I know you've got them. Usually it's that Sofia. But you've joined up with her haven't you?

EMMY. No Vera. You not to say that.

VERA. I can and I am. Because it's true. And you're not invited!

EMMY. What?

VERA. I said you're not . . .

   Enter SOFIA.

   . . . invited!

EMMY. Vera.

VERA (*pointing at* SOFIA). And that bitch! Your new friend. Who you're taking half way round the world to see the daughter she stole from you, the daughter I found for you – she, her, the bitch, I hope she gives you exactly what you deserve. (*To* SOFIA.) You finally got what you wanted. You finally got her.

SOFIA. What're you on about now?

VERA. You! You're trying to leave me on my own; trying to leave me all alone. But I won't be. Not even for a minute. Because, I'm marrying Tucker, so I won't be. I won't be . . .
I'll do anything not to end up like you.

EMMY. Oh Vera.

SOFIA. But you have, haven't you?

VERA. I have not.

SOFIA. I mean, look at your hair Vera.

VERA. There's nothing wrong with my hair.

SOFIA. No there isn't. Pity it's not yours.

VERA. You liar. He said it enhanced my beauty and Finnbar would never lie.

EMMY. No him wouldn't Vera and you hair lovely.

VERA. Just like me, Finnbar said. He had a masterful hold right here in the small of my back. Great big huge man. He had a face like . . . I remember . . .

SOFIA. The time you had your 'infants'?

EMMY. Oh Miss Sofia!

VERA. I used to know that. I did, I used to know what his face looked like . . . It was, like something but I can't remember what now. If I screwed my eyes up I could see him. I could see them all . . . My infants too. Because you see, Finnbar once had eyes and a mouth, perhaps even a little dimple – but it's all gone now – all of them gone into a black hole where I can't follow . . . I often wonder what became of him . . .

SOFIA. I used to wonder why you called them 'infants'.

VERA. They have nothing to do with this.

SOFIA. Then I knew.

VERA. Shut up.

SOFIA. It's how you remember them.

VERA. Shut up! Shut up!

EMMY. Miss Sofia . . .

SOFIA. You don't have any!

VERA. Liar! I'm not listening.

SOFIA. You gave them all away.

VERA *fumbles about putting her head-sets on.*

VERA. Don't any of you listen. I'm not listening!

VERA *sits in a chair with her head-sets clamped over her ears.*

SOFIA. I know you can hear me. I know! You gave them all away.

KATE (*to* SOFIA). What're you doing?

SOFIA. They hate you!

VERA. Liar!

SOFIA. Don't they?

VERA. Liar!

SOFIA. Sure you remember how many infants you had?

KATE. Stop it!

SOFIA. Had being the operative word of course.

VERA. Where are my batteries?

KATE. Vera it's okay. It's okay.

VERA. Six! Six babies Kate. Six! And they do love me. And it is my hair, Kate. It is. Comb it and see. Comb my hair, Kate. Here . . . here . . . comb . . .

VERA *fumbles about in her handbag and shoves the comb in* KATE's *hand.*

Here . . .

She suddenly stops and looks in her handbag and takes out two batteries.

Here they are . . . Where they belong . . .

VERA *collapses sobbing into a chair.*

EMMY. Why you do that Sofia? It never important to anyone except Vera . . .

SOFIA. What?

EMMY. We all know 'bout each other. But it never important.

EMMY *comforts* VERA. SOFIA *and* KATE *look on.*

SOFIA. Emmy . . . ?

LOVE STORY
OF THE CENTURY

by Märta Tikkanen
adapted by Clare Venables
from the translation by
Stina Katchadourian

MÄRTA TIKKANEN was born in Helsinki, Finland, in 1935 and still lives there. She belongs to the Swedish speaking minority of Finland and writes her books in Swedish. They are translated into Finnish. She has a BA (fil.kand.) from the University of Helsinki (Swedish Literature, Swedish Language, English Language) and has worked as a journalist, a High School teacher of Swedish and as the Director of an Adult Education School. Since 1979 she has been a full-time writer. She was married to the artist and writer Henrik Tikkanen who died in 1984. She is the mother of two sons and two daughters.

She has published ten books and edited two anthologies. The most successful books are *Man Rape* (1978) and *The Love Story of the Century* (1978). Together they have been translated into sixteen languages, the Scandinavian languages and Finnish, English, German, French, Spanish, Japanese, Serbian, Estonian, Dutch, Greek and Greenlandic. She has also written some plays and several of her books have been dramatised. *Man Rape* was filmed by Jörn Donner in 1977.

A note on the production

Like the original poem, the piece is a fluid emotional journey.
The narrative is not a linear or literal account of a woman's life,
but a complex and contradictory internal dialogue. In order to
dramatise this the woman is played by two performers, GILLIAN
and MARY, who compliment, contradict, challenge and react to
one another as the woman's story is told. Although they
frequently observe, or are aware of one another, they avoid direct
contact. It is only finally that they can comfortably acknowledge
each other.

The set is a grey room; two walls set at a right angle to each
other, with three tall sets of shutters. On the stage right wall the
shutters are open to reveal a large window. On the upstage wall
both sets of shutters are closed. Behind one is a cupboard in two
sections. The main section is filled with books, empty alcohol
bottles, and various household items which are used during the
piece. The top section of the cupboard conceals a mass of white
roses. Behind the third set of shutters is a second large window
which remains hidden until the end of the play.

The room is sparsely furnished; a table and two chairs. On the
table is some paper, a pen, and a half eaten bowl of rice crispies.
A vase and a bunch of white roses are set downstage on a pile of
books. There is a pile of large stones in the corner. Along the
upstage wall is a trail of small objects – a bag, some broken toys,
a book. Everything in the room is devoid of any real colour –
clear glass bottles, grey and brown books, faded toys.

Love Story of the Century by Märta Tikkanen was adapted for the stage by Clare Venables from a translation by Stina Katchadourian. It was first performed by Monstrous Regiment on 8 February 1990 at the Strode Theatre, Street, transferring to the Traverse Theatre, Edinburgh on 13 February 1990. Its tour ended on 24 March 1990 at the Chapter Theatre, Cardiff.

It was performed by Gillian Hanna and Mary McCusker

Directed by Debbie Shewell
Designed by Moggie Douglas
Lighting Design by Tina MacHugh
Original Music by Joanna MacGregor
Technicians: Lizz Poulter and Greta Millington
Administrators: Rose Sharp and Carin Mistry
Photographer: Sean Hudson
Graphic Design: Jo Angell at Paton Walker Associates

Daylight. GILLIAN *sits at the table, writing. Behind her, crouched on the stones, is* MARY. *They are dressed in dark clothes that are similar but not identical.*

GILLIAN. My mother's grandmother
  used to write secretly during the night
  at her white Empire desk

  but her diary
  could never be published
  it was too indiscreet
  and at seventeen I was not allowed to read it.

  I read it of course
  but thought it was boring
  I did not understand what she was all about.

  Why did she not get a divorce
  from that domestic tyrant?

  A couple of times a year
  my mother got her attacks
  her forehead seemed high and she looked past us
  with a strangely shrill and monotonous voice
  she avoided our
  anxious and irritated questions.

  A few days later
  when someone could get her to speak
  she would always say the same thing –
  that she did not have a desk
  where she could sit and write.

  Father was sitting with tears in his eyes
  in his study
  arranging the pencils in order of length.

But she knows we don't have the space
for yet another desk he said
now that you're all growing and need your own nooks.

When yet another day had passed
mother came out with her usual forehead
and said in her usual voice
that father was so kind
and that she had been silly again
and she hugged us all.

We heaved a sigh of relief
and everything continued
and everyone could go on doing their homework
at their respective desks
and, occasionally, take a break to talk
to mother
sitting there in the easy-chair of the living room
which opened up to other rooms, and was telephone-room,
    coffee-room, and parlour.

My mother held her typewriter
in her lap
when she wrote.

MARY (*interrupts screaming in rage and pain*). Nobody ever
    hit me.

Nobody ever hit me
and never was I
physically afraid
that someone might
hit me

until you hit me
the feeling
of being deserted
with no turning back
with no options
not to have strength
not to have control
not to be able to do anything

not to be able to do anything.

MARY *gets up and picks up the bag from the floor. She goes to the table
and starts to pack the bag with the small items lying around – the cereal
bowl, the toys, some stones.*

GILLIAN *moves away from her, and busies herself with arranging the roses in the vase.*

GILLIAN. For me it was easy
to begin with
one would simply love.

MARY. But then everything
gets only more difficult.

Then the question comes:
Why don't you leave?

GILLIAN. Innumerable times I've been
on my way

if this drinking bout isn't
the last
then I'll leave

if his malice affects
the children
then I'll leave

if he also starts
to lie
then I'll leave
and if he ever uses force
on me
then I'll leave

when the children can no longer
take it
then I'll simply have to.

During this, MARY *has unpacked the bag and returned the objects to their original places.*

MARY. And all of it happened.
Still, I didn't leave.

Why?

GILLIAN *opens the cupboard to reveal rows of bottles. She lines a large number of them up on the floor and feverishly arranges and re-arranges them.* MARY *watches her, snatching some of the bottles away each time she speaks, and stacking them against the back wall.*

GILLIAN. An alcoholic's wife
  that's someone
  who is always wrong
  whichever way she turns.

  If she understands and understands
  and forgives
  and smooths things out
  and keeps the relatives at bay
  and quiets the children
  and admires
  and comforts
  and believes and believes and believes
  and hopes

MARY. then she is a self-righteous bitch
  who's always so goddamn perfect
  and wonderful

  an almighty one
  who thinks she can move mountains
  and offer forgiveness for every sin.

  Good God
  one could vomit
  when one sees her shining face.

GILLIAN. And if she asks and pleads
  and hides the bottles
  and pours out half through the window
  and into the flower pots
  and refuses to lie to the relatives
  and blame it on the stomach flu once more
  for the colleagues
  and turns a deaf ear
  to the five hundred and ninetieth round
  of the unhappy childhood
  and the unforgettable war
  and the jealous colleagues

MARY. then she is a dangerous one
  scheming and vindictive
  and I'll be damned
  if it isn't she
  when it comes right down to it

who gets those conspiracies
going all around
and the slander and the mudslinging campaigns.

It is of course she
who is behind everything.
Who else knows so well
all those details that get thrown
into one's face
she it is who's sitting there like a spider in the web
all puffed up with malice, Jesus.

GILLIAN *crouches over her remaining bottles, protecting them.*

GILLIAN. And if she realises
   that she has her own life
   to live
   and that, anyway, she can't ever live
   someone else's life
   and not carry someone else's burdens
   even if she wanted to
   ever so much

MARY. then she is a hard devil
   a goddam careerist
   who gets herself involved in anything
   and with anyone
   only not with the person who's closest to her
   and who needs her the most
   and whom she has promised, moreover
   to love for better for worse
   now we're through with the better
   as soon as things get somewhat worse
   now she's all over the place
   and dedicates herself to all kinds of nonsense
   and mostly to herself
   and her own success
   whatever that might be, hell

MARY. but somebody else has to pay the price
   remember that
   although she probably won't give a damn
   the bloody bitch.

GILLIAN. And if she finally gives up
  and stands there alone
  with her torn nerves
  and the children's torn nerves
  and a thousand pangs of conscience
  because she loved too little
  or even loved too much,
  because she did this and not that
  which might have saved everything,
  if she had been human enough
  to understand a little better

MARY. then one can bet one's life
  that soon she'll have found
  the next man
  to put her claws into
  and torture and pester
  and dominate
  and play guardian angel to
  until nothing else remains
  for that poor devil either
  but the bottle . . .

MARY *kicks the bottles over, angrily.*

A beat.

GILLIAN *goes to the cupboard and gets out a wadge of notes, which she carefully arranges in nine piles on the floor.*

GILLIAN. I'm reading my notes
  from nine books
  on alcoholism

  I recognise everything
  I know
  that the person who's grown up without love
  doesn't think
  that love exists.

  I know all the tricks
  needed to satisfy
  insatiable demands
  more and more and more
  it's never enough.

I gradually get to know
the rules of the game
only too well
now coddled
now bawled out
feeling guilty about everything
and nothing
and above all about the drinking
the glory of the hangover
that finally provides punishment, longed for
and staged.

MARY *sits at the table flicking through a book.*

MARY. I'm reading my notes
about the controlling wives
of alcoholics
who must have a weak man
to keep down
and to hate through the kids
so she herself won't go under
and I read about how the wife
ingeniously seeks to thwart
all improvement.

She rips the pages from the book and throws them on the floor.

GILLIAN *scrabbles around the floor, trying to retrieve the screwed up pages. She gives up.*

GILLIAN. I get extremely tired.

Why is it
that I'm holding on
if, in addition,
it is I
who sit here
and prevent you
from becoming
human?

MARY. Such an honest account
of alcoholism
say the wise men in the book review sections.

Strange, that none of them
feel there's something missing –
like the smells,
for example.

The sharp penetrating brandy smell
that stabs you in the gut
as soon as you come through the door.

The lukewarm bulging stench
of cognac diluted by gastric juices
when you've vomited it all up.

MARY *empties the dregs of a bottle onto* GILLIAN's *notes.*

Rough redwineink
sour whitewinebelch
sweet slush of sherry
gooey vermouth.

MARY *takes a bowl from the cupboard and empties it onto the notes. It is full of vomit.*

But most disgusting of all
the smell of putrid hops
you breathe over me
when for the five thousandth time
you think beer enhances your sexual power.
The smell of rancid dregs hovering above everything
in the bedroom
after you've passed out with your clothes on
across both beds.

the saliva
that beerbrown runs down across your chin
The diarrhoea that follows
without fail
can be felt in the house for several days
along with that drastic purge
which makes your teeth so white.

Just that
Just the smells.

A beat. GILLIAN *moves away and sits on a chair by the cupboard.*

GILLIAN. Of course it hasn't escaped me
  that there is

a rather nasty
aspect
to this thing:

You're lying there
blabbering
with your clothes on
unless I take them off.
Now I can use
whatever tone of voice I prefer
when I prevent
those who call you
from speaking to you.
Now you can't reach me
with some nasty sarcasm
which drives me to despair
because I know
why you're saying it –

you are scared
of me!

GILLIAN. Now you realise
that if you're going to make it
through this
one more time
it'll depend on
my giving you
the medications
exactly when you need them

that I don't give you
more booze
just when you claim
you simply can't
do without it
that I see to it
you ingest
salt and proteins
when the electrolyte balance is disturbed
that I call an ambulance
and don't let you
have your way
when you refuse to lie down on the stretcher
despite the fact that you just asked
to be admitted to the hospital

MARY. and that I sit there, then
    and hold your hand
    just when I really don't want
    to hold your hand
    or even see
    you at all.

GILLIAN. Somehow
    it is quite awful
    all of this –

    to have the upper hand
    the power
    and to be quite pleased
    about that.

    Most awful to know
    that both of us
    realise it.

MARY. Somehow
    it is quite awful
    all of this –

    to have the upper hand
    the power
    and to be quite pleased
    about that.

    Most awful to know
    that both of us . . .

GILLIAN (*interrupting*). You're telling me
    how you fell asleep on the landing
    resting your head on your dog many nights
    how you biked around and cried
    when your dog died
    that the dog meant more
    to you
    than your father and your mother
    who were never home or sober
    and who did not know
    what they wanted you for.

    It is sad
    and you cry.

MARY. I'm sitting in the chair opposite you
and I've got time to think a lot
because the story is not short
and it isn't the first time
I'm hearing it.
You talk
and I sit and wonder
why you don't say anything
about the nights when your kids
haven't dared to go to sleep
but have sneaked around the corner
and spied on you –
Dad hasn't started drinking again, has he?

How's Dad?

Are you really sure he won't drink
tonight?

While you're crying yourself to sleep
because you feel sorry for yourself
who had a father who was
an alcoholic

I sit wondering when
my hatred
will burn you
to white ashes

while you're lying there, sobbing
without thinking for one second
that your kids, too, have
a father.

GILLIAN. Kids
are not usually the ones
who'll take responsibility when something happens.
In our family
the seven-year-old took the bottle of red wine
and hid it, half-emptied, behind the policeman's back
once when you were drunk at the wheel.

MARY. Kids
don't hide their jealousy
they pinch their siblings, take their
toys, tell on each other.

In our family
kids have had to put up with
your tearing a favourite book apart
slandering their friends
and mocking the socialism they believe in.

GILLIAN. Kids
don't normally protect
they are the protected ones
as long as they are helpless and small.
In our family
the kids are the ones
who protect and comfort you
when you're racked by fears
and need the strength of others.

MARY. Kids
should gradually grow
into the adult world
learn to give and take
and experience but master fear.
In our family
everything was there in excess from the start
but their tenderness grew all the more
for you, the child
so early given them.

GILLIAN. She crawls into my lap
smelling of sleep
downy baby hair on her neck
words stumble eagerly:

MARY (*as a child*). Guess what.
I had such a strange dream last night.
I dreamt that I was drinking one whole week
and I drank and drank
and got all dizzy
but then I went to the doctor
and the doctor took a blood test
and then I went home to my house
and then I drank another whole week
and then I got dizzy again.

Guess what
then I suddenly noticed
that I'd become a wolf.

I was ferocious and wild and crazy.
I only wanted to fight
but then my wolf daddy was coming
and we rolled in the grass
and were biting each other
but then I bit him to death you know
and then I stopped fighting right away.

MARY *moves abruptly to the table, sits down, and stares at* GILLIAN.

GILLIAN. At the breakfast table
she tells her dream again
to everybody
all the way to the wolf daddy, there she stops abruptly
quickly smiles at me from the corner of her eye

MARY. and that was it,

GILLIAN. she says and continues to nibble her rice crispies.

MARY *takes a man's shirt from the back of the chair. She stands at the
table folding and smoothing the shirt, repeatedly shaking the shirt out and
folding it again.* GILLIAN *sits on the chair by the cupboard, writing.*

MARY. Earlier
you were nasty and sardonic
only when you drank.

Nowadays you are
even nastier and more sardonic
when you are sober.

GILLIAN. One would think that you wouldn't
need to drink
now that you can be nasty anyway.

MARY. It begins on about the second or third day
of your hangover
when you're starting to realise
who you are
and where you are
and that you have a family
that has been walking around you
like ghosts
or accusations
or like distorted monsters
as long as you were drinking.

At that point you think
it's time
to take everyone to task.

GILLIAN. discipline at the table
the cushions of the sofa must be straight.

MARY. I guess I can still
take your remarks
about the cleaning

GILLIAN. because nothing is working
in our house.

MARY. ok, it isn't perfect
but then
there have been other things
to think about the last few days

GILLIAN. and obviously it is only me
who does any cleaning at all
in this house.

MARY. I actually have never seen you
touch a vacuum cleaner
ok anyway about the cleaning

GILLIAN. you cannot handle the children
at all.

MARY. That's when I feel
the explosion coming.

MARY. But when the kids
get roughed up
if one of them happens to forget
that it's impolite to reach
at the table
or serve himself before you
when they are told
that they are impossible, horrible
and spoiled
and should be ashamed
and sent from the table
and that you won't have anything to do with them
as ill-bred
and degenerate as they are

then my patience runs out

and then I let it spill out
it's really the limit
to strike out at them
when they've been putting up with everything
everything
for ten days
and have helped and comforted
and held you
and been
deeply unhappy
for your sake
and that now it is they
who have to suffer the consequences
of your violent guilt
and your need to put some order
in your life.

She hurls the shirt against the wall, then throws herself against the wall and stand shaking.

SHAME ON YOU.

GILLIAN *continues to write, furiously.*

GILLIAN. And all this anger
that I cannot heap on you
direct and unpadded
now that you're having trouble anyway
in managing to face the world
and when the worst finally is over
and you are on your way back
to life.
All this anger
will have to take this detour
but you're the one it's aimed at
and it surges over you

and I truly hope
that it will drown you forever
AMEN.

She takes the piece of paper and rolls it up very tightly, grabs a bottle, and stuffs the 'message' into it. Suddenly she realises what she is doing. She stops, aware that MARY is staring at her. Their eyes meet for a moment before they break from each other.

Night. Dull light in the room.
The sound of heavy rain.
MARY *picks up the bowl of rice crispies from the table and moving to the*
window sits on the ledge and eats them.
GILLIAN *picks the shirt up and carefully folds and smooths it on the*
table.

MARY. You must be strong
  people
  occasionally say
  to me.

GILLIAN. There was a letter:

  I assume
  that you'll survive
  in spite of everything

  that was enough.

MARY. And I think about
  all that's happened
  – maybe
  I'm strong.

  Yes, I suppose that's it
  I suppose I'm strong.

  Strong people don't bend.

GILLIAN. They break.

  GILLIAN *leaves the shirt on the table and turns to the flowers and*
  books.

  If I hadn't loved you
  so immensely
  and if I had not always believed
  your words
  about this being the last time
  definitively and irrevocably
  the very last time
  that you drank
  then perhaps it would have been easier
  to put up with
  the times that followed.

  But you see I always believed
  in what you said

and loved you
and was convinced that
you really wanted nothing else
but to stop drinking
and never start again.
That actually seemed
completely logical
because who would voluntarily
want to go through the hell
that you went through every time
and in addition each time always seemed
a bit worse
than the previous god-awful time.

She sits with her back against the wall.

A beat. Daylight returns. MARY *sits at the table.*

MARY. Sometimes when I despaired
   I would ask you
   why you hadn't quit
   though you had promised for sure
   that you would
   the previous time.

   Then you answered
   that you really
   hadn't wanted to stop
   deep down
   that time or any other time.
   But, you said, now you wanted to
   in a really different
   and completely new way.
   Now you really
   never again
   wanted to drink.
   And did I believe you?

GILLIAN. Of course I believed you
   now that you wanted
   really deep deep down.
   And I loved you, didn't I ?

MARY. As time went on
   I guess I really no longer
   believed you
   when you assured me

that you would stop
but I noticed
that I'd been going around
hoping anyway
because each time
I got so terribly
disappointed.

Of course one should
neither believe nor hope
only just love
and be just as
surprised
and grateful
each sober evening
after a sober day.

GILLIAN. But that's not the way it is
no, it's not like that at all.

MARY. When I no longer believe
and no longer have the strength to hope
I don't give a damn
whether you're sober
or drunk.

I step over you
when you lie there, drunk
I keep the kids at a distance
move my mattress
sleep on the floor in another room
continue
with my work.
I live my life
and the kids live theirs.

She stands and takes the chair over to the cupboard.

yes, you're bothering us
the hours you're awake
stumbling around
nagging
but you don't concern us

MARY *sweeps the shirt off the table.*

you are no longer
part of our lives.

She drags the table over to the cupboard, and using the furniture,
barricades herself in.

Now you may believe and hope
completely by yourself
we're fed up with
being disappointed
we no longer exist.

GILLIAN *looks at her.*

GILLIAN. Of all the ways
we have tried
this one seems to be the only one
that really works.

MARY. Only too bad
it came too late
for me.

So it was
my indifference
you needed
while my love apparently
only hurt you.

GILLIAN. So it was
my indifference
you needed
while my love apparently
only hurt you.

A beat.

GILLIAN (*brightly*). At one time
I was hiding bottles
and quickly emptying
dregs
into flower pots and ashtrays
and through the window
as soon as you turned your back.

Nowadays I don't give a damn
The quicker you pour the stuff into yourself
the sooner you'll pass out.

Besides, it isn't necessary
to wait long anymore
since you get drunk

on just a few drops
and vomit right away
and pass out.

Practical.
One saves both time
and money.

MARY. You work methodically
and finish your jobs
for the two weeks ahead
and set up only unimportant meetings
that you've never thought of going to
you calmly lay away a supply
of everything that you might need
in order for a binge to proceed
pleasantly
and according to plan.

You get brandy
a superior kind for the beginning
and then an inferior one, cheaper,
an emergency ration of beer
and light beer from the supermarket
and finally you ask me
to renew your prescription
of that drastic purge and your sleeping pills.

Then suddenly you find yourself
with a glass in your hand
voicing your surprise
over your metabolism
which demands that you start drinking
on this ordinary weekday morning
completely without warning.

You who are such a bohemian
and absolutely can't remember
a phone number,
you never miss one single detail
when you are preparing
for your unexpected
drinking bouts.

She goes to the window and closes one of the shutters. There is daylight
outside but the room is now dark, like a sick room. From the window

MARY *watches as* GILLIAN *tiptoes toward the cupboard and gets out
a child's tea set.* GILLIAN *sets out the tiny cups and saucers and has a
'tea party'.*

GILLIAN (*whispering*). Now I don't have to
be scared anymore
one of them says
that he'll start
drinking
now that he's started
we can only wait
till he stops.

Now I don't have to
come home for dinner
on time today
says another
now that he's drinking
he won't notice
if I skip
dinner today.

Bye,
I'm leaving
says a third
takes off
gets home only
after dark
whispers on the sofa
half an hour
now that for once
we've got time
just the two of us.

To a fourth one
I read a double-length story.
I can well afford to do it
since he has
passed out
and doesn't sit there
hoping it'll be his turn
sometime.

I myself have a nice long
telephone conversation
where I don't have to be careful

with my words
or my inflections
now that there's no one
pricking up his ears
to listen
and try to
misunderstand.

Then I stay up
half the night
and write and write and write
now that there's no telling
what I'm up to
and when I don't first
have to go to bed
and wait
until he's sleeping.

MARY. As long as we are this far
the second day or so
into a drinking bout
when he can still sleep
and while no devils
chase him yet along the walls
all of us are doing
pretty well.

GILLIAN *angrily sweeps the tea set off the table.*
Together they confront the husband, MARY *advancing gradually*
downstage, challenging.

GILLIAN. You're so goddamn perfect
you hiss
so damned flawless
always so strict
and demanding
restrained superior
you always accuse me.

MARY. Yes
I accuse you
for the fact
that you don't see me
as the person I am
but are trying to shape me
according to your needs

into someone who is never wrong
and who therefore cannot create disorder
in your authoritarian world.

GILLIAN. into someone who demands that you
know your place
when you yourself don't want to stay put
but don't dare to leave
either

MARY. into someone who wants to force you
to look yourself in the eyes
and admit
that you don't want to be responsible
for your life

GILLIAN. into someone who erects barriers
around you
so that you feel you have a freedom
above and beyond

MARY. into someone who'll only raise her eyebrows
when you hurl your invectives
against the world
that's always against you

GILLIAN. into someone who'll furnish the arguments
you know are correct
and that you therefore don't dare
to listen to

MARY. into someone who accuses
when your guilt overwhelms you
and the only thing that can lighten your burden
for a while
is punishment and suffering.

GILLIAN. Still a five-year-old, you're asking me
to be the one you never had
fifty years ago –
Your Mother, the Almighty.

A sudden light change. MARY *stands rooted to the spot in a shaft of light.* GILLIAN *throws herself into the corner. She crouches on the stones, trying to protect herself.*

MARY. In slow motion
  you raise your hand
  that will strike me.

  Many thoughts
  pass through my mind
  before your hand
  reaches me.

  The thought
  of all women
  in all times
  who have known this second
  the one before the hand strikes

  the fear
  that paralyses
  making me unable
  to get away
  bite kick flee
  I can't open my mouth
  I don't scream
  the feeling
  of being deserted
  with no turning back
  with no options
  not to have strength
  not to have control
  not to be able to do anything

  not to be able to do anything

  and finally
  the incredible
  in what's happening to us –

  it is inconceivable
  it won't happen
  it can't happen

  you
  cannot hit
  me.

GILLIAN *flinches, as if from a violent blow. Crouched on the stones, her position mirrors* MARY's *at the start of the piece.*

MARY. Even before your hand
  reaches me
  I already know:
  this comes to us not
  from lack of love
  but from love's despair

  still
  it is hard to comprehend
  impossible to forget.

GILLIAN. Nobody
  could have begun life more secure
  than I.

  Nobody
  could have been more hopeful
  than I.

  Nobody
  could have loved more devotedly
  than I.

  Nobody
  could have been more unsuspecting
  than I.

  Nobody nobody
  could have been
  more fateful
  for somebody else
  in her all-embracing understanding
  in her self-effacing forgiveness

  than I.

  A long beat.
  In the darkened room a crackly recording on 'I can't give you anything
  but love' is overtaken by harsh piano music.
  Dull daylight gradually returns.

MARY. For me it was easy
  to begin with
  one would simply love

  I love you so immensely
  you said
  no one has ever been able to love like me

I have built a pyramid of my love
you said.
I have placed you on a pedestal
high above the clouds.
This is the love story of the century
you said
it will last forever
in eternity it will be admired
you said.

I had difficulty sleeping
the first seven hundred and thirty nights
after I'd realised
how immensely you love
your love.

GILLIAN. We moved in together
not because we
wanted to
but because we
couldn't help it.

It probably wasn't at all true
that you fell in love
with my blue striped cotton dress
because I looked so innocent
which I was
or that I became deeply enamoured
of your brilliant expressions
and your genius
which hit me
twenty years before it hit the world.

MARY *takes a stack of framed photographs from the drawer in the table,
and sets them out on the floor, the vase of roses at the centre like a shrine.
The photographs are all of the same man – the husband.*

GILLIAN. but only that
your needs fit mine
– to need and to be needed –
and that both of us
completely lacked
all sense of moderation.

Thus, at the starting point
we were
completely equal

if later on things went wrong
the fault was
entirely our own

MARY. if later on things went wrong
the fault was
entirely our own.

GILLIAN. This is the love story of the century
you said
it will last forever
in eternity it will be admired.

MARY. you said

you said

you said

GILLIAN. my blue striped cotton dress

MARY. your brilliant expressions.

GILLIAN. I love you so immensely
you said.

MARY. how immensely you love

GILLIAN. your love.

MARY. You who love
can't you some time
try to tell me what it is you mean
when you say
that you love me?

GILLIAN. Early on
I hid my vulnerability
from you.

Why would I want to hurt you
by showing you
how much
you had hurt me

that way I managed to prevent
both you and me
from growing.

You who love
can't you some time

try to tell me what it is you mean
when you say
that you love me?

MARY. You are asking me
what you mean to me
and suddenly it seems
difficult
for me to answer.

GILLIAN. You were my yearning
to take and to give
one single huge answer to my need
to be needed.
You were the one I wanted
to stand equal with
and to have confidence in
the one I wanted to trust
and never let down
whatever happened.

You were a challenge so enormous
it seemed inevitable
you were a task
which was too difficult
and therefore necessary
and you were the one I wanted
my children to look like.

You were every possibility
and development and future
you were mutual struggle
and the impossible hope
for change.

You were fathomless
and I was fathomless
and together we would drown.

MARY *is rummaging through the cupboard. She opens the top section
and a cascade of white roses falls around her.*

MARY. But somewhere along the years
something has happened.

Today you are the person
I live with.

She kicks at the roses at her feet.

Dialogue is no longer possible
we have lost the language
we have no dictionary
we can't even read a text
and the rules of grammar we have never learned
– we improvised as we went along

now mouths jabber without sound
arms gesticulate
feet stamp their emphasis
we throw up our arms
we still grasp nothing.

But still for some time
we will keep on trying
in despair and hopelessness

until finally we realise
that we have already given up
a very long time ago.

Oh yes, we know each other so well
only too well
for us to remain silent is also
a message
confidence has a thousand ways
to show
that it doesn't exist
treacherous solicitude
stabs you in the back
the mustard gas of suspicion
creeps insidiously along
the ground
filling each crack
with its stench.

All the words
that we throw out
which should be communication
are camouflage
but neither of us
still manages to hide
anything
from the other.

MARY *is kneeling by the piles of notes covered in vomit.*

Even honesty
is a weapon
in our hands.

We'll never get away
from each other.

She lets herself fall head first into the mess on the floor. GILLIAN *looks
at her as she lies there.*

GILLIAN. For me it was easy
  to begin with
  one would simply love
  there was nothing to it
  to love
  when one had always been surrounded
  by love
  and when one had learned early on
  that love was the biggest
  and the happiest
  and the best there was.

  As long as it was love
  things went well.
  But then it became hate
  and hate was not allowed
  when I was little.

  What are you supposed to do
  about a hatred
  that mustn't exist?

  You don't use any dirty words.
  You don't swear.
  You don't hit.
  You don't shout.
  And by no means do you slam the door.
  You don't make any faces.
  Of course you don't throw
  anything.
  You try to be really friendly
  when you're hating.

  You swallow your hatred
  eat it up

don't show it
never admit it.

For me it was not easy
to hate
but the disastrous thing was
not to do it.

She looks at MARY, *waiting for her to respond.*
Finally MARY *responds*.

MARY. But the disastrous thing was
not to do it.

GILLIAN *opens the shutters. The room is flooded with bright daylight.*
MARY *slowly gets up. Fetching an old towel she dries her hair.*

GILLIAN. One whole day
we keep squabbling

that I never told you
that you should have helped me
with the kids
and the house
that of course I told you
and told and told and told you
but that you never listened
or understood
or cared to
understand
what I was trying to say

that you never tried to read
my five hundred page letter to you
when you were away
because you couldn't see
how it might contain anything
that would be as important
as the fact that you returned
to me

MARY. that the only thing you apparently
needed
was my body
not me
not my thoughts

that you never seemed to have had
any use for
by the way

that in case it really only
was the body
then by God
the world is full
of other bodies

that if that's the case
well do as you please
go go go.

You hoist the sails
of your old tub
and steer it
seething with anger
into the reeds.

I'm chopping up kindling
so the splinters
fly
I stick out my tongue
at you.

GILLIAN. I hate you I hate you I hate you
I can only imagine
how you're cursing
and repudiating me
and my body and my thoughts
out there on the bay.

When you return
you sit quietly on the rock, sneer ironically:
'Since I only seem to utter
stupidities
I guess I'd better
just
shut up.'

MARY. By all means
byallmeans byallmeans

I go in and start
dinner

I always I
of course I
and dinner.

GILLIAN *looks out of the window*.

GILLIAN. I chance to look out
see those sad eyes of yours.

I walk around you
on the shore.
You idiot, I say
you goddamned stupid idiot.
I give you a kiss.

You stupid jerk, you say
reluctantly
give me a kiss
seven thousand volts
you rush off and pull in
four pikes
from the sea
give a lecture
on Van Gogh and Georgia O'Keeffe
talk talk talk.

We talk
talk talk.

MARY. Well my goodness
how we must
love each other.

I feel
that you have failed me
since you've had
no use for me the way I am
but rather have made me into a spiritual being
who doesn't have character traits
or thoughts or a voice
but who only exists as a casing
around the enormous selfish
masochistic
love
that turns its back to the world.

She kicks at the heap of roses.

You feel
that I have failed you
that I have been in sympathy
with your enemies
that I do not want to see
your intentions
that I do not receive
your love

which exists only for me
and never has needed anything else
in the world.

GILLIAN. I don't know
how I'll get over
my disappointment.

You don't know
how you'll get over
your disappointment.

MARY. So here we stand
showing off
our disappointments
and struggling over
whose are the greatest
and the heaviest.

GILLIAN. Actually, it is
only now
that we fail.

GILLIAN *retrieves the man's shirt. She hugs it.*

While I was away
you used to go to her in the mornings
and sleep with her
and tell her about yourself
but you wanted to be loyal to me
you said
so you lied to me when I came home

and said that you'd only been chatting a bit
about your job mainly
with her.

You only did that because you felt
so loyal towards me
and you didn't want me
to get upset.

She and I
used to meet sometimes
and occasionally talk on the phone
and we also talked about you
and how you felt
that you wanted to be loyal
and so you lied

MARY *sits at the shrine of photographs. Carefully she snips the heads off the roses one by one with a pair of scissors, and puts the stalks back in the vase.*

GILLIAN. and a pretty long time passed
but then I asked you
why
you think it's better to lie
and you said you loved me so much
that you wanted to be loyal to me
you understand that, you said.

I said I really did not understand
why you slept with her at all
if you loved me so much
that you even wanted to be loyal to me
and then you said
oh well one's got one's erotic habits
as you know, you said

and then you asked me how I knew
that you slept with her
and I said that we talked about that too
when we met
or talked on the phone together

and you got extremely upset.

That goddamned liar
you said
doesn't she have any feelings at all
about loyalty?

MARY. Feel contempt for women, you?
  Never in this world
  have you heard anything
  so absurd.

  You who've always only appreciated
  the women
  you've had, well,
  dealings with.

  Felt contempt for them
  you really haven't ever.
  Not even the whores
  have you felt contempt for
  you say
  proudly.

  Not
  even
  the whores

  you said.

A round starts, gradually at first, each woman building her own rhythm.
GILLIAN beats the back wall with the man's shirt. MARY stabs at a
photograph with the scissors. Their anger mounts with each line, building
to a scream of rage.

GILLIAN. } Keep your roses
MARY   } clear the table
            instead

            keep your roses
            lie a little less
            instead

            keep your roses
            listen to what I say
            instead

            love me less
            respect me more.

            Keep your roses!

They stop abruptly. MARY has completely destroyed the photograph.
Silence. The two women cannot look at each other.

MARY (*calmly*). How can I explain
the paradoxical fact
that I need a job
that takes too much of my time
because I have you
who take the rest of the time.

As long as I've got the job
I have a context
to belong to
a connection with some of my dearest friends.

As long as I've got the job
I would at least have accomplished something
this day of my life
regardless of what you look like
this particular day.

As long as I've got the job
I've got the way there and back
which is my own.

GILLIAN. Seventeen minutes in the bus
when I have time to read
or turn a poem over in my head
or just mull over something difficult
connected with the place
that's just demanded
all of me
before the next place
that demands all of me
would have devoured me.

As long as I've got
my demanding stimulating
numbing job
I've still got some place

where I can be
without you
so that I'll have the strength
to come home again
to you.

MARY. Keep your roses
clear the table
instead

keep your roses
lie a little less
instead

keep your roses
listen to what I say
instead

love me less
respect me more.

Keep your roses!

It is not by the great shortcomings
that love is killed
love expires
from quite small and almost imperceptible
faults.

When you all these years
without ever noticing
let me handle
responsibility and garbage
by myself
love has trouble
surviving.

About ten years ago
when in desperation
and with my reserves of strength as a young mother
almost depleted
I tried to talk to you
about doing your share
and taking responsibility
for what is
both of ours
you never listened to me
but said
that I was petty
making a fuss
when you were so busy
creating a name
for yourself.

GILLIAN. What I never understood was
why you insisted
on saying

that you loved me
when you did not even notice
that pretty soon
there would be
nothing left of me to love.

MARY. You forced me into a compartment
where I never belonged
you put a mask over my face
which gave you the expressions you needed
as an answer.

GILLIAN. A sunny and protected Mediterranean harbour

MARY. a repulsive creature who drove her husband to his death

GILLIAN. recipient of seven ejaculations in one night, carefully
registered and accounted for

MARY. a nodding doll who'll deliver infidelity when necessary

GILLIAN. a flower-pot to sow brilliance into

MARY. a laying hen that hatches beautiful children with the
proper genes

GILLIAN. an ornament which moreover is useful, offers orgasms
and admiration
a mirror and an echo, sounding-board and background

MARY. a fence without which no freedom exists on the other side

GILLIAN. a hole and an understanding and a forgiveness
and fourteen or forty-four or four hundred and forty cunts
without face or personality.

MARY. Elevated to a pedestal among the clouds, worshipped and
threatening,
or else trodden underfoot in utter contempt

GILLIAN. but they were never my expressions
behind the mask was never me

MARY. never ever
the person one stands equal with
every ordinary day

GILLIAN. never ever
the person one stands equal with
every ordinary day

MARY. What sort of influence do I have on you
  when I've made you believe
  that all the thoughts I think
  are hostile towards you?
  How can you have gotten the idea
  that my road to freedom
  goes over your body?
  Who gave you the thought
  that my life
  is death for you
  and the death of our love?

GILLIAN. How loudly must I shout
  how wordlessly breathe into your ear
  for you to grasp
  what I'm trying to tell you –

MARY. I don't threaten you
  my freedom does not hurt you
  my love does not trample you
  it does not fight against you

  but for us

GILLIAN. How slowly do I have to talk
  for you to hear –

  it is very very urgent now
  if we're going to survive.

MARY. Long have I felt
  the danger
  that's hanging over you and me.
  Many times I have wondered why
  it hasn't yet
  fallen down on us
  and crushed us.

  GILLIAN. The Chinese write
    the word 'crisis'
    with the sign for 'danger'
    and the sign for 'possibility'.

The room darkens. It is early morning, just before dawn. The room is lit only from the window.
MARY *lights a cigarette, and paces restlessly by the window.* GILLIAN *is huddled in the corner.*

MARY. I was sitting next to my mother
   holding her hand
   when her light blue eyes grew dim.

   That moment I promised her
   that I would never
   say what she had said:
   I haven't had the chance.

   What I will say
   if I have to, is:

   I didn't take the chance.

   The older I get
   the more I love
   my mother
   the more I miss her
   the better I understand her
   the more of her characteristics
   I find to my surprise
   in myself.

   I would like to write
   about my mother
   and about my mother's grandmother
   and my maternal grandmother
   and my paternal grandmother
   and my father's grandmother.

GILLIAN. I would like to write
   about the mothers.

   I would like to write
   about their legacy
   and what they saw and knew and felt
   all they were able
   to put up with
   all they believed in and hoped for
   and loved.

GILLIAN *fetches a pen and paper and an open can of beans from the cupboard. She settles herself on the table, ready to write.*

MARY. They had been married nineteen years
   and every Wednesday night
   she packed his black bag
   for that's when he went to the other one

and when he returned home again
on Saturday
she unpacked his black bag
and put his clothes to soak

but one night
she ran out into the forest
and thought that she would die.

When the children found her in the morning
she said that she wouldn't pack the bag
never ever again
will she pack his bag
and she'll never see him again.

He cried a bit
because he would gladly have continued
to live with her
from Saturday to Wednesday each week
and then of course
there was that laundry
that winter she thought
she would die.

When the delivery-boy from the florist came
in the spring
with twenty red roses on their anniversary
and a card that said
THANK YOU FOR TWENTY HAPPY YEARS
she said nothing
but took the roses
and tore every leaf off them
and smashed
the stems
and slowly and resolutely
she dumped everything on the delivery-boy.

GILLIAN *wolfs the beans down straight from the can. She stops suddenly, caught in the act.*

GILLIAN. Sister
you say you're a compulsive eater
and emotionally undernourished
and your equilibrium a refusal to pry deep
sister.
I eat compulsively

to be able to stand my great common sense
and my big feelings sit forlornly beside me
all my feelings
and I
through the nights on my sofa.

MARY. What is happening to us?
Did you know her? The one who shot herself
last Tuesday
at dawn
after a sleepless night?

All her acquaintances
were surprised
and upset of course
but most of all surprised.

GILLIAN. She who was so strong
She who was always happy and outgoing
very active in the community
and the whole big family.

She seemed to have got over that thing with her husband that
    he left her
that she was left alone in a house that was too big
an impressive house, nine rooms
the finances apparently were a bit of a problem
the house was hard to sell.

MARY. but she had got over it everyone says
and seemed strong and happy like before
and had started working full time
seemed to be in fine shape last autumn
say people who knew her.

I never even met her
and I know nothing of her last night
or the spring or the summer and autumn
or all the white nights of this past winter
when it snows and snows
and snows
throughout the nights

GILLIAN. but her dawn
sister
both you and I recognise.

Cold dawn light, which builds to daylight. GILLIAN *kneels on the floor, poised to write.*

MARY. When I wake up in the morning
a poem sits in my head
singing.

I'll write it down right away
so I won't forget it
it's got such a good rhythm
that poem.

GILLIAN *looks up from her work.* MARY *rushes round the room setting the furniture to rights, laying and clearing the table.*

GILLIAN. I'll just
fix some tea and eggs and cereal
set the table
eat with the others
clear the table and clean up
put things back in the fridge
find something
to occupy big and small ones
when it rains
and then make myself a pot of coffee
I can enjoy
while I'm sitting
at the typewriter.

MARY. How was it again that it started
that poem?

GILLIAN. Someone gets angry
because I said
that I'm the one who runs
everything in this house
another one because I hadn't
covered the ping-pong table
and then it rained
last night

one comes and wants to
talk.
What is it that you're writing
all the time?

two start a fight
one is crying
needs lots of hugs to feel better
then three sit and draw pictures
and talk constantly about
what they're drawing.
What do lilacs look like?
Does it go straight out
on both sides
and at the top too
in lilacs?

then they sing
three different songs
at the same time.

MARY *moves to the window.*

MARY. That's when I go outside to pick
a branch of lilacs in the rain
and hope that perhaps it
might find the rhythm
for my poem.

Lilacs do grow straight out
at the top
but those flowers couldn't care less
about my
poems.

I won't allow
my work to take time
away from my family
this I promised myself
when I escaped from suburbia
just in time.

That's why I smooth out the lines
on my forehead
when I go through the doorway
in the evenings
the smoother my forehead
the more tired I am.

GILLIAN. That's why I often smile
when I'm home

the more I smile
the bigger the troubles I've got
to deal with on the job.

That's why I read stories
with a mild voice
and sit for hours on bedsides
and listen to ABBA
The more I'm predicting scores
of ice-hockey matches
the more absorbed I am
in my own problems.

MARY *gets a cardboard box from the cupboard and puts it on the table.*

MARY. I almost totally manage
to hide from my family
the fact that I, too
have a life of my own
to live.

*She takes a bright bowl of oranges from the box and puts it on the table.
The colour is startling in the colourless room. She takes one from the bowl.
As she moves away* GILLIAN *comes to the table and takes an orange.
orange.*

GILLIAN. Without those
who share my working-days
it would be hard for me
to work
impossible
to live

In a world of
greyish white
greyish blue
greyish brown
a hostile world
a rejecting world
which at best could be said to be
on guard

were her brown eyes.

Together
we bought
two yellow cups with orange designs

a tentative beginning
in order to conquer
the greyish white chill in our office.

Sometimes
things went well
then we got ourselves
– wild with joy –
the yellow curtains
in a room that we made
green as sea water.

Sometimes everything stood still
or went
backwards.
Then we shed salty tears together into the yellow cups.

But always when the going was really tough
it still was she and I
only she and I

the yellow cups
and her brown eyes.

GILLIAN *slips the orange into her pocket. She goes to the cupboard and takes out another box. In it is a small portable typewriter. She sits hugging it on her lap.*

MARY *begins to set up an area for herself to write in. She chooses the objects she wants – a few books, one photograph.*

MARY. Every day
that I lived with you
I did so
because I wanted to.

Every time
that it was you
and no one else for me
it was because it was you
I wanted.

Always
when I came back to you
it was because it was
together with you
and no one else
that I wanted to be.

Only
when you dare to believe
that this day
and all other days
are a free choice for me
– you or not you –

can you and I go on
living
together.

GILLIAN. Though I'm aware
that people die
from lack of other people.

I almost cannot stand
the shouts and voices
laughter and talk
demands and love
closeness and crowding
everything that spills over me
every second.

Shrewd and cunning
revolutionary and bold
I then struggle for my right
to those hours of solitude
on the sofa
in the middle of the night.

MARY *writes her poems on pieces of paper which she sticks to the walls.*
Hugging the typewriter, GILLIAN *is still unable to write.*

MARY. Happy
about people
I get close to

love them to pieces.

You warn me –
people simply are not
that wonderful.

Doesn't bother me
at all
so much more reason
to love
until I get disappointed.

Naive
you say.

That's right
I say.

go on loving.

GILLIAN. They think it is courage
which makes me
choose the struggle

compulsion it is
to try to change things.

They think it is my will to fight
that makes me
choose the challenge.

dread it is
that everything will just continue.

They think I am thick-skinned
because I struggle and challenge

cry is what I do

can't help doing what I'm doing.

MARY. Everywhere
I looked for you
who were everywhere
in my world.

I tried to change
my world
so it would fit you
looked for you everywhere

but the one I finally found
was myself.

GILLIAN. It is time
for us
to scrap
our guilty conscience, sisters

this society
lives
off our guilty conscience

no need at all
to bother about
oppressing us
as long as we
oppress ourselves.

This is enough

MARY. What would happen . . .?

GILLIAN. Now it is time
to scrap
our guilty conscience, sisters.

Now we have
got to
allow ourselves

the disappointment
the anger
the rage
the hate.

MARY. What would happen . . .?

GILLIAN. When we're done hating
we'll get up
and go.

What's done
while the hands are still shaking
in indignation
in anger
is perhaps not the greatest
or eternal.

MARY. What would happen . . .?

GILLIAN. step by step
we are making progress

that's the way it is.

MARY. What would happen.
If I could suddenly speak
so you could hear
and understand?

What would happen
if suddenly we would
dare
to trust each other?

What would happen
if neither of us
ever again
lied?

step by step
we are making progress

that's the way it is.

GILLIAN. When the ground is heaving
I take small small steps
almost entirely
imperceptible ones
maybe then I can
maintain my balance.

MARY. When the seconds
pile up
and then come rushing over me
all at once
I am very severe with them.
I have to be.
One by one, one by one
they get permission to pass me
and the endless hours
until morning.

MARY *opens the third set of shutters. The second window is revealed.*
The room is flooded with daylight.

GILLIAN. When pages and passages
and sentences
seem impenetrable
I take the words
one after the other
and hold them up to the light
so they become
transparent.

MARY. Then I gather together
  the miniscule remains
  of my courage
  and whisper quietly.

The two women are finally able to look at each other, easily and comfortably. For the first time they speak directly to each other.

GILLIAN. but only to those
  with their ears close to the ground
  and who

            are

MARY.   slowly

GILLIAN.   creeping

MARY.   forward

GILLIAN. like

BOTH.   me

GILLIAN *starts to type rapidly as the lights fade.*